James Payn

Prisons, Asylums And Hospitals

Miscellaneous Reports

James Payn

Prisons, Asylums And Hospitals
Miscellaneous Reports

ISBN/EAN: 9783744758949

Printed in Europe, USA, Canada, Australia, Japan

Cover: Foto ©ninafisch / pixelio.de

More available books at **www.hansebooks.com**

Contents.

1. N.J. Home for Disabled Soldiers. 1868.
2. Woman's Hospital. Philadelphia.
3. N.H. House of Reformation 1866–'67.
4.   ,,   State Prison. 1866–'67.
5.   ,,   Insane Asylum. 1866–'67.
6. California Insane Asylum. 1865.
7. Petition of Cal. Prison Commission, 1868.
8. Rep. & Pet. of Managers of Magdal. Asylum of San Fransisco. 1864 to Febr. 1868.
9 & 10. Cal. State Prison. Reports 1867 & 1868
11. Ohio Inst. for the Blind. 1868.
12. Ark.   ,,   ,,   1868.

ANNUAL REPORT

OF THE

NEW JERSEY

Home for Disabled Soldiers,

SITUATED AT NEWARK,

FOR THE YEAR 1868.

TRENTON, N. J.:
PRINTED AT THE TRUE AMERICAN OFFICE.
1869.

OFFICERS.

MANAGERS,

MARCUS L. WARD,
DANIEL HAINES,
WILLIAM A. NEWELL,
CHARLES S. OLDEN,
RYNIER H. VEGHTE.

PRESIDENT,

RYNIER H. VEGHTE.

SECRETARY.

DANIEL HAINES.

COMMANDANT AND SURGEON,

COL. ALEX. N. DOUGHERTY.

SUPERINTENDENT,

CAPT. WM. WAKENSHAW.

MATRON,

MRS. WAKENSHAW.

MANAGERS' REPORT.

NEW JERSEY HOME FOR DISABLED SOLDIERS,
NEWARK, November 30, 1868.

To His Excellency Marcus L. Ward,
Governor of the State of New Jersey:

SIR:—I would respectfully present herewith the third annual report of the New Jersey Home for Disabled Soldiers.

The principal new item to enter is the fact that, owing to your Excellency's efforts, an arrangement has been in operation during the year with the National Asylums, by which a sum has been realized, which has gone far towards supporting the institution, and, to a corresponding extent, of course, has relieved the State treasury.

This arrangement has made our Home a temporary *quasi* branch of the National Asylum; and we have, accordingly, received by order of the National Asylum authorities, from time to time, disabled soldiers of other States.

The accompanying reports of the executive officers show a reduction of the cost of the ration from 36c., as in the last report, to 30.7-10c. per man, also of the total cost per day from 56.7-10c. to 42½c. per man.

The average number of beneficiaries has been 204 against 144 last year, while the amount expended was $30,913 38 against $29,991 33 last year.

The officers in charge have fulfilled their duties in a satisfactory manner.

During the year a vacancy occurred in the Board of Managers, occasioned by the death of Edwin A. Stevens, Esq. This vacancy has been filled by the appointment of Hon. Wm. K. McDonald, State Comptroller.

I have the honor to be, your obedient servant,
R. H. VEGHTE, *President*

The following resolutions were passed by the Board at its annual meeting, December 23, 1868, and ordered to be appended to the above report:

WHEREAS, The Board of Managers of the New Jersey Home for Disabled Soldiers have been deprived by death of the presence and valuable services of Edwin A. Stevens, their late associate in said Board; therefore,

Resolved, That this Board, and the institution under its care, have sustained loss, great if not irreparable, in the death of Mr. Stevens, who, from its organization to the time of his death, had been an efficient manager thereof, and was ready at all times to contribute his efforts, and wisdom and influence, in aid of the objects of this institution, and in behalf of the comfort and contentment of its beneficiaries.

Resolved, That this expression of sentiment in regard to Mr. Stevens, together with the sympathies of this Board, be tendered to his family and relatives.

Resolved, That a copy of these resolutions be sent to his widow, and also entered on the minutes.

COMMANDANT'S REPORT.

NEW JERSEY HOME FOR DISABLED SOLDIERS,
NEWARK, November 30, 1868.

Hon. R. H. Veghte, President of Board of Managers of New Jersey Home for Disabled Soldiers:

SIR:—The report of the Superintendent, herewith transmitted, conveys pretty much all the information needed as to the operations of the Institution for the last year. Little remains for me to add, except in my capacity of Surgeon.

The health of the beneficaries has continued good; the large death list is due to chronic disease, chiefly pulmonary consumption, contracted long before admission.

The total number of soldiers and sailors cared for or aided during the year is 573. Of these 23 were regulars; 13 belonged to the navy; 53 with one arm; 51 with one leg; 139 were disabled by gunshot wounds received in the service; 12 totally or partially blind; 2 insane.

One hundred and seventy-three have been treated in hospital during the year of the following diseases:

Phthisis Pulmonalis,	44
Rheumatism,	24
Wounds,	25
Urinary disorders, as strictures, &c., including one case of stone in bladder,	14
Ulcerations,	7
Bright's Disease,	7
Ophthalmia,	5
Sprains,	5
Amputation of fingers,	1
Reamputation of leg,	1
Fever,	5

8 REPORT OF HOME FOR DISABLED SOLDIERS.

Dislocations,	2
Heart Disease,	2
Epilepsy,	3
Paralysis,	4
Asthma,	2
Chills,	1
Anchalasis,	1
Fracture,	1
Diabetes,	1
Various complaints,	18
	173

Whole number died during the year, 26, of the following diseases:

Pulmonary Consumption,	19
Bright's Disease.	2
Sunstroke,	1
Suicide,	1
Chronic Cystilis,	1
Gangrene of Lungs,	1
Chronic Diarrhœa and General Debility,	1
	26

NAMES.

1. John Smith, Company D, 8th New Jersey Volunteers; admitted July 17, 1867; died December 8, 1867; chronic diarrhœa and general debility.

2. John Welcher, Company F, 33d New Jersey Volunteers; admitted July 13, 1866; died February 25, 1868; pulmonary consumption.

3. Joseph O. Ewing, Company M, 2d New Jersey Cavalry; admitted September 29, 1866; died January 18, 1868; pulmonary consumption.

4. John Frayner, Company C, 12th United States Infantry; admitted July 24, 1867; died February 10, 1868; pulmonary consumption.

5. Joseph McLaughlin, Company C, 35th New Jersey Volunteers; admitted February 6, 1868; died February 17, 1868; pulmonary consumption.

6. William Chauncey, Company G, 1st New Hampshire Cavalry; admitted March 10th, 1868; died March 17, 1868; dropsy, from Bright's disease of the kidneys.

7. John McCarty, Company A, 1st New Jersey Artillery; admitted November 4, 1867; died March 29, 1868; chronic cystilis.

REPORT OF HOME FOR DISABLED SOLDIERS.

8. Horace Edgar, Company A, 1 New Jersey Volunteers; admitted April 11, 1868; died April 13, 1868; pulmonary consumption.
9. James Concannon, Company G, 26th New Jersey Volunteers; admitted April 30, 1867; died May 24, 1868; pulmonary consumption.
10. Patrick McCarty, Company B, 1st New Jersey Artillery; admitted September 12, 1867; died June 4, 1868; pulmonary consumption.
11. Thomas Hogan, Company H, 13th New Jersey Volunteers; admitted January 4, 1867; died July 13, 1868; sunstroke.
12. Henry Martin, Company I, 13th New Jersey Volunteers; admitted July 7, 1868; died July 22, 1868; pulmonary consumption.
13. Louis C. Follar, Company B, 8th New Jersey Volunteers; admitted August 6, 1866; died July 25, 1868; pulmonary consumption.
14. Matthew Schwartz, Company C, 68th New York Volunteers; admitted August 10, 1868; died August 10, 1868; pulmonary consumption.
15. Peter Sutphin, Company E, 15th New Jersey Volunteers; admitted January 4, 1868; died August 17, 1868; pulmonary consumption.
16. Jacob Cook, Company B, 33d New Jersey Volunteers; admitted August 18, 1868; died August 22, 1868; gangrene of the lungs.
17. Bernard O'Donnell, Company E, 73d New York Volunteers; admitted August 22, 1868; died September 1, 1868; Bright's disease.
18. Bernard Moore, Company K, 162d New York Volunteers; admitted February 21, 1868; died September 11, 1868; pulmonary consumption.
19. Joshua Bertinshaw, Company C, 33d New Jersey Volunteers; admitted November 18, 1867; died September 27, 1868; pulmonary consumption.
20. Robert McDonald, Company C, 33d New Jersey Volunteers; admitted October 28, 1867; died September 28, 1868; pulmonary consumption.
21. Samuel Adams, gunboat Philadelphia; admitted January 23, 1867; died September 30, 1868; pulmonary consumption.
22. Nathan Willard, Company F, 5th Maine Volunteers; admitted July 14, 1868; died October 3, 1868; pulmonary consumption.
23. David G. Jones, Company I, 7th Rhode Island Volunteers; admitted July 14, 1868; died October 11, 1868; pulmonary consumption.
24. Philip Markhart, Company I, 35th New Jersey Volunteers; admitted March 26th, 1868; died November 3, 1868; pulmonary consumption.
25. William R. Stelling, Company I, 33d New Jersey Volunteers;

admitted August 16, 1866; died November 5, 1868; suicide in city prison.

26. John Hill, Company E, 1st New Jersey Volunteers; admitted November 20, 1868; died November 27, 1868; pulmonary consumption.

Largest number on sick list at one time, 54; smallest, 18; average, 44. Average proportion of sick to average inmates, between ¼ and 1-5.

Number of prescriptions, 5,469.

Average monthly cost of drugs and liquors, $79.48, against $110.84 last year.

Average monthly cost of drugs per patient on sick list, $1.81, against $3.69 last year.

The whole No. of beneficiaries between 20 and 30 yrs. of age are 194
" " " " 30 " 50 " " 306
" " " " 50 " 70 " " 71
" " " over 70 " " 2
                                                                      ———
                                                                      573

Whole number married, with wives and minor children, or either, still living, 195.

Whole number native born, ... 204
" " foreign " . . . 369
                                                       ———
                                                       573

The following surgical operations have been performed during the year:

Amzi W. Brown, amputation of three fingers of right hand.
Christian Hoemlein, reduction of dislocation of left shoulder.
Thomas Beatty, reamputation of right leg.
Wm. Cockroft, lithotomy—removal of an iron ball, incrusted with urinary salts, from the bladder. This patient was wounded April 2, 1865, in the final assault on the forts at Petersburg, Va., by a bullet contained in a shrapnell shell. The ball worked its way into the bladder, and becoming a source of annoyance, was removed by operation August 31, 1868, he having been admitted to the Home a short time before, for the purpose of undergoing the operation. His health is much improved, and he has been discharged, feeling competent to earn a livelihood.

The specimen when recent weighed one ounce, twenty-three grains avoirdupois, and at the request of Surgeon General Barnes has been presented to the Army Medical Museum at Washington, D. C.

With regard to the general affairs of the Institution, I have only to say that they have, on the whole, been satisfactory.

Due economy has been practiced in all departments. Indeed, in this respect, I think the New Jersey Soldiers' Home will compare more than favorably with any similar institution in the country.

We have made constant and unwearied efforts to maintain discipline with at least partial success, by liberal use of our authority to expel from the Institution for gross infraction of the rules.

Even this, however, has not sufficed entirely to prevent occasional disorder, caused by the surreptitious introduction of intoxicating liquors.

These are, of course, never allowed to be used, except on medical prescription.

I have only to renew my expression of thanks to Captain and Mrs. Wakenshaw for their faithful, earnest and successful efforts to conduct the Institution in a creditable manner.

I am, very respectfully,
Your obedient servant,
ALEX. N. DOUGHERTY,
Surgeon, Brv't. Col. and Commandant.

SUPERINTENDENT'S REPORT.

NEW JERSEY HOME FOR DISABLED SOLDIERS, }
NEWARK, November 30, 1868.

Col. A. N. Dougherty, Surgeon and Commandant:

SIR:—I have the honor to submit the following report as Superintendent for the year ending November, 30, 1868.

The large increase of beneficiaries during the year has greatly added to my duties, but I am happy to state that all worthy applicants have been admitted and amply provided for. The number supported during the year is nearly one-third greater than heretofore, while at the same time the expenses have not increased in proportion, which the following tables will show:

Number of beneficiaries last report,		157
Number of beneficiaries received during the year ending November 30, 1868,		416
Total,		573
Honorably discharged,	243	
Expelled,	23	
Transferred to National Asylums,	27	
Died,	26	
		319
Number of beneficiaries November 30, 1868,		254
Average number of beneficiaries per day for year,		204

FINANCIAL.

Cash received for the year ending November 30, 1868.

Balance on hand,	298	10
Sundry warrants on M. L. Ward, Treasurer,	31,130	80
Pasturage,	6	00
Total,	$31,434	90

REPORT OF HOME FOR DISABLED SOLDIERS.

Cash expended for the year ending November 30, 1868.

Allowances to out patients,	$6,560 25
Salaries,	2,360 00
Wages,	1,776 75
Buildings,	150 43
Furnishing Home,	1,575 19
Stationery and printing,	164 28
Provisions,	11,947 70
Fuel, lights and soap,	1,748 50
Clothing,	1,002 70
Drugs and medicines,	996 54
Tobacco,	654 24
Lands rent,	600 00
Burial expenses,	751 50
Incidentals,	562 62
Cash in hands of Superintendent,	521 52
Farm stock,	67 68
Total,	$31,434 90

Congress having passed an act to issue one complete uniform to each invalid soldier, inmates of a Soldiers' Home, a requisition was made on the Quartermaster General in accordance with said act, for one hundred and fifty-two (152) uniforms, which were received and issued to the men without expense to the State, but as the number of beneficaries has been so large, we have been compelled to purchase supplies to meet the necessities of the inmates.

The number of out patients has increased in nearly the same proportion as that of the inmates; the sum of six thousand five hundred and sixty dollars and twenty-five cents has been disbursed in monthly installments of from four to eight dollars per month, as their several cases required, and has relieved the pressing wants of worthy disabled soldiers in all parts of the State, and in my opinion is the best appropriation of funds that noble charity ever devised. New Jersey has ever been proud of her soldiers, and acts like these prove that she does not forget them.

The number of sick has also been large, many cases requiring constant care and attention. Everything was done for their comfort that was possible, and I would here add that the kindly assistance rendered by many of the inmates at times of greatest distress is worthy of praise.

Death has been a frequent visitor, and is rapidly thinning the ranks of the scarred and crippled veterans who so gallantly defended our country during the great rebellion. Twenty-six have gone to that bourne from whence no traveler returns.

The majority of them are buried in the Soldiers' Burying Ground at Fairmount Cemetery, a beautiful spot, sacred to the patriotic heart.

Here are buried those who died in hospitals in this vicinity during the war. They have been honorably remembered by the President of the Cemetery, Chas. S. Macknet, Esq., who has, at great expense, erected marble headstones to mark the graves of the heroes.

The farm has produced a good crop of potatoes, corn and hay, together with other vegetables, which have materially assisted in reducing expenses.

I have only to say that the greatest economy has been practiced in every department.

The total expense per day for each beneficiary during the year, is forty-two and one-half cents, (42½). The average cost of ration per day for the year is thirty and seven-tenths (30 7-10) cents.

Our facilities have been increased by building a large brick oven. which enables us to bake all our own bread, which has proved a great saving to the Institution.

To the clergymen of Newark and vicinity we are under renewed obligations for conducting religious services nearly every Sabbath in the Chapel.

Acknowledgments are due to E. Hooker, Esq., of Orange, New Jersey, for a large donation of magazines, and to George B. Sears, Superintendent of Public Schools, for a valuable donation of a blackboard and school books; also the proprietors of the *Newark Evening Courier, New York Methodist, Christian Advocate, Staats Frei Zeitung, West Jersey Press* and *State Gazette* for supplying the Home gratuitously with their valuable papers.

I cannot close my report without mentioning the valuable assistance of our efficient bookkeeper, Dennis Cahill, who has been constantly at his post, and performed every duty to my entire satisfaction.

I would respectfully state that I have endeavored, to the best of my ability, to enforce discipline in accordance with your instructions, and in all respects to advance the interests of the Institution.

I am, very respectfully,
Your obedient servant,
WM. WAKENSHAW, *Superintendent.*

TREASURER'S REPORT.

NEWARK, N. J., Nov. 30, 1868.

To the Board of Managers of the New Jersey Home for Disabled Soldiers :

The Treasurer submits the following report of receipts and payments for the year ending November 30th, 1868:

January 20, 1868.—Received from Major General B. F. Butler, President of the National Asylum for Disabled Volunteer Soldiers,	$7,460 00
February 13th, 1868.—Received from Hon. Howard Ivins, State Treasurer,	2,211 48
March 12th, 1868.—Received from Hon. Howard Ivins, State Treasurer,	5.217 39
June 16th, 1868.—Received from Hon. William P. McMichael, State Treasurer,	6,967 69
October 6th, 1868 —Received from Hon. William P. McMichael, State Treasurer,	2,241 94
November 2d, 1868.—Received from Captain William Hicks (donation),	100 00
	$24,198 50
November 30th, 1868.—Paid drafts of Superintendent for year ending November 30th, 1868,	30,965 92
Balance due Treasurer,	$6,767 42

MARCUS L. WARD, *Treasurer.*

SIXTH ANNUAL REPORT

OF THE

Board of Managers

OF

THE WOMAN'S HOSPITAL
OF PHILADELPHIA,

Connected with the Medical

NORTH-COLLEGE AVENUE AND TWENTY-SECOND STREET,
(NORTH OF GIRARD COLLEGE.)

JANUARY, 1867.

PHILADELPHIA:
THOMAS WILLIAM STUCKEY, PRINTER,
624 WEAVER STREET.

SIXTH ANNUAL REPORT

OF THE

Board of Managers

OF

THE WOMAN'S HOSPITAL OF PHILADELPHIA,

NORTH-COLLEGE AVENUE AND TWENTY-SECOND STREET,
(*NORTH OF GIRARD COLLEGE.*)

JANUARY, 1867.

PHILADELPHIA:
THOMAS WILLIAM STUCKEY, PRINTER,
624 WEAVER STREET.

MANAGERS.

Mrs. Elizabeth W. Lippincott,	538 North Sixth street.
" Martha G. Richardson,	124 North Tenth street.
" Caroline R. Yarnall,	120 South Twelfth street.
" Anna G. Gilpin,	312 South Broad street.
" J. P. Crozer,	Upland.
Miss Mary A. Tyler,	426 Marshall street.
Mrs. Richard G. Stotesbury,	314 South Tenth street.
" Anna J. Steel,	2034 Green street.
" Martha Ann Warner,	Germantown.
Rebecca L. Fussell, M.D.,	910 North Fifth street.
E. H. Cleveland, M.D.,	Hospital.
Mrs. Maria W. Horton,	320 South Fourth street.
" Hannah W. Richardson,	522 Arch street.
" Sarah T. Price,	
" Benjamin Griffith,	1904 Arch street.
" Sarah T. Rogers,	323 North Eleventh street.
Ann Preston, M.D.,	148 North Eleventh street.
Mrs. Enoch Turley,	1819 Mt. Vernon street.
" T. Morris Perot,	1810 Pine street.
" E. F. Halloway,	315 Marshall street.
Miss Anna E. Massey,	1537 Filbert street.
" Mary Jeanes,	1023 Arch street.
Mrs. Lydia E. Turnpenny,	410 South Broad street.
" Edwin Greble,	128 South Nineteenth street

OFFICERS.

PRESIDENT,
M. H. STOTESBURY.

VICE PRESIDENTS,
E. W. LIPPINCOTT,
E. C. GRIFFITH.

CORRESPONDING SECRETARY,
ANN PRESTON, M.D.

RECORDING SECRETARY,
E. F. HALLOWAY.

TREASURER,
HANNAH W. RICHARDSON.

BOARD OF ADVISERS.

ISAAC BARTON,
REV. ALBERT BARNES,
JOSEPH JEANES,
HON. WM. S. PIERCE,
MARMADUKE MOORE,
REDWOOD F. WARNER,
T. MORRIS PEROT,
PHILIP M. PRICE,
CHARLES D. CLEVELAND.

MEDICAL BOARD.

RESIDENT PHYSICIAN,
EMELINE H. CLEVELAND, M.D.

CONSULTING PHYSICIANS,
ANN PRESTON, M.D.,
J. GIBBONS HUNT, M.D.,
D. STANLEY GLONINGER, M.D.,
ISAAC COMLY, M.D.,

MATRON,
MRS. J. E. THOMPSON.

COMMITTEE ON ADMISSION OF PATIENTS,
ANN PRESTON, M.D., 148 North Eleventh Street.
H. W. RICHARDSON, 522 Arch Street.
E. H. CLEVELAND, M.D., at the Hospital.

REPORT.

The accompanying Report of the resident Physician of the Hospital gives all needful information in regard to the Medical Department.

More than six years ago, without a house or capital, the Managers of the Hospital took the first steps for its organization, strong only in the conviction of its urgent necessity, and in the faith that an Institution so imperatively needed would commend itself to the sympathy of the benevolent and rightly-judging, and would secure the means for sustaining its operations. The result so far has more than justified these expectations.

Through the earnest and unwearied exertions of a few active workers, not only has the valuable property of the Hospital been paid for, but thirteen thousand dollars have been secured to the endowment fund, nearly four thousand of this since the date of last Report.

This generous opening of hearts and purses has not only enabled the Managers to continue their work, but it has also strengthened their spirits and renewed their confidence in that Divine Power who permits no earnest effort for the good of humanity to be made in vain. Some have contributed of their abundance, and valuable donations of clothing and other articles have been given by generous co-workers who could not bestow large gifts of money.

A few hundred dollars have been received during the year from patients able to make remuneration for board in the house; but others without money, whose best claim has been their urgent necessities, have been received with as kind a welcome; and it is believed that the influence of the Institution tends to foster in the young lady students, and others connected with it, that reverence for humanity, irrespective of persons, which gives moral beauty to the character of the physician, and every where makes kindness and courtesy an easy and habitual manifestation.

The number of ladies, students of the Female Medical College of Pennsylvania, anxious to reside in the house, as a means of becoming familiar with diseases and the action of remedies, is greater than can be received; and in extending the resources of the Hospital, and increasing the number of the recipients of its bounty, larger opportunities for observation and experience are at the same time secured to these medical students.

In taking their annual retrospect, the Managers pause by the vacant chair which was filled a year ago by their honored President, Anne D. Morrison; and they would do injustice to themselves if they did not here pay a passing tribute to her memory. Active in the first organization of the Hospital, and always interested in its success, her originality, directness, force, and nobleness of character made her a valued and influential member of the Board, and the distinctness of her individuality gave a peculiar interest to our meetings.

This lamented friend is not the only efficient supporter of the Institution, who, within the past year, has put off the body, and become to the members of the Board a fresh link with the invisible and spiritual world; and among these it seems proper to mention the name of one who at the first organization of the Hospital proffered a house for its uses, and whose broad sympathies and generous donations have since aided in its work—John P. Crozer, of Upland, Pennsylvania.

These, and others, have gone, but the work is still binding upon those who remain; and deeply grateful for all the aid which from time to time has been given, the Managers would renew their appeal for the means to extend the operations of the Institution, so as to make it in some degree commensurate with the important objects for which it was organized.

REPORT

OF THE

RESIDENT PHYSICIAN.

To the Managers of the Woman's Hospital:—

LADIES:—In submitting the following tabular statement, I would call your attention to the fact that the total number of patients, enjoying the care of the Hospital, has been increased during the year by three hundred and nineteen. The number received, as resident, has been less by two than during the twelve months preceding. The increase has been in the Dispensary department, which numbers four hundred and forty-eight in excess of last year. This has been in part at the expense of the out-door clinic, which we were obliged to limit during the summer, in consequence of insufficient assistance, by demanding the attendance at the Dispensary of all patients at all able to leave their homes.

In admitting patients, we have felt constrained in some instances to violate our rules in reference to incurable cases, and have received several with the hope only of making their lives for a few months or years more comfortable. This hope has generally been realized, while it has been sometimes our sorrow to return the patients to their friends without improvement. Notwithstanding this, we have in general felt satisfied with the results of treatment. In the lying-in department, especially, have we had repeated occasion to congratulate ourselves upon the successful warding-off of threatened complications. But one patient has been seriously ill in this department.

The number of obstetrical cases might have been greatly increased, but for our regulations excluding unmarried women. Frequent appeals have been made to us by such individuals or their friends,—appeals which have sometimes moved us to deepest sorrow. Members of respectable families, women not wholly lost to virtue, as well as many of a baser sort, have besought our pitying charity. All such have been refused, except in two or three instances, where the claims of immediate suffering have seemed paramount to prudential considerations.

The three deaths reported took place early in the year: the first, from pneumonia complicating phthisis; the second, from pyæmia following a grave operation; and the third, from pneumonia coming on after parturition, resulting from exposure preceding the admission of the patient into the hospital.

Among the out-door patients a few deaths have occurred, mainly from cholera infantum. This disease, however, as well as the more pestilential Asiatic cholera, did not prevail extensively in our section of the city.

Grateful acknowledgments are due to the Board of Consulting Physicians, for the promptness with which they have responded to our calls for assistance, and the efficient aid they have rendered us.

E. H. CLEVELAND.

Statement of Cases for the year ending January, 1867.

Patients received into Hospital	76
Patients treated in Dispensary	1986
Patients attended at their homes	384
	2446

Classification of Resident Patients.

Obstetrical cases	36
Medical cases	21
Surgical cases	19

NATIVITY.		CIVIL STATE.	
Americans	43	Married	36
Irish	25	Widows	21
English	4	Unmarried	17
Scottish	2	Children	2
German	2		76
	76		

Discharged (including 10 retained from last year) 76.

CONDITION AT DISCHARGE.

Well	54	Deceased	3
Convalescent	4	Retained	7
Improved	9		10
Not improved	6		
Incurable	3		
	76		

Dispensary and Clinic Patients.

NATIVITY.		CIVIL STATE.	
American	1696	Married	803
Irish	474	Unmarried	309
German	114	Widows	258
English	74	Children	1000
Scottish	7		2370
French	2		
Swedish	2		
Canadian	1		
	2370		

MARTHA A. WARNER* *and* H. W. RICHARDSON, *Treasurers, in account with the* WOMAN'S HOSPITAL OF PHILADELPHIA.
1st month 16th, 1867.

DR.

To cash on hand, at last Annual Report, 1st month, 19, 1866	$ 574	43
" received since, in annual subscriptions	2,265	00
" donations	1,533	50
" contributions for special purposes	926	41
" for board and treatment	402	50
" for private patients and students	1,040	50
" interest on investments	830	82
" premium on gold, sold	232	35
" for rent of Female Medical College	100	00
" apparatus, sold	155	50
	$8,061	01

CR.

By cash paid for house expenses	$3,636	36
" for clinical expenses	637	55
" for salaries and wages	990	04
" for dumb waiter, provision vault, drainage, &c.	501	00
" for fuel	397	50
" for gas	181	40
" for repairs and furniture	118	18
" for water rent	15	00
" for books, stationary, and printing	189	95
" for gardening, porterage, &c.	40	83
" for commissions	193	70
" for premiums on investments	130	38
" balance on hand, 1st month, 16, 1867.	1,029	12
	$8,061	01

ENDOWMENT FUND.

Cash on hand at last Report	$ 857	00
Cash for investment received since	3,693	00

INVESTMENTS AT PAR VALUE.

United States 5-20 Loan	$3,500	00
Ten Shares, Pennsylvania Railroad Company	500	00
Eleven Shares of Lehigh Coal and Navigation Company's Stock (new issue)	550	00
	4,550	00
Investments at date of last Report	8,450	00
Total Hospital Investments	$13,000	00

By appointment of the Board, we have examined the above accounts, and find them correct.

E. F. HALLOWAY,
A. J. STEEL.

* Resigned on going to Europe.

Annual Subscriptions.

S. A. Atkinson	$1 00	Anna G. Gilpin	5 00
Mrs. S. Bancroft	10 00	Martha Gummere	1 00
Rev. Albert Barnes	5 00	Charlotte Guilbert	1 00
Anna M. Biddle	1 00	Mrs. E. C. Griffith	20 00
Joel J. Bailey	10 00	E. F. Halloway	5 00
Washington Brown	5 00	Priscilla Henzey	1 00
Maria Bispham	2 00	Mrs. J. S. Halloway	2 00
Ann M. Boulden	5 00	Anne Haines	3 00
Mrs. Frank L. Bodine	10 00	Rebecca Horner	2 00
Susan Boss	10 00	Mary Hazard	5 00
Catherine W. Brown	5 00	Beulah M. Hacker	5 00
Mary N. Burk, for 2 years	6 00	Maria W. Horton	5 00
M. W. Baldwin	10 00	Samuel Huston	10 00
Leah M. Bodine	2 00	Joseph Harrison, Jr.	25 00
Cash	600 00	Mrs. Jos. Harrison, Jr.	10 00
Dr. R. M. Cooper	5 00	Hannah Hoffman	3 00
Alfred Cope	10 00	C. A. Hoffman	3 00
R. Anna Cope	10 00	Margaret Handy	1 00
Sarah W. Cope	5 00	Anna M. Hopper	2 00
Mrs. J. P. Crozer	100 00	Samuel Jeanes	20 00
Mrs. Samuel A. Crozer	10 00	Joshua T. Jeanes	20 00
Sarah F. Corlies	2 00	Anna T. Jeanes	20 00
Letitia L. Cresson	5 00	Mary Jeanes	10 00
Mary F. Cox	5 00	J. & E. C. Jones	5 00
Beulah Coates	2 00	Anna Johnson	1 00
Mrs. John H. Campbell	1 00	Elizabeth Justice	5 00
Mrs. Enoch Clark	10 00	A. Knox, for five years	
A. E. Carpenter	1 00	(including 1867)	5 00
Cash	600 00	Mrs. Robert P. King	5 00
David Dennison	5 00	Mrs. Joseph Lennig	1 00
Mrs. Frank Drexel	10 00	Emily Lippincott	2 00
Elizabeth Dorsey	5 00	Lydia Longstreth	2 00
Hannah M. Darlington	1 00	Isabella J. Lippincott	15 00
Mary A. Derbyshire	10 00	Elizabeth W. Lippincott	10 00
J. Gillingham Fell	20 00	H. B. Lincoln	2 00
Rebecca Ann Fell	5 00	Joseph S. Lovering	10 00
Eliza Fell	2 00	Mrs. Jos. S. Lovering	10 00
Susan V. Greble	5 00	E. C. K. Latimer	10 00

Mary Lewis	10 00	Thomas Sparks	25 00
Mrs. Linnard	10 00	Mrs. George H. Stuart	10 00
Sidney Ann Lewis	1 00	Dr. George Smith	10 00
Joseph S. Lovering, Jr.	10 00	Mary Smith	5 00
Mrs. Wm. Lewis	5 00	Rachel C. Smith	5 00
Mrs. J. Maris	2 00	Ellen L. Smith	5 00
Hugh M'Ilvaine	10 00	Abby C. Shinn	10 00
Lucretia Mott	5 00	Eleanor Stroud	10 00
Marianna Mott	5 00	Maria B. Smith	5 00
Anna E. Massey	2 00	Anna Shoemaker	2 00
Anne D. Morrison	5 00	Mrs. Professor Stephens	5 00
William Massey	10 00	Lydia Starr	3 00
Mary Ann C. Morris	10 00	Anna J. Steel	10 00
Mrs. J. B. Moorhead	10 00	Adeline Thompson	1 00
Lucy M. Moyer	1 00	Anna Thompson	1 00
E. J. Mellon, M. D.	2 00	Anna M. Taber	1 00
Lydia Newbold	2 00	Anna M. Townsend	2 00
Elizabeth Nicholson	2 00	Mary Tyler	1 00
Hannah J. Newhall	5 00	Emma Taylor	5 00
Mrs. Daniel Neall	2 00	Emily W. Taylor	5 00
Mrs. Nancrede	2 00	Mary Ann Taylor	3 00
R. L. Nicholson	2 00	Mrs. Aaron Thompson	5 00
Harriet Ogden	5 00	Jos. D. Thurston, Ex.	20 00
Almira Pechin	5 00	Henrietta Townsend	2 00
Susan M. Parrish	10 00	Henrietta Troth	1 00
Mrs. Thomas H. Powers	10 00	Joseph C. Turner	10 00
C. N. Peirce	5 00	Eliza S. Turner	10 00
Sarah Price	1 00	Lydia E. Turnpenny	2 00
Sidney Potts	1 00	Elizabeth R. Turnpenny	10 00
Mary Potts	1 00	Margaret Vaux	5 00
Isabella L. Pennock	5 00	Mrs. J. A. Wright	1 00
Edwin M. Parker	5 00	Mary Wharton	5 00
Margaret Robinson	1 00	Anna Wharton	5 00
Mrs. T. Morris Perot	5 00	Mrs. K. H. Wilson	5 00
Julianna Randolph	5 00	Lydia White	10 00
Evans Rogers	5 00	M. P. Williams	2 00
A. P. Robinson	4 00	M. A. Warner	5 00
Mrs. Raguet	2 00	Ann Warder	3 00
Carrie Rowland	1 00	Deborah F. Wharton	10 00
Mary H. Robinson	4 00	Alan Wood	10 00
Mrs. R. G. Stotesbury	5 00	Ann Wood	5 00
Charles L. Sharpless	5 00	Daniel S. White	5 00
John Saunders	10 00	Mrs. West	5 00
Mary C. Sellers	1 00	Harriett Webb	1 00
Sarah J. Sharpless	2 00	Ann B. Williams	3 00
H. G. Smith	2 00	Charlotte T. Woodruff	10 00
Margaret Saunders	1 00	Caroline R. Yarnall	4 00

DONATIONS.

Mary D. Brown*	$300 00	E. D. Marshall	5 00
Jay Cooke & Co.	100 00	Julianna Randolph	5 00
Robert H. Crozer	100 00	Eliza Pennock	5 00
Geo. H. Crozer	100 00	Abby Scull	5 00
Emma Crozer	50 00	H. C. Feltus	5 00
Eliza P. Gurney	50 00	Richard Wright	5 00
Geo. Stockham	50 00	Rosengarten	5 00
Mary P. Loxley	50 00	Samuel Bispham	5 00
Mrs. Wm. Bucknell	50 00	Wm. Milward	5 00
Mary D. Haines	50 00	Edmund Mitchell	5 00
A. D. Jessup	50 00	E. & A. Souder & Co.	5 00
William P. Wilstach	25 00	Henry G. Morris	5 00
John Sharpless	25 00	G. L. Oliver	5 00
J. V. Williamson	25 00	Henry McCroskey	5 00
J. H. Towne	25 00	Ann Haines	5 00
Israel W. Morris	20 00	S. Smith	5 00
John Robbins	20 00	Lydia White	5 00
C. H. Rogers	20 00	Edward Parrish	5 00
William W. Justice	20 00	E. S. Buckley	5 00
Cash per M. W. Horton	10 00	Wm. P. Cresson	5 00
Wm. A. Drown	10 00	John Thomas	5 00
J. B. Elliston & Sons	10 00	B. H. Shoemaker	5 00
Réné Guillou	10 00	James E. Caldwell	5 00
J. R. Carpenter	10 00	Evan Randolph	5 00
Susan Boss	10 00	Wm. Gaul	5 00
Hannah Morris	10 00	G. S. Fox	5 00
M. & J. Painter	10 00	J. E. Mitchell	5 00
Jehu Jones	10 00	Henry Sloan & Son	3 00
Charlotte S. Lewis	10 00	Stuart & Peterson	5 00
Stephen Colwell	10 00	Newhall & Borie	5 00
Geo. Vaux	10 00	Susan V. Greble	5 00
Edward Lewis	10 00	Geo. Milliken	5 00
A. H. Whildin & Sons	10 00	Charles E. Smith	5 00
J. W. Patten	10 00	J. K. & S.	5 00
G. W. Child	10 00	S. & T. Flanegan	5 00
M. S. Waln	10 00	J. R. Ingersoll	4 00
Isaac Winslow	10 00	M. A. W.	3 50
Rachel Haines, Md.	10 00	A Friend	2 00
Mrs. A. E. Carpenter	5 00	M. Regester	3 00
" B. Griffith	5 00	Anna Neall	3 00
" Elizabeth Lye	5 00	C. Lewars	2 00
James Allen	5 00	C. Linnard	1 00

* Through Ann Preston and Mary Jeanes.

Endowment Fund.

Cash received since last Report,

Sallie L. Crozer	$1000 00	John Mason	10 00
J. Lewis Crozer	500 00	J. F. Way	10 00
Alfred Cope	500 00	J. C.	10 00
R. Anna Cope	300 00	J. B. Myers	10 00
H. W. Richardson	437 38	Chas. Ellis	5 00
Susan Boss	100 00	Frederick Collins	5 00
Cash	167 62	Peter Williamson	5 00
S. J. Solms	100 00	E. W. Bailly	5 00
Wm. Houston	100 00	J. Wright	5 00
Anna M. Powers	100 00	Hannah Flickwir	5 00
William Sellers	50 00	G. B. Roberts	5 00
Henry Bowers	25 00	A. R. Perkins	5 00
Richard M. Marshall	25 00	T. J. Husband	5 00
Isaac Lea	25 00	Joseph Jones	5 00
Morris, Wheeler & Co.	25 00	R. Norris & Sons	5 00
Tatham & Brother	25 00	D. L. Brown	5 00
Mellor, Bains, & Mellor	25 00	F. Brown	5 00
Samuel French	25 00	E. C. Knight	5 00
Cooper & Graff	25 00	Alan Wood	5 00
Samuel Norris	10 00	J. K. Barclay	2 00
Chas. Sharpless	10 00	D. L. Collier	1 00

Donation for incidental expenses, paid . $30 97

The Managers return their cordial thanks for the following Donations, in articles:—

From Eliza S. Turner, $80, for the better remuneration of domestic service in the Hospital.

From W. H. & G. W. Allen, two dozen knives and forks; one doz. tea-spoons; one doz. table spoons; one ladle; one meat fork.

Thomas H. Powers, drugs, valued at $75 47.

Frederick Goos, one bushel pears.

A. Felton, garden plants.

Mrs. Mead, knives and forks.

Frederick Zais, matches.

Jane Mather, two bed-chairs and table.

Rebecca White, garden plants and shrubs, sorghum, pitcher, &c.

H. W. Richardson, two stoves, infants' clothing, &c.

Mary Jeanes, six bed-spreads.

Mr. M. Guire, one load kindling wood.

Mrs. E. Hatfield, three dozen bottles.

Large box of bottles from Mrs. C. S. Shinn.

Ladies of Darby, through Sarah Pearson, one pair of blankets, forty-eight pillow cases, thirty-five muslin garments.

Ridge Avenue Railroad Company, complimentary ticket.

REPORT

OF THE

BOARD OF TRUSTEES

OF THE

HOUSE OF REFORMATION,

FOR JUVENILE AND FEMALE OFFENDERS AGAINST THE LAWS,

TOGETHER WITH THE REPORTS

OF THE

SUPERINTENDENT AND TREASURER.

REPORT

OF THE

BOARD OF TRUSTEES

OF THE

HOUSE OF REFORMATION

FOR JUVENILE AND FEMALE OFFENDERS AGAINST THE LAWS,

TOGETHER WITH THE REPORTS

OF THE

SUPERINTENDENT AND TREASURER.

CONCORD:
GEORGE E. JENKS, STATE PRINTER.
1867.

OFFICE OF THE SECRETARY OF STATE,
Concord, New-Hampshire, June 1, 1867.

SIR: By virtue of authority vested in me by chapter 2398, Pamphlet Laws of this State, I hereby authorize you to print fifteen hundred copies of the Reports of the officers of the House of Reformation for the use of the State.

      WALTER HARRIMAN,
           Secretary of State.

GEORGE E. JENKS, *State Printer.*

OFFICERS OF THE INSTITUTION.

TRUSTEES.

HORTON D. WALKER, Esq., Portsmouth.
WILLIAM P. WHEELER, Esq., Keene.
D. C. CHURCHILL, Esq., Lyme.
DAVID GILLIS, Esq., Nashua.
JOSEPH KIDDER, Esq., Manchester.
MOSES HUMPHREY, Esq., Concord.
OLIVER WYATT, Esq., Dover.

HORTON D. WALKER, *President*.
JOSEPH KIDDER, *Secretary*.
CHARLES H. BARTLETT, *Treasurer*.
ISAAC H. JONES, *Superintendent*.
MRS. LOUISA J. JONES, *Matron*.

REPORT OF THE TRUSTEES.

To His Excellency the Governor and the Honorable Council:

GENTLEMEN :—In conformity with the act establishing the House of Reformation for Juvenile and Female Offenders against the Laws, the Board of Trustees have the pleasure herewith to present their

ELEVENTH ANNUAL REPORT.

In reviewing the history of the past year, we are impressed, at every turn, that whatever of success has crowned our labors, must be ascribed to Him who rules over all and is blessed for ever more. If Paul plants and Apollos waters, in the discharge of duty, God alone gives the increase. We most religiously believe in the truth of this sentiment; and in the performance of the high and responsible trusts committed to our charge, we have aimed to keep this thought uppermost in our minds. And now, as we trace the *Good Hand* that has directed so many, and, in some instances, perhaps, conflicting interests to a successful issue, for the year has been one of prosperity in the affairs of the Institution, our hearts fill with gratitude and thanksgiving for untold mercies.

At the time our last report was made, the Institution was really in distressed circumstances. Our large and handsome building was a heap of blackened ruins, an unsightly vestige of its former fair proportions. The *General Stark House* that furnished temporary accommodations for a portion of the children, was also in ashes, by the hand of an incendiary. Mr. Shattuck, who had stood at the head of the Institution from its first inception, and who, with his estimable lady, had done much to extend its popularity and usefulness, during ten years of difficult administration, with scanty means, had resigned his position to his successor in office. And children, officers and assistants, were huddled together at the Gamble house, with only such miserable accommodations for sleeping as made the Legislative Committee shudder as they passed into the hot and poorly ventilated attics to examine the premises, on the occasion of a flying visit to the Institution. The intellectual arrangements for the inmates were largely broken up; and regular, moral and religious training, in a measure necessarily dispensed with, although absolutely essential to the healthy discipline which should obtain in all reformatory institutions. The increased expenditures, in consequence of repeated disasters, had drained the treasury of the last dollar, and left a debt of some five thousand dollars, for which no provision had been made. Such was our condition on the first day of May, 1866. But as the summer advanced our prospects brightened. The rebuilding of the Institution had been entrusted to faithful and competent parties. Mr. Hilas Dickey had charge of the mason work, and Mr. Alpheus Gay was boss carpenter. Both these gentlemen fulfilled their contracts in a very satisfactory manner. The Legislature, seeing our pressing needs, was generous in its appropriations. And the new Superintendent, Mr. Isaac H. Jones, of Derry, entered upon his new and arduous labors with the will of one who means to succeed, no matter what obstacles are in the way. A gentleman of considerable experience in kindred institutions, humane and sympathetic in disposition, a good disciplinarian, and possessed of general intelligence, he soon brought order out of chaos, and established himself in the confidence of the Trustees, and all who had intimate knowledge of the school. So well satisfied were the Board with his management, under trying and difficult circumstances, that he was unanimously reëlected at the annual meeting in May, to take charge of the Institution for the current year. We trust he will in no wise disappoint those who are interested in the success of the school.

The new buildings were finished and occupied in October last. Some very valuable improvements were introduced and important additions made. The buildings are more thoroughly and completely finished than before. The steam and water works are greatly improved. A large and excellent oven has been built in the basement. Several new rooms have been partitioned off where there were none before. These are found to be very useful. A substantial brick addition, in place of a tumble-down wooden building, answers now the double purposes of a shed, and work-shop for the children engaged in sewing stockings. These, and many other changes, have enhanced the value of the property over and above what it was worth at the time of the fire, on the 20th of December 1865, in the estimation of the Board, not less than five or six thousand dollars. It is to be hoped that His Excellency, the Governor, and His Honorable Council, together with both Houses of the Legislature, will visit the Institution during the session, and witness, for themselves, what has been done since the last Legislative visit two years ago. We are confident you will be satisfied the money has been judiciously expended.

The crops raised upon the farm last year were very satisfactory, both in quantity and quality. The income from hay alone, as may be seen from the report of the Superintendent, was quite a large sum, after reserving enough for the use of the stock. And, by the way, we are glad to mention that there has been also a marked improvement in the extent and quality of the stock. While we are no advocates of *fancy farming*, yet, for the credit of the State, we confess to some degree of pride in making and keeping the Reform School farm so far a model in its culture, stock, and vegetable products, as to lead those who visit the Institution to copy the example set before them. Beside, the moral influence upon the children is a matter of no small magnitude. If the inmates are accustomed to see neatness, order, and thrift around them, as the result of well organized and well directed labor, it will beget in them corresponding habits whose influence will be exerted upon them, to a greater or less extent, so long as they shall live. Hence we hope the appropriations will always be large enough to carry on ample farming operations, with more and better stock than has heretofore been the case—having an eye to the best breeds, all things considered, to be found in the country. Good stock generally indicates a good farmer.

The fences are sadly out of repair. Indeed some parts of the farm are not fenced at all, nor have they ever been, so far as we are able to ascertain. It is important that the fences should be thoroughly repaired, and kept so at all times. Slovenly fences are a positive disgrace to any farmer, and it is not less discreditable to the State to allow her Reform School lands to remain without substantial and sightly inclosures. Heretofore, lack of means has been the assigned reason for this neglect. We trust this excuse will not be valid much longer. It is the opinion of the Board that the means should be sufficient to make some permanent improvements upon the grounds every year, so long as they shall be needed.

The earnings of the Institution, for the past year, compare favorably with former years. If not so large as some might think they ought to be, it may be said, in reply, that the children do not average as old or as large in size as was the case five years ago. Many of the older and stouter boys, filled with a commendable spirit of patriotism, went to the war and performed faithful service for their country in its time of peril. The terms of others have expired by limitation; while not a few, whose labor was the most valuable, have been honorably discharged by the Board. A good per cent of the latter class now find employment in useful and honorable stations in life. Having been started on the right track, we may reasonably expect that they will hereafter reflect credit, both upon themselves and the Institution.

Formerly, under the act establishing the Institution, " boys under the age of eighteen years," and "females of any age," convicted of crime, might be sentenced to the House of Reformation. Under this provision, at least one female, nearly forty years old, became an inmate; and there is reason to believe that many boys, older than the law provided, to escape a severer alternate sentence in prison, understated their ages and gained admission to the House. Subsequently, the act was amended, and now " no person above the age of seventeen years " can be lawfully admitted. Beside, the courts having jurisdiction in these matters, and men interested in the reformation of juvenile offenders, begin to see that children between the ages of eight and twelve years are more susceptible to reformatory influences than those between fifteen and seventeen; while the presence of the latter class, if hardened in vicious ways, counteracts the moral force of the teachers, and exerts a deleterious power on the younger inmates. Hence the more "juvenile" the "offenders against the laws" are, the more hope there is that the House of Reformation will accomplish for them its highest and truest mission.

The House of Reformation, we would impress upon the courts and police justices, as well as our citizens generally, is not to be regarded as simply a place of punishment.

Fines are imposed, and imprisonments in jails and penitentiaries are secured for this purpose; while the Reform School is designed, in accordance with the plan of its benevolent founder, Hon. JAMES MCKEEN WILKINS, to reform, educate and save our wayward youth from the fearful consequences that follow continued criminal action. For, let it be remembered, many of those sent to our Institution are more the victims of unfavorable circumstances, than of innate depravity and vicious dispositions. Look over the tables presented in the Superintendent's report, and observe how many of our children have lost either father or mother, or both, at tender ages, and are left with none to care for them and lead them in paths of peace; or having parents, were really in a worse condition than if they were helpless orphans. How many have come from the highways and by-ways of life, where their homes were but hovels, and all their surroundings of the most vicious character. Poverty and idleness, coupled together, as they often are, with ignorance added, beget crimes, and draw children of weak moral perceptions, into the slippery paths of temptation. Now, these children of misfortune, we would redeem and restore to the State; and if our efforts are successful, a term of one to ten years at the Reform School is a great blessing, rather than a punishment and a disgrace. No boy, or girl, who goes out with good habits firmly established, and high aims to lead him on in life, need ever look back with sorrow or shame to his connection with this excellent Institution. To him it will be the starting point of a noble career; and may God bless all such graduates.

There are many children in the State, deprived of the advantages of this Institution, simply because the towns, through their officers, refuse to incur the expense of one dollar per week, in payment for board and clothing. These "fathers of the town," allow children to grow up in idleness and ignorance until arrested by the strong arm of the law, in preference to subjecting the town to a small tax. We regard this as an unwise policy, in every respect. It is poor economy in the long run, and leaves the child to pursue a ruinous course of life unchecked, until the commission of some glaring crime that startles the whole community. To obviate this difficulty, the people must be enlightened in regard to the nature and purposes of reformatory institutions, or else the State must assume the entire management of the Reform School and defray all its expenses. Were the latter plan adopted, there is no doubt that the number of inmates would be more than doubled within a single year. With the present accommodations, the number might be largely increased, without a proportionate additional expense. It would require no more officers than are now necessarily employed about the Institution.

Intimately connected with this topic is another which has escaped general attention, but which is often brought to our notice. It is of frequent occurrence that a lad is arrested and thrown into jail to await his trial. This is delayed, sometimes for weeks and even months. It may have been the boy's first grave offense. He may have been induced to commit the offense by older and more wary parties. Perhaps he did not realize the guilt that attached to his conduct. His former associates may not have been of the vilest sort. But lodged in jail, he mingles with every grade of criminals, and possibly is put into a cell with the most hardened villains. Here he becomes familiar with every ingenious and well-laid plan for robbing and stealing. The whole vocabulary of the jail is poured into his ears only to poison his heart. And when, at last, he comes to trial, and is sentenced to the House of Reformation, it may require years to undo what he has learned of his vile companions in jail. How long will those having the care of our jails thus put in jeopardy the highest interests of those in their charge who are young and comparatively innocent? To the honor of the State these remarks do not apply to all our jails.

Several of the clergymen of Manchester have rendered essential service, the past year, as in former times, in conducting religious services on the Sabbath, in the presence of the children. We are aware that this " labor of love " is a tax upon the time and energies of the ministry of the city, for which we can return no just equivalent. Their reward must be found in the sweet consolation of having contributed to the success of a noble cause. Among those to whom we are under especial obligations, we would mention Rev. Dr. C. W. Wallace, Revs. T. P. Sawin, A. M. Haskell, S. L. Roripaugh, N. C. Mallory, W. H. Thomas, J. A. Knowles, N. Brooks, and Rev. Mr. Wilkins, of Rochester. We thank these gentlemen most sincerely for the services rendered, and trust it will be a pleasure to them to respond to any similar demand that may hereafter be made upon them. In passing, we would say that on the last Sabbath in April, *thirty clergymen* from the *Methodist Conference* visited the Institution, several of whom made interesting and appropriate remarks. We cordially invite ministers of all denominations to visit the School at their convenience, and become interested in this reform enterprise.

For a long time it has been the opinion of the Board, and many friends, that the " Gamble estate " would be a valuable acquisition; but various difficulties were in the way of obtaining it. The various parties owning it were not agreed upon a price for which they would dispose of it. The place, originally, was a part of the Gen. Stark Farm. It would give us a straight and continuous line on the south from the Merrimack to the old road. It embraces some five or six acres of excellent land, and would make the westerly half of the farm a "square lot." There is upon it a large house, barn and out-buildings. They are the premises occupied by us, for nearly a year, while waiting for the new buildings. Some time ago a committee was appointed to get a proposition from the owners to sell. We finally succeeded, and now hold a bond for a deed running until the first of next September. It will be for you, and the coördinate branches of the government, to say whether the purchase shall be completed. It can be bought only by act of the Legislature. Price $2,590. We believe it to be a desirable purchase.

One of the great losses, occasioned by the fire, was the interruption and suspension of the regular school exercises for nearly a whole year. On the first of December last, the school was reorganized and opened under favorable circumstances. The children were all very backward in the primary branches. They could read but poorly, as a general statement, and had but little knowledge of spelling, geography or arithmetic. Only two or three of the boys could write a legible hand. But under the patient and persevering efforts of Miss Rogers and Miss Wilkins, the progress made in these several departments was marked and satisfactory. All things considered, the school never appeared to better advantage on examination day, than it did this year. This is the testimony, so far as we know, of all the visitors in attendance, and many distinguished gentlemen were present. Two interesting features of the occasion were the presentation of prizes, offered by *Mrs. Moody Currier*, to those who made the greatest proficiency in their studies, and whose average deportment was the best, and the honorable discharge of three of the children. Their names are George Welland, of Dover, Thomas Haley, New Salem, and Ellen Whidden, Manchester. This latter ceremony was performed by the President of the Board, Hon. HORTON D. WALKER, in the most feeling and impressive manner. We trust that the words of wisdom that dropped eloquently from his lips, will not be without a salutary influence. Several other gentlemen made interesting and appropriate remarks.

We can not close this Report without reiterating our belief that the institution, committed to our charge, is one of the most important and useful in the State. Thus far it has succeeded beyond the expectations of its most sanguine friends. The strong opposition that once existed against it, in many parts of the State, has ceased; and those unfriendly to the enterprise, in its earlier stages, becoming familiar with its aims and operations, may now be ranked among its warmest advocates. Indeed, it is now felt to be a necessity, as much so as the Asylum for the Insane. While the one treats physical and mental maladies, the other seeks to cure moral infirmities, and to open to its juvenile inmates a future full of usefulness and unsullied joy. It removes the temptations that lurk in the paths of idleness; it cultivates habits of industry; stimulates a love of labor, as a means of livelihood, and taste for study; and more than all, it subjects the children to a course of healthy discipline, and brings them under the influence of moral and religious training. Impressed with the importance of this great work, we invoke the aid and sympathy of the Legislature, and commit the Institution, with all its varied interests, to the care and protection of our Heavenly Father, in full faith, that he who suffers not a sparrow to fall to the ground without his friendly notice, will not neglect these precious ones, who "are of more value than many sparrows."

JOSEPH KIDDER,
Secretary of Board of Trustees.

Manchester, May 31, 1867.

SUPERINTENDENT'S REPORT.

To the Honorable Board of Trustees of the House of Reformation for Juvenile and Female Offenders against the Laws:

GENTLEMEN:—The tenth annual Report of this Institution is herewith respectfully submitted.

TABLE No. 1,

Shows the number received and discharged and the general state of the school for the year ending April 30, 1867.

	Boys.	Girls.	Total.
In the House April 30, 1866,	61	27	88
Committed since,	29	3	32
Escaped inmates returned,	6		6
Whole number in the House during the year,	96	30	126
Honorably discharged before expiration of sentence,	6	3	9
Discharged at the expiration of sentence,	9	5	14
Discharged to the care of friends,	9	2	11
Sent to alternate,	4		4
Escaped,	9		9
Remaining in the House April 30, 1867,	59	20	79

Average time of detention of 34 children discharged in 1866–7, 1 year, 10 months, 8 days.

TABLE No. 2,

Shows by what Authority Committed.

	1867.	Previously.	Total.
By Supreme Judicial Court,	9	47	56
By Concord Police Court,	5	22	27
By Dover Police Court,		17	17
By Nashua Police Court,		36	36
By Manchester Police Court,	7	97	104
By Portsmouth Police Court,	1	24	25
By Somersworth Police Court,	3		3
By Justices of the Peace,	7	138	145
State Prison sentence commuted by Executive,		1	1
	32	382	414

TABLE No. 3,

Shows term of Commitment.

	1867.	Previously.	Total.
During minority,	13	145	158
For ten years,		1	1
For eight years,		3	3
For seven years,		9	9
For six years,		8	8
For five years,	4	12	16
For four years,		15	15
For three and one half years,		1	1
For three and one fourth years,	1		1
For three years,	4	55	59
For two and one half years,	2		2
For two years,	2	63	65
For one and two thirds years,		1	1
For one and one half years,	1	4	5
For one year,	5	64	69
For six months,		1	1
	32	382	414

TABLE No. 4,

Shows the offenses for which committed.

	1867.	Previously.	Total.
Assault,	1	10	11
Barn-burning,		2	2
Drunkenness,		5	5
Horse-stealing,		8	8
House and shop-breaking,	5	22	27
Lewdness,		7	7
Poisoning,	1		1
Runaway,		2	2
Stealing,	14	155	169
Stubbornness,	3	76	79
Street begging,		1	1
Truancy,	4	24	28
Vagrancy,	4	70	74
	32	382	414

TABLE NO. 5,

Shows the Alternate Sentence.

	1867.	Previously.	Total.
State Prison 7 years,		2	2
" 6 "		1	1
" 5 "	3	2	5
" 4 "	1	3	4
" 3 "		14	14
" 2 "	2	21	23
" 1½ "		1	1
" 1 "	1	5	6
Jail 2 years,		4	4
" 12 months,	1	2	2
" 9 "		1	1
" 6 "		14	14
" 4 "		2	2
" 3 "	2	56	58
" 2 "	1	23	24
" 1½ "		2	2
" 1 "	4	45	49
" 25 days,		1	1
" 10 "		1	1

House of Correction	6 months,			7	82	89
"	"	4	"	1	3	4
"	"	3	"		9	9
"	"	2	"		9	9
"	"	1	"	1	25	26
Fined,				2	45	47
No alternative,				6	9	15
				32	382	414

TABLE NO. 6,

Shows Nativity.

	1867.	Previously.	Total.
Born in Canada,		4	4
" Connecticut,		1	1
" England,	1	4	5
" Germany,		1	1
" Ireland,		18	18
" Kentucky,		1	1
" Maryland,		1	1
" Maine,		15	15
" Massachusetts,	3	51	54
" New-Hampshire,	23	224	247
" New-York,	2	10	12
" Ohio,		2	2
" Prince Edward's Island,		2	2
" Rhode-Island,		3	3
" Vermont,	3	18	21
Birthplace unknown,		27	27
	32	382	414

TABLE NO. 7,

Shows Age when committed.

	1867.	Previously.	Total.
Eight years old,	1	11	12
Nine years old,	2	21	23
Ten years old,	3	19	22
Eleven years old,	2	44	46
Twelve years old,	5	46	51

Thirteen years old,	4	51	55
Fourteen years old,	4	72	76
Fifteen years old,	6	46	52
Sixteen years old,	5	63	68
Age unknown,		9	9
	32	382	414

Average age, 13 years 3¾ months.

TABLE NO. 8,

Shows moral, social and home influence before commitment, gathered from their statements, and other sources.

	1867.	Previously.	Total.
Have lost fathers,	8	132	140
Have lost mothers,	7	92	99
Have lost both,	2	29	31
Have step-fathers,	1	28	29
Have step-mothers,	4	32	36
Have intemperate fathers,	16	138	154
Have intemperate mothers,	4	46	50
Have fathers without a regular occupation,	11	105	116
Who were mostly idle previous to commitment,	17	204	221
Who were profane,	19	242	261
Who had not regularly attended Sabbath-school,	17	215	232
Who had not regularly attended church,	16	316	332
Who have slept in barns, sheds and similar places,	12	173	185
Who had used tobacco,	16	140	156
Who had used intoxicating drinks,	10	136	146
Arrested once before,	6	58	64
Arrested twice before,	3	48	51
Arrested three times before,	3	25	28
Arrested more than three times,	2	36	38

The above table can not be perfectly accurate, but it gives an approximate statement.

TABLE No. 9.

Office and Library.

Tables and chairs,	$28 00	
Sofa and lounge,	12 00	
Stamping press,	5 00	
Library books,	50 00	
Clock,	30 00	
Books and stationery,	20 00	
		$145 00

TABLE No. 10.

Reception Room and Guest Chamber.

Carpet,	$100 00	
Center and side-tables,	9 00	
Curtains,	8 00	
Sofas and chairs,	50 00	
One set chamber furniture,	40 00	
Bedding,	55 00	
Chamber carpet,	15 00	
		$277 00

TABLE No. 11.

Officers' Rooms and Hospital.

9 bedsteads, beds and bedding,	$360 00	
3 wardrobes,	24 00	
Other furniture,	60 00	
		$444 00

TABLE No. 12.

School-rooms.

40 settees,	$180 00	
50 double desks and 100 chairs,	300 00	
36 double desks, with chairs damaged,	175 00	
Teacher's desk and chairs,	24 00	
Melodeon,	18 00	
School books,	230 00	
Lamps,	7 00	
		$934 00

TABLE No. 13.
Workshop.

58 chairs,	$14 50	
Work-table,	10 00	
Lamps,	4 00	
Clock,	2 00	
Shears, needles, &c.,	3 00	
	———	$33 50

TABLE No. 14.
Shoe-shop.

46 pairs new shoes,	$92 00	
Leather and findings,	12 00	
Lasts and tools,	16 00	
	———	$120 00

TABLE No. 15.
Children's Cook Room and Dining Hall.

Cooking stove and furniture,	$40 00	
Wash-dishes,	3 00	
Crockery,	20 00	
Tin ware,	55 00	
Wooden ware,	5 00	
Iron ware, baking pans, &c.,	12 00	
1 clock,	3 00	
Bread trough and table,	12 00	
97 stoves,	48 50	
14 tables,	42 00	
1 movable closet,	8 00	
	———	$248 50

TABLE No. 16.
Sleeping Halls.

126 iron bedsteads,	$157 50
84 mattresses,	168 00
100 single blankets,	150 00
100 pairs blankets,	275 00

264 sheets,	211 20	
100 spreads,	150 00	
Other bedding,	80 00	
Furniture,	6 00	
		$1,197 70

TABLE No. 17.

Family Cook Room, Dining Room and Pantry.

Cook stove and furniture,	$50 00	
Crockery, glass, tin and wooden ware,	55 00	
Knives and forks,	13 00	
Dining table and chairs,	32 00	
Tables and movable closets,	30 00	
Refrigerator,	4 00	
		$184 00

TABLE No. 18.

Bath Room, Wash Room and Laundry.

Bathing tank,	$100 00	
Towels and rollers,	8 00	
2 wringers,	24 00	
Pails and brushes,	8 00	
6 wash tubs,	4 00	
2 rinsing tanks,	8 00	
30 pairs drying bars,	30 00	
32 flat-irons and stands,	11 00	
Laundry stove,	10 00	
Tables,	9 00	
		$212 00

TABLE No. 19.

Provision and Store Room.

2½ barrels flour,	$33 00	
216 pounds ham,	38 88	
14 gallons kerosene,	7 70	
12 gallons molasses,	7 20	
10 gallons vinegar,	5 00	
30 bushels corn,	37 50	
26 bushels potatoes,	19 50	
275 pounds pork,	34 37	
4½ bushels beans,	13 50	
6 stoves, not in use,	30 00	
		$226 65

TABLE No. 20.

Girls' Sewing Room.

1 work table,	$8 00
Clock,	2 00
20 chairs,	5 00
Buttons, thread, &c.,	8 00
Cloth on hand,	34 00
Boys' clothing,	48 00
18 caps, $9; 16 hats, $2 50;	11 50
72 pairs socks, new,	26 00
60 pairs socks, old,	6 00
12 new shirts,	12 00
Girls' clothing,	85 00
Other articles,	7 00
	$247 50

TABLE No. 21.

Stock and Farming Utensils.

4 cows,	$280 00
2 pairs oxen,	530 00
3 horses,	395 00
11 shotes,	170 00
Poultry,	8 00
2 ox carts,	80 00
1 horse cart,	50 00
2 farm wagons,	90 00
1 buggy wagon,	60 00
1 express wagon,	80 00
2 sleighs,	90 00
1 hay rack,	12 00
Stone drags,	5 00
Harnesses and robes,	78 00
2 wheelbarrows,	14 00
5 plows, 3 harrows, 1 cultivator,	54 00
2 grindstones, 1 seed sower,	22 00
7 manure forks, 5 iron bars,	14 50
15 scythes and snaths,	21 50
Hay-cutter and feed boxes,	11 00
12 shovels, 11 spades,	13 50
26 hoes, 2 bog hoes,	8 00

1 hoe, 2 picks,	4 00
Scale beam,	7 00
Stone hammers and drills,	14 00
Rope and blocks,	5 00
Pitchforks and rakes,	9 00
Axes, saws and wedges,	9 00
Other small tools,	7 00
3 ox yokes,	13 00
Chains,	11 00
Fanning mill,	11 00
	$2,176 50

TABLE No. 22.

Amount and estimated value of Produce raised.

7 tons corn fodder,	84 00
38 tons hay,	950 00
315 bushels corn,	354 37
640 " potatoes,	480 00
166 " carrots,	84 00
27 " beans,	67 50
1696 heads cabbage,	66 84
20 bushels beets,	10 00
2 tons squashes,	30 00
Peas and other vegetables,	35 00
Osier willows,	36 50
Apples, 40 bushels,	20 00
Pork slaughtered, 3115 lbs.	
Milk, 3500 quarts (estimated).	
	$2,218 21

Summary.

Furniture and bedding,	$3,420 70
Farming tools and stock,	2,176 50
Clothing,	324 50
Provisions and groceries,	196 65
Books, stationery, &c.,	300 00
Stock and tools in shoe shop,	28 00
	$6,446 35

The steam apparatus for heating, cooking, and washing, as also the water-pipes, sinks, &c., being regarded as fixtures of the house, are not inserted in any of the foregoing tables. Their approximate value is about $5000.

DETAILED EXPENDITURES.

Salaries and Wages.

J. H. Jones, Superintendent,	$800 00
Joseph M. Rowell, Overseer,	176 38
J. A. Davis, "	325 00
Daniel Readey, "	347 66
Leonard N. George, "	14 00
Watson C. Atwell, "	41 50
F. W. Smyth, Steward,	172 00
Noah Glover, "	76 92
Charles Shattuck, "	222 50
Henry T. LeBosquet, Watchman,	120 00
C. P. Connelly, "	84 00
David A. Wilson, "	4 50
John Conner, "	54 00
A. C. Rogers, teacher,	77 00
H. M. Wilkins, "	61 25
M. J. Eaton, book-keeper,	174 50
E. A. Rose, teacher boys' sewing room,	157 00
M. E. LeBosquet, teacher girls' sewing room,	81 50
Cora E. Wingate, " " " "	72 86
Jennie A. Osgood,	69 86
Mrs. A. D. Glover, cook for family,	53 25
E. M. Howard, " "	18 00
Hattie Dockham, " "	7 50
	$3,163 18

Groceries and Provisions.

Wm. Starr, bread and crackers,	1,311 11
J. S. Kidder, flour, grain, fish,	764 75
French, Hall & Co., flour and meal,	245 63
J. Abbott & Co., meal,	60 18
Lewis Rice, groceries,	35 90
John S. Folsom,	13 62
Kidder & Chandler,	1,039 73
H. B. Putnam,	8 83
Cook & Miller, butter and cheese,	110 22
Mrs. Sleeper, eggs, fish,	19 50
J. Rowley, potatoes,	14 64
Merrill & Drake, coffee, pepper, &c.,	48 94

Charles Shattuck, dried berries,	3 25
Mrs. Yeaton, eggs,	2 65
A. H. Glines, coffee,	1 00
J. M. Rowell, butter,	5 63
Horace A. Hill, apples,	7 00
J. B. Ellinwood, apples,	14 12
Brown & Flanders, ice,	4 00
H. & H. R. Pettee, flour and oats,	40 50
J. S. Holt, soap,	45 50
R. W. Lang, soap,	1 00
M. C. Eastman, soap,	51 25
	$3,848 95

Dry Goods.

Barton & Co., cotton cloth, gingham, &c.,	379 37
Kidder & Chandler, cassimere, cotton cloth, &c.,	442 43
Jackson & Co., dry goods,	32 25
G. S. Holmes, "	3 68
Fearing & Co., stockings, &c.,	8 90
J. T. Wiggin, caps, straw hats,	49 28
J. Truesdale, straw hats,	4 10
L. W. Eastman, girls' hat,	2 55
John Brugger, stockings,	48 50
Mrs. Cheney, skirts,	10 30
J. Peabody, girls' hats, thread, needles, &c.,	40 20
A. B. Page, ribbon,	1 25
	$1,022 76

Meats.

James O. Clark, beef,	616 34
Cook & Miller, meat and fish,	346 33
Mrs. Yeaton, pork,	14 16
Mrs. Sleeper, pork, poultry,	38 91
O. Gage, making sausages,	2 85
	$1,018 59

Medicines and Medical attendance.

Leonard French, medical attendance,	$57 50
Josiah Crosby, " "	2 50
A. F. Perry, medicines,	29 94
J. R. Hanson, "	87
	$90 81

Postage and Freight.

Post-office, stamps, box rent,	$14 01
C. M. & L. Railroad Cor., transportation,	41 29
Hill & Co., "	17 48
Thos. Chase, freight paid out,	1 44
Vermont & Boston Telegraph Co., telegrams,	1 40
	$75 62

Farm Stock.

Ward Parker, oxen,	$225 00
Oliver Bailey, "	305 00
George Davis, "	250 00
Hiram Colby, horse,	175 00
J. S. Holt, "	160 00
Daniel Shirley, heifer,	68 00
Ezra Kimball, pig,	7 00
	$1,190 00

Books and Stationery.

H. C. Tilton, stationery,	$84 25
Wm. H. Fisk, "	7 04
J. W. Moore, singing books,	1 32
John B. Clarke, printing blanks,	4 00
A. Quimby, ink powders,	2 40
	$99 01

Fuel and Lights.

D. G. Roberts, wood,	$733 89
J. P. Rowell, "	43 00
E. P. Johnson, coal,	191 10
Kidder & Chandler, kerosene and sperm oil,	183 93
L. H. James, drawing wood,	487 75
	$1,639 67

Trustees' Expenses.

Horton D. Walker,	$52 15
D. C. Churchill,	72 00
Wm. P. Wheeler,	33 68
R. N. Ross,	17 50
	$175 33

Boots and Shoes.

T. L. Hastings, shoes,	$9 85
Geo. W. Dodge, "	11 75
J. M. Robinson, boots and shoes,	105 65
Kimball & Dow, " "	138 27
Durgin & Dodge, women's boots,	2 00
J. Stickney, leather and shoe findings,	131 71
Ezra Kimball " " " "	40 25
	$439 48

Building Improvements.

T. R. Hubbard, lumber,	$415 55
Gay & Dickey, extra plastering, partitions, &c.,	842 98
Haines & Wallace, lumber,	20 05
Amoskeag Manufacturing Co., grates, rods, iron door frame,	30 87
John B. Varick, iron for rods,	89 33
J. F. Woodbury, making rods,	28 00
J. M. & S. F. Stanton, iron door and labor,	52 67
Wm. W. Hubbard, columns, caps, &c.,	12 50
Hartshorn & Pike, sink, faucets, labor, &c.,	19 01
J. C. Young, repairing roof,	18 75
Daniels & Co., locks, paint, glass, &c.,	145 14
J. Q. A. Sargent, pipe, findings, gage, labor,	58 08
H. M. Bailey & Son, plaster,	90
A. Wicom, laying floor,	25 00
H. A. Davis, plastering,	11 25
	$1,770 08

Farm Expenses.

Timothy Sullivan, manure,	$40 00
J. G. Eaton, "	30 44

William Parker, manure,	14 12
George W. Cheney, "	80 00
Patrick O'Brien, shoveling manure,	30 00
Michael Daulton, "	30 00
Patrick Hagerty, "	6 00
Daniels & Co., phosphate lime, seeds, &c.,	40 51
B. P. Rice, seed potatoes,	33 30
D. G. Roberts, "	8 00
Fisher & Cram, tomato plants, farm seed,	13 52
J. G. Colt, arbor vitæ,	34 40
Davis & Chadwick, tile,	9 60
French, Hall & Co., cement,	5 50
J. Bradley, drain pipe,	87 40
Edwin Branch, repairing harness,	20 77
J. S. Kidder, cement,	2 75
George W. Gould, painting cart,	5 00
R. Bunton, bridge stone,	8 25
H. & H. R. Pettee, cement,	3 00
	$502 56

Tools and Implements.

Amoskeag Axe Co., axes,	$4 25
John B. Varic, tools, farm implements, &c.,	93 16
Daniels & Co., tools,	107 63
J. E. Wilbur, "	13 75
Kidder & Chandler, farm tools,	33 53
J. M. & S. F. Stanton, repairing vise,	2 84
William P. Ford, farm implements,	4 75
Plumer & Chandler, sewing machine,	65 00
F. N. McLaren, curry combs, brushes, &c.,	1 50
Edwin Branch, whips,	4 37
Hartshorn & Pike,	24 00
Peter Kimball,	2 50
J. McCrillis, plank for carts,	9 16
Haines & Wallace, lumber for carts,	17 64
A. Wicom, making carts,	26 33
	$410 41

Blacksmithing.

J. F. Woodbury,	$48 21
Fellows & Co.,	45 14

J. E. Wilbur,	8 50
Charles Bunton,	60 21
	$162 06

Insurance.

N. E. Morrill, Agent,	314 75

Furniture and Bedding.

Lewis Rice, lanterns,	$3 00
Hartshorn & Pike, kitchen furniture,	79 58
Robert Gilchrist, crockery, lamps, &c.,	100 11
Barton & Co., spreads and blankets,	49 50
H. M. Bailey, cooking utensils, lamps, &c.,	3 93
G. F. Bosher, bedsteads and bedding,	116 60
Albert Webster, clock,	30 00
Charles A. Smith, crockery and lamps,	33 54
Kidder & Chandler, blankets,	33 00
David Libbey, seating chairs,	5 85
A. O. Parker, bedroom furniture,	220 39
Jackson & Co., quilts,	6 75
D. F. Straw, clocks, &c.,	29 31
	$711 56

In consequence of Fire.

Gay & Dickey, building boiler-house, shop, oven and tank,	$3,319 73
J. Q. A. Sargent, steam works,	2,016 59
W. H. Wentworth, plumbing,	628 15
Hartshorn & Pike, sinks, water closets, lead pipe, &c.,	148 10
Gregg & Dodge, disconnecting pipe,	16 40
Kidder & Chandler, sheeting, ticking, paints,	216 52
G. B. Fogg, spring locks, &c.,	63 00
Levi D. Green, painting and varnishing desks,	11 00
R. Bunton, stone,	14 25
J. C. Young, roofing,	97 35
Wm. O. Haskell, school furniture,	624 20
Fellows & Co., fitting iron bedsteads,	37 55
George W. Gould, painting blackboards,	5 25
Conant, Woods & Co., blanketing,	209 25
M. Charles & Co., counterpanes,	159 58

Barton & Co., sheeting, gingham, ticking,	200 00
H. C. Tilton, school books,	191 93
N. H. Bible Society testaments,	20 00
N. P. Kemp, hymn books,	4 00
Wm. Starr, cost of baking bread,	560 00
John B. Clarke, advertising reward,	9 00
Henry Clough, reward for apprehending Wiggin,	100 00
A. G. Fairbanks, board of boys at jail,	47 37
E. Gambrell and S. S. Abbot, rent of house,	310 00
	$9,009 22

Miscellaneous.

James E. Rand, returning boy,	3 25
P. B. Putney, fire-crackers,	4 25
Thos. G. Banks, returning boy,	6 00
John Prince, removing body to Raymond,	3 00
J. H. Jones, incidentals,	79 33
R. W. Lang, washing,	190 15
W. G. Hoyt, horse hire,	2 50
Isaac Aldrich, returning runaway,	15 00
J. A. Davis, sundries,	6 40
C. W. Harvey, examining accounts,	10 40
Henry Clough, police services,	21 37
Hill & James, horse hire,	1 50
Wilton Manufacturing Co., interest on bill,	2 80
W. H. Elliot, repairing melodeon,	8 50
Mrs. Sleeper, sundries,	15 19
H. C. Hunton, teaming,	4 75
Amoskeag Manufacturing Co., grate bars,	55 16
Brooks Shattuck,	695 00
	$1,124 55

SUMMARY OF EXPENDITURES.

Salaries and wages,	$3,163 18
Groceries and provisions,	8,848 95
Dry goods,	1,022 76
Meats,	1,018 59
Medicines and medical attendance,	90 81
Postage and freight,	75 62
Farm stock,	1,190 00

Books and stationery,	99 01
Fuel and lights,	1,639 67
Trustees' expenses,	175 33
Boots and shoes,	439 48
Building improvements,	1,770 08
Farm expenses,	502 56
Tools and implements,	410 41
Blacksmithing,	162 06
Insurance,	314 75
Furniture and bedding,	711 56
In consequence of fire,	9,009 22
Miscellaneous,	1,124 55
	$26,768 59

Resources.

Board of children,	$4,097 68
Stockings made,	1,034 50
Stock sold,	966 21
Hay sold,	590 91
Wood sold,	304 92
Balance insurance,	1,000 00
Sundries,	92 02
	$8,086 24

BALANCE SHEET.

The entire expenses for the current year amount to $26,768 59.

From this deduct bills not properly belonging to the running expenses; namely,

Extra expense, in consequence of fire,	$9,009 22
Building improvements,	1,770 08
Farm improvements,	110 50
Farm stock,	233 00
Furniture,	456 24
Miscellaneous,	695 00
Leaving for running expenses,	$14,485 55
Earnings of Institution,	8,086 24
Balance against Institution,	$6,402 31

Claims against the Institution,	$3,997 94
Due the Treasurer,	2,000 00
	$5,997 94
Amount due the Institution,	2,852 75
Balance against the Institution,	$3,145 19

At the date of the last annual report, the children were crowded together in close and uncomfortable quarters, at the Gamble House, where it was almost impossible to obtain proper ventilation.

We continued there during the summer, fearing sickness, but fortunately were spared, and the general health of the inmates was very good.

On the 27th of October we occupied our newly erected and repaired building, and were relieved from the inconveniences attending our narrow quarters.

Our time was fully occupied until winter, in regulating and fitting up the inside and clearing round the outside of the house.

The schools, after a vacation of twenty months, were commenced the first week in December; the boys, in charge of Miss A. C. Rogers and Miss E. A. Rose; the girls, under the care of Miss H. M. Wilkins. These ladies labored faithfully during the winter, as the advancement made by the pupils showed satisfactorily.

·The subjoined tables show the classification of the schools and the promotions during the term.

The school commenced Dec. 3, 1866. Number of boys at commencement of the term, 58. Sixteen boys have been received during the term, making the whole number under instruction, 74. They were classed as follows:

Reading.

In primer,	25
In 2d reader,	12
In 3d "	21
In 4th "	11
In 5th "	5
Total,	74

Arithmetic.

Primary Arithmetic,	50
Intellectual "	24
Written, "	11
Deducting those twice numbered,	11
Total,	74

Geography.

Colton & Fitch's Introductory Geography,	24
" " Modern "	19

History.

United States History,	6

Spelling.

All spell by oral, written or printed exercises,	74

Writing.

All receive instruction in writing, either in Payson & Dunton's writing books, or on the black-board.

Promotions during the term.

In Reading.

From Primer to 2d Reader,	21
" 2d to 3d "	6
" 3d to 4th "	6
" 4th to 5th "	3

Arithmetic.

From Primary Arithmetic to Intellectual,	12

Girls' School.

Number of girls under instruction,	21

Classification in reading.

Commenced the primer,	2
" " 2d reader,	3
" " 3d "	3
" " 4th "	5
" " 5th "	8
Total,	21

In Arithmetic.

Commenced Primary Arithmetic,	9
" Intellectual "	10
" Written "	9
Deducting those twice numbered,	9
Total,	19

Geography.

Commenced Introductory,	8
" Modern,	8
Total,	16

History.

Number studying History,	6

Writing.

In books,	20

Promotions during the term.

To 2d reader,	1
" 3d "	2
" 4th "	3

The annual examination was held April 10, and was fully attended. Gentlemen who were present expressed themselves pleased and satisfied with the appearance of the school.

By vote of the Trustees, the school is to be continued through the summer, giving to each pupil three hours a day for study. Miss A. C. Rogers has charge of both the schools at the present time—the girls during one portion of the day and the boys in another.

The children who come to us are (most of them) very little advanced in scholarship. Many of them will receive but little school instruction after leaving this place. Hence, it is of the greatest importance that, while here, they should be advanced in education as far as possible. It is hoped that, in the future, all who leave the school will at least have a fair knowledge of the common branches of study.

The school is an important aid—one hardly to be over-estimated—in the reformation of its pupils, and, under its present management, we may reasonably expect the best results.

GENERAL REMARKS.

A large portion of the time the last season was employed upon the ruins of the old house, and clearing away the *debris* around the new one, cleaning brick, &c. This, beside the regular farm labor, left but little time for improvements.

We have built two substantial stone bridges over the the brook north-east of the house, giving ready access to the field beyond. About thirty rods of stone drain have been laid, which is doing good service in draining the land upon which our corn is planted the present season. A stone-pipe drain has been laid from the barn-yard, which discharges with beneficial results over the mowing ground south of the barn. Seven or eight acres of the Stark hill have been cleared of bushes and stones, and burnt over, to be planted with potatoes the present season.

We have sold hay to the amount of more than $600,

and have expended about one half the sum in manure for the farm.

We have cultivated about thirteen acres of ground, with the results given in a preceding table. In the shop, the small boys, under the care of Miss E. A. Rose, have been employed, as formerly, in making stockings, and have earned the sum of $1,116.16.

The girls have been busy in the regular work of making, mending, and washing the clothes of the inmates. An extra amount of sewing was necessary to make good the losses by the fire. This has been performed, and we have now all needful clothing, bedding, &c., for our present number.

LIBRARY.

Another year of wear upon the remnant of our library leaves it sadly in need of replenishing. Its books are still read with interest and benefit to the scholars, but an addition is greatly needed, and we trust it will be remembered.

ACKNOWLEDGMENTS.

We would tender our thanks to the publishers of the following papers for copies gratuitously furnished for the use of the school: Manchester Daily Mirror, Concord Daily Monitor, Independent Democrat, Portsmouth Journal, New-Hampshire Gazette, Granite State Free Press, Claremont Eagle, Morning Star, Waltham Free Press; also to Mr. White, of Concord, for the Anti-Slavery Standard. The Sabbath at Home also reaches us regularly.

We have for some years received regularly four copies of the Sunday School Gazette; the number has been increased to twenty-five for the past year; the unknown sender will please receive our thanks.

The children have, at different times, received from H. C. Tilton, Esq., of Manchester, numbers of magazines, illustrated papers, &c., which have been a source of much pleasure to them, and for which they wish to express their gratitude.

Our thanks are due to A. M. Eastman, Esq., for a quantity of plants, roots, &c., sent for our flower garden; also to Miss M. O. Cilley, Mrs. Yeaton, Mrs. Sleeper, and others, for plants and bulbs; to George Clark, Esq., for nuts sent the children at Christmas.

Joseph Kidder, Esq., and J. M. Rowell, Esq., have each donated to our Library copies of the History of Manchester.

Since our removal, religious exercises have been conducted by the clergymen of Manchester and elsewhere, whenever circumstances permitted. We are under obligation to Messrs. Sawin, Wallace, Brooks, Thomas, Roripaugh, Mallory, Knowles and Haskell, of Manchester, and to Rev. Mr. Wilkins, of Rochester, who have been with us to conduct services. Sabbath school and religious instruction have been attended to throughout the year, and the children have learned many portions of Scripture from the New Testament and Psalms—all who can read possessing a copy.

The first year of my labors here has closed. Its trials and discouragements have been many, but it has had its encouragements also. It is a pleasing fact that all of those who have been honorably discharged, so far as heard from, are now doing well. Several have visited us, and their appearance is much in their favor. Many of those now here show a marked improvement in character. My labors are continued in hope and in the belief that, by the blessing of God, they may benefit many who, if not restrained here, would press on in the road to ruin.

ISAAC H. JONES, Superintendent.

PHYSICIAN'S REPORT.

To Isaac H. Jones, Esq., Superintendent of the House of Reformation:

DEAR SIR—For five years I have been the physician in the House of Reformation. As another man is now to take my place, I desire to express my thanks to the past and to the present Superintendents and officers of the institution, for their uniform courtesy to me. By their co-operation, my services have been made pleasant and successful.

The health of the children, for the past year, has been remarkably good. There has not been so little sickness in any one year since my connection with the school. Very few have needed medical treatment. No death has occurred among them. In the summer, when they were crowded together in the old house, we feared there might be sickness. But by care on the part of the officers, and by a kind Providence, disease was prevented.

The present Reform School House is well adapted and located for the comfort and health of its inmates. With the improvements which are made from year to year, and with what the school is doing for an unfortunate class of children, our State may feel that what it gives for its support and enlargement is, and will be, a blessing to multitudes.

LEONARD FRENCH, M. D.

May 20, 1867.

TREASURER'S REPORT.

To His Excellency the Governor and the Honorable Council of the State of New-Hampshire:

The Treasurer of the House of Reformation respectfully presents his

NINTH ANNUAL REPORT.

1866.			
May 1.	Balance of last year's account,		$6 10
July 17.	Cash received from	State Treasurer,	3,000 00
" 27.	"	"	7,000 00
Aug. 27.	"	"	2,000 00
Oct. 26.	"	"	3,000 00
Nov. 25.	"	I. H. Jones, Supt.,	1,000 00
1867.			
March 7.	"	"	1,200 00
"	"	State Treasurer,	2,000 00
April 30.	"	I. H. Jones, Supt.,	2,000 00
May 17.	"	"	4,312 39
			$25,518 49

Recapitulation.

Balance in hand,	6 10
Appropriation by State,	17,000 00
Received from I. H. Jones, Superintendent,	8,512 39
Total receipts,	$25,518 49

He discharges himself by the following payments:

1866.

			No. voucher.	
July 17.	David Gillis, trustees' expenses,		1	$32 10
	Wm. P. Wheeler,	"	2	63 07
	D. C. Churchill,	"	3	100 80
	Moses Humphrey,	"	4	22 50
	Joseph Kidder,	"	5	50 70
	Horton D. Walker,	"	6	92 65
	William Shepherd, hack hire, &c.,		7	67 00

July	25.	L. H. James, drawing wood,	8	487 75
		H. G. Wilson, sundries,	9	7 79
		J. E. Wilbur, painting and repair,	10	7 50
Aug.	4.	Charles Williams, goods and labor,	11	26 93
		Aaron Mears, watchman,	12	154 50
		Kidder & Chandler, groceries,	13	101 04
		" "	14	143 61
		J. T. Folsom, "	15	39 07
		Barton & Co., dry goods,	16	149 36
		" "	17	92 88
		John B. Varick, hardware,	18	153 10
		J. M. Robinson, boots and shoes,	19	48 22
		A. O. Parker, bedsteads,	20	16 50
		" wood-stools,	21	58 00
		J. M. Robinson, shoes and leather,	22	19 67
		A. F. Perry, medicines,	23	28 57
		French, Hall & Co., meal,	24	55 30
		Brooks Shattuck, salary,	25	250 00
		R. W. Lang, labor,	26	73 56
		G. B. Fogg, sundries,	27	11 45
		E. M. Howard, labor,	28	15 00
		William Shepherd, coach hire,	29	45 00
		G. F. Bosher, furniture,	30	62 96
		William Starr, provisions,	31	438 37
		J. E. Wilbur & Co., repairs,	32	5 25
		Robert Gilchrist, crockery,	33	31 47
		Thomas R. Hubbard, lumber,	34	54 69
		" "	35	200 53
		J. F. Woodbury, blacksmithing,	36	35 55
		Ezra Kimball, leather, &c.,	37	40 25
	24.	Cook & Miller, Meat,	38	90 55
		" "	39	63 62
		David F. McGilvray & Co., mattresses, &c.,	40	165 50
		D. F. McGilvray & Co., bedsteads,	41	156 25
		M. C. Eastman & Co., soap,	42	27 00
		Hartshorn & Pike, goods and labor,	43	309 02
		" goods,	44	7 56
		A. G. Fairbanks, board,	45	96 94
		" fees,	46	9 50
		" board,	47	18 58
		" beans,	48	45 90
		" 1 cow,	49	70 00
		" fees,	50	50
		Mrs. Wm. Cheney, clothing,	51	19 35
		J. W. Moore & Co., sundries,	52	4 88

Aug. 24.	E. Paige & Co., groceries,	53	19 39
	C. R. Colley, paints, &c.,	54	76 96
	" setting glass,	55	4 60
	Daniels & Co., hardware,	56	16 82
	" "	57	34 51
	John T. Chase, watching,	58	6 00
	E. M. Lee, labor,	59	30 50
	" "	60	32 50
Sept. 5.	Brooks Shattuck, salary,	61	600 00
	" reward,	62	85 00
	" sundries,	63	60 00
Oct. 9.	J. Rowley, potatoes,	64	10 80
	R. W. Lang, labor,	65	108 74
	Daniels & Co., hardware,	66	89 13
	Durgin & Dodge, boots,	67	2 00
	John Prince, box and express,	68	3 00
	J. A. Davis, labor,	69	97 50
	I. H. Jones, sundries,	70	38 16
	" salary,	71	200 00
	William Parker, Jr., manure,	72	14 12
	E. A. Rose, labor,	73	30 00
	Elizabeth Yeaton, provisions,	74	16 81
	J. M. Rowell, labor,	75	34 50
	Chas. Shattuck, provisions,	76	3 25
	" labor,	77	98 75
	Daniel Readey, "	78	91 58
	J. F. Woodbury, blacksmithing,	79	50 46
	J. S. Holt, 1 horse,	80	160 00
	" soap,	81	20 75
	L. W. Eastman, clothing,	82	2 55
	M. E. LeBosquet, labor,	83	39 00
	M. J. Eaton, "	84	45 50
	John Connor, "	85	54 00
	E. M. Howard, "	86	18 00
	J. S. Wiggin & Co., hats,	87	6 75
	B. P. Putney, provisions,	88	4 25
	Post-office, postage,	89	1 00
	" "	90	8 73
	William Starr, provisions,	91	209 76
	" "	92	236 06
	" "	93	198 79
	Merrill & Drake, provisions,	94	3 50
	Lewis Rice, provisions,	95	33 42
	J. Truesdale, hats,	96	4 10
	V. & B. Tel. Co., telegraphing,	97	1 40
	J. G. Colt, arbor-vitæs,	98	34 40

Oct.	9.	J. Rowley, provisions,	99	3 84
		H. Sleeper, "	100	19 32
		" "	101	6 63
		J. G. Eaton, manure,	102	30 44
		Ezra Kimball, 1 pig,	103	7 00
		D. G. Roberts, potatoes,	104	8 00
		John B. Clarke, bills,	105	4 00
		" advertising,	106	9 00
		Amoskeag Ax Co., axes,	107	4 25
		B. P. Rice, potatoes,	108	10 80
		" "	109	22 50
		J. E. Rand, expenses,	110	3 25
		A. B. Page, goods,	111	1 25
		J. Stickney, hardware,	112	3 49
		Timothy Sullivan, manure,	113	40 00
	20.	J. Q. A. Sargent, repairs,	114	1,356 21
		" "	115	535 38
	26.	W. H. Wentworth & Co., goods and labor,	116	628 15
	27.	W. O. Haskell & Son, furniture,	117	603 70
		T. W. Parsons, labor,	118	18 00
		Thos. Chase, provisions,	119	18 00
		J. S. Kidder, "	120	208 00
		" "	121	60 13
		" "	122	219 25
		Fellows & Co., repairs,	123	6 81
		W. H. Fisk, stationery,	124	7 04
		Cook & Miller, provisions,	125	124 66
		Kidder & Chandler, provisions,	126	33 53
		" "	127	172 23
		H. C. Tilton, stationery,	128	12 86
		Barton & Co., dry goods,	129	177 88
		Kimball & Dow, boots and shoes,	130	52 22
		A. F. Perry, medicines,	131	12 77
		Fisher & Cram, seeds,	132	13 52
		Hill & Co., express,	133	16 15
		John S. Folsom, groceries,	134	13 62
		J. E. Wilbur, farming tools,	135	13 75
		Jackson & Co., dry goods,	136	23 09
		Kidder & Chandler, provisions,	137	229 12
		Hartshorn & Pike, hardware,	138	14 54
		J. M. Robinson, boots and shoes,	139	34 63
		J. Peabody, goods,	140	10 16
		J. B. Varick & Co., hardware,	141	111 63
		Thos. G. Banks, fees,	142	6 00
		J. C. Young, repairs,	143	18 75

Oct. 27.	Amoskeag Man. Co., repairs,	144	7 00
	Concord railroad cor., freight,	145	6 00
	" "	146	11 38
	" "	147	11 08
	" "	148	1 30
	" "	149	1 40
	N. E. Morrill, insurance,	150	150 00
	S. & S. C. Eastman, insurance,	151	50 00
	Henry Clough, reward,	152	100 00
	David A. Wilson, labor,	153	4 50
	W. G. Hoit, horse hire,	154	2 50
	George Davis, oxen,	155	250 00
	A. H. Glines, provisions,	156	1 00
	Watson C. Atwell, labor,	157	41 50
	I. H. Jones, salary,	158	200 00
	Charles Shattuck, labor,	159	91 25
	Joseph M. Rowell, "	160	94 38
	J. A. Davis, "	161	96 25
	Daniel Readey, "	162	92 75
	M. E. LeBosquet, "	163	39 00
	E. A. Rose, "	164	36 00
	Mary J. Eaton, "	165	45 50
	H. T. LeBosquet, "	166	37 33
	R. W. Lang, "	167	81 41
Dec. 17.	Haskell & Son, furniture,	168	20 50
20.	Gay & Dickey, building,	169	2,383 97
	" building tank,	170	100 00
22.	J. Q. A. Sargent, hardware,	171	125 00
1867.			
March 7.	Fearing & Co., clothing,	172	2 40
	Conant, Woods & Co., blanketing,	173	209 25
	Lewis Rice, provisions,	174	4 09
	Hannah Sleeper, "	175	8 25
	" board,	176	15 19
	Daniels & Co., hardware,	177	104 11
	French, Hall & Co., goods,	178	82 90
	Kimball & Dow, boots and shoes,	179	23 65
	J. Peabody, dry goods,	180	6 82
	Robt. Gilchrist, crockery,	181	37 67
	J. M. Robinson, boots, &c.	182	43 47
	F. W. Smith, labor,	183	36 00
	John B. Varick & Co., hardware,	184	82 34
	Hartshorn & Pike, sundries,	185	161 55
	Kidder & Chandler, groceries,	186	272 67
	" "	187	186 14
	Thos. R. Hubbard, lumber,	188	197 25

March 7.	Barton & Co., dry goods,	189	159 29
	T. L. Hastings, boots and shoes,	190	9 85
	H. M. Bailey & Son, sundries,	191	2 08
	J. E. Wilbur, repairs,	192	5 00
	A. F. Perry, medicine,	193	7 07
	G. F. Bosher, blankets,	194	12 00
	Leonard French, medical attend'e,	195	17 50
	" "	196	15 00
	Thomas Chase, freight,	197	1 44
	John S. Kidder & Co., provisions,	198	219 85
	Cook & Miller, "	199	132 58
	J. W. Morse, sundries,	200	1 32
	H. B. Putnam, provisions,	201	6 73
	Plumer & Chandler, sew'g m'chine,	202	65 00
	Hill & Co., express,	203	1 33
	M. Charles & Co., dry goods,	204	159 58
	William Starr, provisions,	205	229 59
	Gambrell & Abbott, rent	206	310 00
April 30.	J. Stickney, sundries,	207	19 92
	M. E. LeBosquet, labor,	208	3 50
	Concord, Manchester & Lawrence Railroad, freight,	209	8 00
	William P. Ford & Co., hardware,	210	4 75
	Joseph M. Rowell, provisions,	211	5 63
	J. Bradley, pipe,	212	87 40
	Horace A. Hill, apples,	213	7 00
	J. S. Wiggin, caps,	214	42 48
	Robert Bunton, stone,	215	22 50
	J. Abbott & Co., meal,	216	5 60
	Concord, Manchester & Lawrence Railroad, freight,	217	1 00
	A. D. Glover, labor,	218	15 25
	Hannah Sleeper, provisions,	219	17 77
	" "	220	6 44
	J. B. Ellinwood, apples,	221	4 50
	F. N. McLaren, sundries,	222	1 50
	Charles Shattuck,	223	32 50
	N. E. Morrill, insurance,	224	50 00
	N. P. Kemp, books,	225	4 00
	Albert Webster, clock,	226	30 00
	O. Gage, provisions,	227	2 85
	Isaac Aldrich, fees,	228	15 00
	Post-office, postage,	229	2 15
	J. B. Ellinwood, apples,	230	4 62
	Daniel Shirley, cow,	231	68 00
	J. B. Ellinwood, apples,	232	5 00

April 30.	New-Hampshire Bible Soc'y, books,	233	20 00
	Ward Parker, oxen,	234	225 00
	H. C. Tilton, stationery,	235	208 73
	J. M. & S. F. Stanton, hardware,	236	52 67
	J. Stickney, sundries,	237	80 47
	H. & H. R. Pettee, cement,	238	3 00
	J. Q. A. Sargent, B. & R. fittings,	239	53 58
	Wm. W. Hubbard, lumber,	240	12 50
	Kidder & Chandler, dry goods,	241	197 23
	" groceries,	242	407 22
	David Libbey, repairs,	243	5 85
	Edwin Branch, sundries,	244	4 87
	Fellows & Co., hardware,	245	14 98
	I. H. Jones, salary,	246	200 00
	F. W. Smyth, labor,	247	60 00
	J. A. Davis, "	248	98 75
	Noah Glover, "	249	50 00
	Henry T. LeBosquet, labor,	250	56.67
	Charles A. Smith, crockery,	251	12 74
	A. C. Rogers, teacher,	252	31 50
	H. M. Wilkins, "	253	28 00
	Mary J. Eaton, book-keeper,	254	38 00
	E. A. Rose, overseer,	255	45 50
	Cora E. Wingate, labor,	256	36 86
	A. D. Glover, "	257	22 00
	J. A. Osgood, "	258	30 86
	J. A. Davis, expenses,	259	6 40
	Jackson & Co., dry goods,	260	15 91
	J. Peabody, "	261	15 52
	Leonard French, medical attend'e,	262	12 50
	Kimball & Dow, sundries,	263	34 80
	H. M. Bailey, & Son, "	264	90
	Thomas R. Hubbard, lumber,	265	72 70
	J. M. Robinson, boots, &c.,	266	27 55
	Mrs. Cheney, clothing,	267	3 30
	J. P. Rowell, wood,	268	43 00
	J. O. Clark, meat,	269	115 41
	A. F. Perry, medicines,	270	2 46
	Merrill & Drake, coffee, &c.,	271	10 40
	Charles Bunton, blacksmithing,	272	20 37
	R. N. Ross, trustee expenses,	273	17 50
	Wm. Starr, provisions,	274	265 64
	" "	275	223 46
	Fearing & Co., dry goods,	276	6 50
	J. F. Woodbury & Co., horse-shoeing,	277	10 00

April 30.	G. S. Holmes, dry goods,	278	3 68
	Concord, Manchester & Lawrence Railroad, freight,	279	65
	Fellows & Co., blacksmith,	280	52 44
	Merrill & Drake, provisions,	281	19 07
	Gregg & Dodge, pipe,	282	16 40
	Josiah Crosby, physician,	283	2 50
	H. C. Hunton, sundries,	284	4 75
	George W. Dodge, boots and shoes,	285	11 75
	W. H. Elliott, repairs,	286	2 50
	John Brugger, hose,	287	48 50
	J. O. Clark, meat,	288	161 57
	Daniel Readey, labor,	289	82 83
	I. H. Jones, incidentals,	290	16 09
May 17.	Daniels & Co., hardware,	291	51 65
	John B. Varick & Co., hardware,	292	27 36
	Robert Gilchrist, crockery,	293	48 52
	Cook & Miller, provisions,	294	114 08
	D. F. Straw, sundries,	295	29 81
	William Starr, provisions,	296	6 88
	George W. Gould, repairs,	297	10 25
	Hill & James, horse hire,	298	1 50
	A. G. Fairbanks, board,	299	2 54
	" "	300	44 83
	Brown & Flanders, ice,	301	4 00
	Haines & Wallace,	302	25 05
	A. Quimby, ink,	303	2 40
	J. F. Woodbury, blacksmithing,	304	4 00
	Peter Kimball, ox yoke,	305	2 50
	Post-office, postage,	306	2 13
	William Starr, provisions,	307	271 08
	" "	308	213 30
	" "	309	7 72
	W. H. Elliott, repairs,	310	6 00
	D. G. Roberts, wood,	311	554 50
	" "	312	179 39
	Mrs. Cheney, clothing,	313	7 00
	Concord, Manchester & Lawrence Railroad, freight,	314	48
	J. R. Hanson, medicine,	315	87
	J. M. & S. F. Stanton, repairs,	316	2 84
	R. W. Lang, soap,	317	1 00
	J. E. Wilbur & Co., repairs,	318	3 50
	G. F. Bosher & Co., sundries,	319	60 70
	H. B. Putnam, groceries,	320	2 10
	Haines & Wallace, lumber,	321	12 64

May 17.	Oliver Bailey, oxen,	322	305 00
	Hattie Dockham, labor,	323	7 50
	Henry S. LeBosquet, labor,	324	26 00
	I. H. Jones, Superintendent, salary,	325	200 00
	A. D. Glover, labor,	326	16 00
	Noah Glover, "	327	26 92
	J. A. Davis, "	328	32 50
	J. M. Rowell, "	329	37 50
	David Readey, "	330	82 50
	J. M. Rowell, "	331	10 00
	L'n'rd N. George, "	332	14 00
	F. W. Smyth, "	333	76 00
	C. P. Connolly, "	334	34 00
	A. C. Rogers, "	335	45 50
	Mary J. Eaton, "	336	45 50
	E. A. Rose, "	337	45 50
	C. E. Wingate, "	338	36 00
	H. M. Wilkins, "	339	33 25
	J. A. Osgood, "	340	39 00
	Patrick O'Brien, "	341	30 00
	Michael Dalton, "	342	30 00
	Patrick Hagerty, "	343	6 00
	A. F. Perry, medicines,	344	7 64
	George W. Cheney, manure,	345	80 00
	H. A. Davis, labor, &c.,	346	11 25
	Levi M. Green, painting,	347	11 00
	Leonard French, physician,	348	12 50
	Merrill & Drake, groceries,	349	15 97
	J. F. Woodbury & Co., bl'ksmithing,	350	2 00
	N. E. Morrill, insurance,	351	64 75
	Hiram Colby, horse,	352	175 00
	H. M. Bailey & Son, tin ware,	353	1 85
	Kimball & Dow, boots and shoes,	354	28 10
	Alonzo Wicom, labor,	355	51 33
	Reed P. Clark, expenses,	356	8 00
	Sarah Griffith, labor,	357	4 00
	C. W. Harvey, expenses,	358	10 40
	J. O. Clark, meat,	359	213 96
	" "	360	27 67
	" "	361	78 63
	" "	362	149 88
	Davis & Chaddick, hardware,	363	9 60
	Wilton Manufacturing Co., yarn,	364	59 05
	A. O. Parker, sundries,	365	220 39
	J. S. Kidder & Co., provisions,	366	84 95

May 17.	H. C. Tilton, stationery,	867	54 59
	Hartshorn & Pike, sundries,	868	55 09
	Fellows & Co., repairs,	869	4 35
	" "	370	2 23
	" "	371	11 63
	J. C. Young, roofing,	372	97 35
	Amoskeag M'f'g Co., castings,	373	79 03
	Henry Clough, expenses, &c.,	374	21 87
	I. H. Jones, incidentals,	375	25 08

Total expenditures, $27,338 31
Receipts, 25,518 49

Due the Treasurer, $1,819 82

CHA'S HENRY BARTLETT, *Treasurer.*

Council Chamber,
Concord, N. H., May 31, 1867.

The undersigned, having this day carefully examined the foregoing account of the Treasurer of the House of Reformation, hereby report that we find the same correctly cast and properly vouched.

ISAAC SPALDING,
LUTHER B. HOSKINS, } *Auditors.*

AUDITOR'S REPORT.

Concord, N. H., June 7, 1867.

Having been appointed by the Trustees of the Reform School to examine the account of Isaac H. Jones, I submit the following report:

I find the account to have been properly and correctly kept, and that he has received for board, products of the farm, and work of the children, $8,509 04, and that he has paid out for incidental bills, and to the Treasurer, for which he has the Treasurer's receipt for $8,512 39, leaving a balance to his credit of $3,35.

C. W. HARVEY.

REPORT

OF THE

WARDEN OF THE N. H. STATE PRISON,

FOR THE YEAR 1867.

REPORT

OF THE

WARDEN

OF THE

NEW-HAMPSHIRE STATE PRISON:

ACCOMPANIED BY REPORTS OF THE

CHAPLAIN AND PHYSICIAN,

TOGETHER WITH OTHER

DOCUMENTS RELATING TO THE AFFAIRS OF THE PRISON.

JUNE SESSION, 1867.

CONCORD:
GEORGE E. JENKS, STATE PRINTER.
1867.

OFFICE OF THE SECRETARY OF STATE,
Concord, New-Hampshire, May 20, 1867.

SIR: By virtue of authority vested in me by chapter 2398, Pamphlet Laws this State, I hereby authorize you to print twenty-one hundred copies of the Report of the Warden of the State Prison, and Synopsis of Inventory, for the use of the State.

WALTER HARRIMAN,
Secretary of State.

GEORGE E. JENKS, *State Printer.*

OFFICERS.

WARDEN,
JOSEPH MAYO.

DEPUTY WARDEN,
AUGUSTUS BEAN.

PHYSICIAN,
A. A. MOULTON.

CHAPLAIN,
Rev. SULLIVAN HOLMAN.

OVERSEERS,

ALVAH H. BICKFORD,
    Overseer of Prison Hall and Cook Room.
AUGUSTINE L. GALE, *Overseer of the Shoe Shop.*
CHARLES ELWELL, *Overseer of First Cabinet Shop.*
CHARLES H. ORDWAY,
    Overseer of Second Cabinet Shop.
FRANCIS W. KILBOURN,
    Instructor in the Cabinet Shop.

GUARDS.

ORRISON DUDLEY,
Z. T. CUTLER,
LEVI R. LANEY,
GEORGE SNOW,
G. H. CHADWICK, *Night Watchman.*

WARDEN'S REPORT.

To the Honorable Senate and House of Representatives in General Court assembled:

GENTLEMEN:—In conformity with the requirements of the laws of the State, I have the honor of presenting to you my Annual Report of the affairs, management, and present condition of the State Prison, appended to which is a full and true statement of all the receipts and expenditures connected with the prison, for the year commencing May 1, 1866, and ending April 30, 1867.

I am happy to be able to state that the affairs of the Prison are in a prosperous condition, it being substantially self-sustaining, and, under the new contracts for the labor of the prisoners, which will soon be in operation, a degree of prosperity will be attained that has hitherto been unknown in the history of the Institution. For the next, and, for several succeeding years, the earnings of the prisoners will be many thousand dollars in excess of the expenditures; so that, instead of being a burden upon the State, they will be a source of large and increasing revenue. The State, of course, would gladly forgo the profits, if the commission of crime could thereby be stayed; but, while crime and the necessity for its punishment exist, it is a cause of congratulation that the earnings of honest industry are not to be taxed to support its perpetrators.

In justice to the prisoners, I should state that, with few exceptions, during the past year, they have labored zealously, and even cheerfully; more so than could well have been expected, considering the unhappy circumstances in which they are placed. I have endeavored to inspire them with fortitude, and with hope for the future; and, as a part of the means to accomplish this, they have had granted to them all the indulgencies deemed consistent with their position; more especially as to the quality of their food, which has been improved at a somewhat increased cost.

So far as the prisoners are concerned, it is my aim to render them as contented and happy as circumstances will permit, being satisfied that unnecessary severity, by rousing resentful feelings, fails to accomplish what all desire to see attained, the reformation of the criminal. When they realize, as some of them now do, that, in placing them under restraint, the constituted authorities seek not only to protect society from unlawful depredations, but the good of the criminal as well, and not to inflict vindictive punishment, it is to be hoped that those of them, at least, who are capable of reflection, will see the error of their ways, and resolve to conform themselves to the requirements of the laws instituted for their benefit, as well as for the protection of society at large.

I am happy to be able to say that I have always had the hearty coöperation of His Excellency, Gov. Smyth, and of the Honorable Executive Council, in aid of all measures calculated to advance the prosperity of the Institution and to promote the welfare of the prisoners.

CONTRACTS.

The labor employed in the Cabinet Shop is still under the control of Messrs. I. Elwell & Son, whose contract (for five years) will expire in August next. As usual, the contractors have fully and promptly complied with the requirements of their contract during the past year.

Realizing that the State was not receiving a full equivalent for the labor of the convicts, under the existing contract (which has been but forty cents per day), with the advice and consent of the Governor and Council, at an early day I caused advertisements to be inserted in newspapers in this and other States, inviting bids for the labor of all the prisoners in the Institution, which led to the formation of new contracts with new contractors.

George T. Comins, Esq., of Lowell, Mass., has contracted for the labor of the prisoners in the Cabinet Shops (comprising three fourths of all the prisoners in the Institution), for a period of five years from August next, at ninety cents per day ; and, at the end of three years from March 15, 1867 (when the contract for the labor of the convicts in the Shoe Shop will have expired), he is bound to employ all the prisoners in the Institution, during the remainder of the time that his contract has to run, at the same price of ninety cents per day.

A contract has also been entered into with the State, by Messrs. Piper & Clough, of Concord, for the labor of the prisoners in the Shoe Shop (comprising one fourth of all the convicts in the prison), for three years from March 15, 1867, at the price of seventy-five cents per day.

The parties to both contracts have given adequate bonds for the full and faithful performance of their several contracts with the State.

In every aspect in which they may be viewed, these contracts may be considered as highly advantageous to the State. They are for a reasonable length of time; the prices are more than double what are paid under the old contract, and higher than ever before received by the State for the labor of the prisoners in this Institution. They also compare favorably with those recently made for the labor of convicts in other State Prisons. In Massachusetts, the prices paid are eighty-three cents and one dollar seven cents per day, averaging a trifle more than is paid here, but which is more than made up to the contractors there, by their proximity to an extensive market, saving of transportation, &c.

Under the old contract, with the present high prices of provisions and clothing, the Institution has but little more than paid its way. Under the new contracts, during the coming year, commencing July 1st, even should the present prices of the principal articles consumed in the prison remain as high as they now are, the earnings of the prison will exceed the expenditures in the sum of about ten thousand dollars, and that, too, after making allowance for unforeseen contingencies.

The difference in the balance of the financial statements, between the past year and that of the first ten months of my superintendence of the affairs of the prison, is owing mainly to the fact that most of the U. S. Government prisoners, formerly confined here, have been discharged, there being now but five remaining. But for that, the balance in favor of the prison would have been about the same as for the previous ten months, when it was $933.19. The balance in favor of the prison for the year just ended is $648.89.

HEALTH.

Through the blessing of Providence the convicts have enjoyed a fair degree of health during the year. There are several cases of chronic disease, induced by previous excesses, the cure of which is quite doubtful. There are also a few cases of general debility among those who have been long confined here; induced, or aggravated at least, by the insufficient ventilation of the prison.

Three of the prisoners have died during the year. Their deaths are more particularly alluded to in the report of the prison physician, Dr. Moulton.

With the exceptions noted, the health of the prisoners has averaged about the same as with an equal number of persons of equal ages, outside the prison.

DISCHARGED CONVICTS.

Since the passage of the act providing for the appointment of an Agent for Discharged Convicts, that duty has been performed by Governor Smyth and myself, aided by the subordinate officers of the Institution, without cost to the State. During the latter part of the year, Rev. Mr. Holman, Chaplain of the prison, has aided in the work. His wide circle of acquaintance, and large experience, enabled him to be of much service in procuring suitable employment for the discharged prisoners.

The first step after their discharge has been to procure their signatures to the total abstinence pledge, in which we have generally been successful.

FEMALE DEPARTMENT.

There have been eight different female convicts in the prison during the year, three of whom were pardoned early in the year. Four were sentenced here during the year, and there are five now remaining in the prison.

The women have been employed in the manufacture and repair of clothing, all of which labor, needed in the prison, has been performed by them.

It is proper for me to add that their conduct has been exemplary, leaving nothing to desire in that particular.

PARDONS.

The subject of executive clemency is one of much interest, especially to the friends of convicts, and forces itself upon our attention, whether we will or no. The pardoning power has been exercised with much caution and discretion by Governor Smyth, and, happily, has been so applied as to leave no jealousies, or ill-feeling rankling in the minds of the remaining prisoners.

Nine pardons have been granted during the year, upon petitions to the Governor and Council. In several cases it was thought that there were fair probabilities, at least, that the parties were innocent, or less guilty than had been supposed; and in one case the fact of innocence seemed to be fully established. Several prisoners were discharged a few days before the expiration of sentence, in order to secure to them the rights of citizenship, of which they were deemed worthy. Governor Smyth has often met the prisoners, and addressed them publicly and privately, with deep feelings of sympathy. He assured them that, although possessing the power to open the prison doors, and feeling for them, as he did, yet they must not generally expect pardons; for, while disposed to be merciful, he must be just. The prisoners all seemed to realize that His Excellency was their friend, and disposed to do all in his power, consistent with duty, to better their condition. In all cases of pardon the Governor has required that one or more of the persons who requested it should be present when the prisoner was discharged, to aid him by council, and otherwise, in withstanding the temptations that encompass the discharged prisoner on every hand. I am glad to be able to state that the prisoners pardoned by Governor Smyth, so far as known, have generally abstained from vicious courses, and are doing well in other particulars. From some of them letters have been received, the tone of which indicates that executive clemency was not misapplied in their behalf.

MORAL CULTURE, SABBATH-SCHOOL, &C.

For more particular information on this subject I refer you to the report of the Chaplain. Although he has had but four months' experience in that office, he has become deeply interested in its duties, and the prisoners have already learned to look upon him as their friend. His stated preaching on the Sabbath, his Sabbath-school, and the week day evening school, bring him into frequent and familiar intercourse with the prisoners, which, with his large experience as a pastor, and his affectionate interest in their behalf, render him peculiarly well qualified to make deep and lasting impressions on their minds.

The evening schools have been commenced recently, for the convenience of which gas fixtures have been put into the Chapel, with the concurrence of Governor Smyth. It is proposed, when the evenings again become long, to have, occasionally, an evening lecture, as a means of instruction.

Our Sabbath-school was continued nine months during the year, with much apparent profit. Without saying how much good has been done — as I know the prejudice existing in regard to State Prison conversions — I would "sow the seed in the morning, and in the evening withhold not thy hand."

The one hundred dollars, appropraited at your last session, has been expended for the purchase of fifty Bibles, at forty cents each; one hundred and fifty Christian Almanacs, at eight cents each; twenty copies of Bunyan's Pilgrim's Progress, in paper covers, at fifteen cents each, and the remainder in books of the American Tract Society; all late publications, containing useful knowledge of a religious character. These books are read with avidity by the prisoners, and are exercising a good influence on their minds.

DISCIPLINE.

The discipline that has characterized this institution has been fully maintained during the year, with the usual mode of punishment—the dark cell, and rations of bread and water—which have been found to be sufficient. The cases of punishment have been less in number than during the previous year, and no cases of insubordination have occurred. The mixed gentleness and firmness with which discipline has been maintained has had the best possible effect in stimulating the industry and promoting the cheerfulness of the convicts. Indeed, the industry and cheerfulness of the prisoners, when at work, had much to do with increasing the price of their labor, as gentlemen who came to examine the prison preparatory to making bids for the labor, observed and commented upon it, as being somewhat remarkable.

Upon the whole, with few exceptions, the conduct of the prisoners has been steadily improving; has been as good, in fact, as could reasonably have been expected.

DISCIPLINE AND CRIME.

The subject of "prison discipline" is one of the questions of the age, in which nearly all persons are interested, since men of all classes desire to see the best possible measures adopted for the prevention of crime and the reformation of the criminal. Philanthropic societies, such as the "New-York Prison Discipline Association," the "Massachusetts Board of State Charities," &c., are instituted and organized for the purpose of preventing crime and promoting the welfare of the unfortunate criminal.

The reports of those and other kindred associations, furnish copious information in relation to the working of the various systems of discipline in operation in this country and in Europe. Yet all, it is acknowledged, fail to accomplish the desired result, excepting in a measurable degree; and all that we can hope for, then, at present, is to approximate nearer and nearer toward the accomplishment of the grand result aimed at.

The Rev. Dr. Wynes, of the New-York "Prison Discipline Association" (with whom I have conversed upon the subject), and whose opinion is entitled to great weight, expresses the belief that no system of discipline can be correct that has not for its end "the prevention of crime and the reformation of the criminal." Dr. Wynes' labors have been blest in the adoption of means for ameliorating the condition of, and furnishing employment for, discharged convicts. May the time soon come when prejudice shall be removed, so that discharged convicts may readily find honorable employment, instead of being tempted to crime, for the want of it. Yet, committals for crime are being increased to an alarming extent, and that, too, from among a class of men who are deserving of a better fate. In the prison there are now confined forty-two returned soldiers, who have been honorably discharged, being over thirty per cent of the whole number of prisoners in the institution. It can no longer be said that the returned soldiers who are sent to prison are those only who were fugitives from justice when they went to the war. I do not say that any are sent here who are entirely innocent, but I am often told, by the officer in charge of them, that this man always bore a good character previous to this, his first offense, and now has a respectable wife, and helpless children, or an aged father, or a widowed mother, who felt that she was doing God's will when she bade her son—perhaps her only one—God-speed, to defend the liberty of her country from the assaults of the minions of slavery; who was proud of her boy who had honored our flag with his battle-scarred body; who never showed himself a coward before the rebel foe; yet possessed not sufficient moral courage to resist the blandishments of the tipling-shop, or the solicitations of those who enticed him to drink; and next we find him violating that law which he had sacrificed an arm, or a leg, perhaps, to maintain.

Now, this is no fancy sketch, but has been of frequent occurrence during the past year. In some cases the disgrace of the state prison might have been avoided, no doubt, by the employment of counsel; in others, a spirit of forgiveness might have been exercised with the happiest results, in the spirit of Him who said, "not only seven times, but seventy times seven, if thy brother offend thee, shalt thou forgive him."

I appreciate the necessity of enforcing the laws by inflicting punishments that shall prove a terror to evil doers; not in a spirit of revenge, but disciplinary in its character, and applied in a manner, and to the extent, that will satisfy the demands of society for the wrong that has been committed.

SUGGESTIONS.

In view of the increased earnings of the Institution it may be proper to suggest that some more efficient means of instruction should be provided for the younger portion of the prisoners, whose education has been totally neglected. There are now here, for a term of years, several boys who have been in the Reform School, and several others who have not been in that Institution, who are ignorant, and are now being taught to read; but they get on slowly, as all the instruction they have received here has been in the Sabbath School, and occasionally at other times, through the grates of their cell doors. It seems to be a matter of importance that these young men should not be sent out into the world ignorant, as they now are, fit candidates to be returned here again; but that they should be instructed in the rudiments, at least, of common school knowledge; and I can perceive no way of accomplishing the work, excepting through the instrumentality of the chaplain of the Prison, which office is filled, since January 1st, by the Rev. Mr. Holman, formerly pastor of the M. E. church in Concord. Mr. Holman is a gentleman of rare ability and of large experience, whose heart is in the work of imparting spiritual and intellectual instruction to the convicts. But the sum now appropriated ($400 per year) is insufficient to secure the permanent services of such a man. I deem it of the highest importance that measures be taken, by direct appropriation or otherwise, to secure to the Institution the services of so earnest and efficient a man as Mr. Holman has already shown himself to be.

I beg leave to call your attention to the importance of better ventilation for the prison. The fact is, that the system of ventilation (or rather of no ventilation) by which it is attempted to supply pure air to the prison, is a total failure. The want of pure air in the cells is a prolific cause of disease, and those who are confined here for any considerable length of time invariably suffer in health from that cause. Bilious diseases are so induced, or aggravated by it, as can easily be demonstrated to the satisfaction of all who investigate the subject. It is hoped that an appropriation, sufficient to defray the cost of providing proper means of ventilation, will be made at the present session of the Legislature.

Few persons will now deny that the general system of management of prisons that is based on the principle of kindness and humanity, and applied with the object of reformation, is the best. Industry and the hope of acquiring mechanical skill have much to do in encouraging the convict to good behavior, and it is thought by many who are interested in this subject that additional incentives to good conduct, and absolute reformation, may be placed before the convict, without at all weakening the efficacy of the law under which he is punished.

I beg leave to call the attention of the Legislature to a system of commutation existing in Massachusetts, Maine, and other States, as well as in Europe, and which, it is said, has been attended with good results. By this system of commutation, convicts, sentenced for a term of years, are allowed to have deducted from their time from one to three days in each month, according to the degree of good conduct and the length of sentence; also, to have subtracted from such deductions as many days as are lost by solitary confinement. In the States where such laws exist their effect has been decidedly good, as I have been assured by wardens and other officers of prisons, in several of these States. The prisoners are usually anxious to have a few days deducted from their terms, in order to retain the rights of citizenship; and much of the time of the Governor and Council is consumed investigating such cases, which might be saved if the convicts could secure that end by their own good conduct. Should the Legislature enact such a law I trust that it will be so framed as to apply to those now in imprisonment, as well as to those who may be sentenced hereafter.

The following is a copy of the law recently passed by the Legislature of Maine:

"The warden of the State Prison shall keep a record of the conduct of each convict, and for every month that such convict shall appear by such record to have faithfully observed all the rules and requirements of the prison, the warden may recommend to the Executive a deduction from the term of service of such convict's sentence, according to, but not exceeding, the following rule and proportion: For a convict under the sentence of two years or less, one day for each month good conduct; three years, or less, and more than two years, two days; four years, three days; five years, four days; seven years, or less, and more than five years, five days; nine years, or less, and more than seven years, six days; ten years, and less than fifteen years, seven days; fifteen years and less than twenty years, eight days; and to all other convicts, except those sentenced to perpetual imprisonment, ten days."

OFFICERS.

There have been some changes among the officers of the prison during the year:

Mr. Charles W. Davis recently resigned the office of Deputy Warden, and Mr. Augustus Bean has been appointed to fill that office. Mr. Bean is well qualified to fill the office, having been an overseer, as well as foreman, in the cabinet shop for two years previous to his present appointment. He is well known in this community as an upright, christian man, and will, no doubt, give satisfaction in the performance of his official duties.

Mr. A. W. Wiggin, formerly overseer of the shoe shop, has recently retired from that position, and Mr. Augustus Gale has been appointed to the place. Mr. Gale was a meritorious soldier during the late war, and for some time acted as a faithful watchman in the prison.

Mr. A. H. Bickford, who has filled various positions in the prison for five years, is still overseer of the culinary and clothing department of the prison, which his experience renders him well qualified to fill.

Mr. Charles Elwell, who has faithfully served the State for years, is still acting as overseer in the cabinet shop.

Mr. C. H. Ordway, formerly a watchman, is now acting as an overseer in the cabinet shop. He received a severe wound in the late war, from which he still suffers, but which does not incapacitate him for the duties of his present position. Mr. Ordway has also had charge of the prison books the past year, and the admirable manner in which they have been kept proves that he well deserved the diploma received from "Warner's Commercial College," as an accomplished pupil of that Institution.

The other subordinate officers, of whom several are returned soldiers, give satisfaction in their several positions.

Mr. C. S. Piper, one of the contractors for the labor in the shoe shop, is himself instructing the men in the employ of his firm. Being thoroughly master of the business, and, withal, kind and gentle with the men, they prove zealous and profitable workmen. All of them now have an opportunity of making themselves good workmen, under Mr. Piper's tuition.

ESCAPES.

There have been but two escapes from the prison during the year. Silas S. Nash, who was on a sentence of five years, and who then had some six months to serve, escaped July 26, 1866. He had been sick for a long time, and pronounced by the prison physician unable to work, and performed but little labor for nine months previous to his escape; consequently he was employed occasionally with light tasks, and, as is customary in such cases, in doing errands about the premises. Having been sent to the barn for some purpose, he escaped, and has not been retaken.

The other escape was that of Mark Shinborn, on December 3, 1866. He was received here February 27, 1866, on a sentence of ten years. He had previously escaped from the Keene jail, after sentence, and was at large for several months before he was retaken. Being aware of his desperate character, unusual precautions were taken for his safe keeping. I caused to be placed upon his cell-door an extra lock, of the most approved construction, the key of which, at night, was kept in my own custody, or that of the Deputy Warden. On the day of his escape the convicts were formed in line, as usual, just before dark, and, while in the act of marching across the yard, toward the prison, Shinborn set his bucket upon the ground and ran for the gate. The alarm was immediately given, and the guard, upon the prison wall, discharged his musket at Shinborn, but failed to hit him. He reached the gate, with a blow removed a portion of one of the planks of which it is composed, passed through, entered a carriage waiting near by, and was quickly out of sight.

The piece of plank displaced from the gate had been perforated with auger-holes bored close together across its whole width, which weakened it so much that a slight blow only was required to break it off. The holes were bored nearly through, immediately under the cross-bar, where they were not observable, and filled with putty of the color of the paint on the gate.

It is scarcely necessary for me to say that I deeply regret the escape of so important a prisoner; but I do not feel that I am deserving of censure for not using due care and diligence as to his safe keeping. In his cell he was perfectly safe; and, while in line with the other convicts, each section being attended by an officer, with armed guards upon the prison wall, he was thought to be secure; more especially as an escape from the line had never before taken place. The plan of escape was well devised and adroitly executed. It is needless to say that it could not have been successfully carried out without concerted action between Shinborn and his confederates. A reward of one thousand dollars was immediately offered for his arrest and delivery here, but he has not yet been retaken. No efforts have been wanting—no proper measures have been, or are now being, left untried to re-arrest him.

My thanks are due to the Legislature for having elected me to fill so important a position. I entered upon the duties of the office last year with more cheerfulness and assurance than I should have done without the experience of the previous year. That experience has enabled me to avoid some errors and mistakes to which I should otherwise have been liable. I can but hope that my course has given satisfaction. Be that as it may, the intention to do right, and to do it in the best manner, has been my governing purpose.

JOSEPH MAYO, Warden.

BILL OF FARE.

List of Rations furnished the Prisoners confined in the State Prison, Concord, N. H.

MONDAY:
    Morning—flour bread, molasses, and coffee.
    Noon—corned beef, vegetables, and brown bread.
    Night—corn meal mush, and molasses.

TUESDAY:
    Morning—meat hash, brown bread, and coffee.
    Noon—salt fish, potatoes, gravy, and brown bread.
    Night—corn meal mush, and molasses.

WEDNESDAY:
    Morning—fish hash, brown bread, and coffee.
    Noon—beef soup, and brown bread.
    Night—flour bread, molasses, and coffee.

THURSDAY:
    Morning—meat hash, brown bread, and coffee.
    Noon—stewed beans, pork, and brown bread.
    Night—corn meal mush, and molasses.

FRIDAY:
    Morning—flour bread, molasses, and coffee.
    Noon—fish chowder and brown bread.
    Night—corn meal mush, and molasses.

SATURDAY:
    Morning—fish hash, brown bread, and coffee.
    Noon—stewed peas, pork, and brown bread.
    Night—corn meal mush, and molasses.

SUNDAY:
    Morning—baked pork and beans, brown bread, and coffee.
    Afternoon—boiled rice, molasses, and brown bread.

FINANCIAL STATEMENT

Of the Transactions of the New-Hampshire State Prison, from May 1, 1866, to April 30, 1867.

Inventory of Property on hand May 1, 1866, as appraised by Messrs. Buffum, Hackett and Currier,	$11,219.14
Inventory of Property on hand April 30, 1867, as appraised by Messrs. Buffum, Hackett and Stevens,	12,348.04
Net gain in inventory,	$1,129.18

New-Hampshire State Prison in Account with the State of New-Hampshire.

Dr.

To inventory, May 1, 1866,		$11,219.14
provisions,	$5,015.19	
clothing and bedding,	1,664.43	
light and fuel,	1,561.47	
hospital stores,	226.51	
furniture,	155.64	
steam engine and fixtures,	2.75	
shoe shop,	5,746.01	
expense,	982.65	
officers' salaries,	4,138.69	
library,	100.00	
discharged convicts,	286.69	
repairs and improvements,	332.85	
		20,212.88
		$31,432.02

Cr.

By inventory, April 30, 1867,		$12,348.18
cabinet shop,	$6,773.20	
visitors,	251.82	

By State appropriation,	100.00	
provisions,	647.87	
clothing and bedding,	24.84	
light and fuel,	5.85	
expense,	190.75	
shoe shop,	11,736.40	
	19,730.73	
		32,078.91
Balance,		$646.89

AUDITOR'S OFFICE,
Concord, May 20, 1867.

I have examined the foregoing statement of the receipts and disbursements of the New-Hampshire State Prison, and the books and vouchers of the Warden, and do hereby certify that said statement is properly made and correctly cast.

D. D. RANLETT, *State Auditor.*

Statement, showing the Financial Condition of the N. H. State Prison, April 30, 1867.

Increase of property on hand,	$1,129.04	
Paid amount due Joseph Mayo, on last year's account,	1,445.95	
Due the prison for board and clothing of U. S. convicts,	738.56	
Due the prison on book accounts,	306.71	
Due the prison on note,	400.00	
Cash on hand,	117.76	
		$4,138.02
Amount due the prison, May 1, 1866,	$670.00	
Amount the prison owes on book accounts,	2,821 13	
		$3,491.13
Balance in favor of the prison,		$646.89

NET PROFITS AND EXPENDITURES OF THE DIFFERENT DEPARTMENTS.

Subsistence.

1866.	May 1.—Stock,	$1,543.65	
	Since purchased,	5,015.19	
			$6,558.84
1867.	April 30.—Stock,	$1,601.42	
	Sales, and due for boarding United States prisoners,	647.87	
			$2,249.29
	Amount expended,		$4,309.55

Clothing and Bedding.

1866.	May 1.—Stock,	$840.88	
	Since purchased,	1,664.43	
			$2,505.31
1867.	April 30.—Stock,	$1,437.35	
	Sales, and due for clothing furnished U. S. prisoners,	24.84	
			$1,462.19
	Amount expended,		$1,043.12

Light and Fuel.

1866.	May 1.—Stock,	$267.50	
	Since purchased,	1,561.47	
			$1,828.97
1867.	April 30.—Stock,	$592.50	
	Sales,	5.85	
			$598.35
	Amount expended,		$1,230.62

Furniture.

1866.	May 1.—Stock,	$2,096.95	
	Since purchased,	155.64	
			$2,252.59
1867.	April 30.—Stock,		2,219.76
	Amount expended,		$32.83

Hospital Stores.

1866.	May 1.—Stock,	$69.05	
	Since purchased,	226.51	
			$295.56
1867.	April 30.—Stock,		36.00

Amount expended, $259.56

Steam Engine and Fixtures.

1866.	May 1.—Stock,	$4,842.40	
	Since purchased,	2.75	
			$4,845.15
1867.	April 30.—Stock,		4,817.00

Amount expended, $28.15

Shoe Shop.

1866.	May 1.—Stock,	$1,317.71	
	Since purchased,	5,746.01	
			$7,063.72
1867.	April 30.—Stock,	$1,425.30	
	Sales,	11,736.40	
			$13,161.70

Net gain, $6,097.98

Expense.

1866.	May 1.—Stock,	$241.00	
	Since purchased,	982.65	
			$1,223.65
1867.	April 30.—Stock,	$218.85	
	Sales, manure, old rags and iron,	190.75	
			$409.60

Amount expended, $814.05

Officers' Salaries.

1867. April 30.—Amount expended, $4,138.69

Library.

1867.	April 30.—Amount expended,	$100.00

Cabinet Shop.

1867.	April 30.—Amount received for labor,	6,773.20

Visitors.

1867.	April 30.—Amount received,	$251.82

Discharged Convicts.

1867.	April 30.—Amount paid out,	$286.69

Repairs and Improvements.

1867.	April 30.—Amount paid out,	$332.85

State Appropriation.

1867.	April 30.—Amount received for library,	$100.00

RECAPITULATION.

GAIN:

Convicts' labor in Shoe Shop,	$6,097.98	
Convicts' labor in Cabinet Shop,	6,773.20	
State appropriation for Library,	100.00	
Visitors,	251.82	
		$13,223.00

LOSS:

Subsistence,	$4,309.55
Clothing and bedding,	1,043.12
Light and fuel,	1,230.62
Furniture,	32.83
Hospital stores,	259.56
Steam engine and fixtures,	28.15
Expense,	814.05

Officers' salaries,	4,138.69	
Library,	100,00	
Discharged convicts,	286.69	
Repairs and improvements,	332.85	
		$12;576.11
Net gain,		$646.89

PRISON STATISTICS.

TABLE No. 1.

The whole number of convicts in the prison, May 1, 1866, was 106 males and 5 females.	111
The whole number received on warrants from courts, from May 1, 1866, to April 30, 1867, was 42 males and 3 females.	45
Whole number in the prison during the year was	156

Discharged between May 1, 1866, and April 30, 1867.

Pardoned by the Executive a few days before expiration of sentence, to save rights of citizenship,	6	
Pardoned, on petition to the Governor and Council, 7 males and 3 females,	10	
Discharged by expiration of sentence,	11	
U. S. Government prisoners discharged by order of the President,	6	
Number escaped,	2	
Number deceased,	3	
		38
Whole number in the prison, May 1, 1867,		118

TABLE No. 2.
Age of Convicts now in the Prison.

From 15 to 20,	19
" 20 to 25,	37
" 25 to 30,	26
" 30 to 40,	17
" 40 to 50,	11
" 50 to 60,	7
" 60 to 70,	1
Total,	.118

TABLE No. 3.
Employment of the Convicts.

Employed in the cabinet shop,	66
" " shoe shop,	32
" as waiters,	4
" as tailor,	1
" as washers,	2
" as hall-sweepers,	2
" as cooks,	3
Invalids,	3
	—113

TABLE No. 4.

Number of Convicts in the Prison, committed, discharged, pardoned, deceased and escaped, in each year, since the establishment of the Institution, in 1812.

Year.	In Prison.	Committed.	Discharged.	Pardoned.	Died.	Escaped.
1812	1	1				
1813	12	11				
1814	22	14	4			
1815	23	14	5	2		5
1816	48	31	5	1		
1817	59	29	13	3	1	1
1818	69	26	16			
1819	72	16	20	1	1	2
1820	61	18	15	2	2	
1821	65	23	15	2	2	
1822	58	16	19	2	3	
1823	66	26	11	5	1	
1824	62	19	17	5	1	
1825	66	24	13	3	1	2
1826	59	13	15	4	1	
1827	48	12	14	7	2	
1828	86	20	8	4		
1829	50	11	9	7	1	
1830	68	31	9	4		
1831	81	24	8	3		
1832	82	19	10	6	1	
1833	81	16	8	9		1
1834	79	13	4	11		
1835	78	23	6	16		
1835	78	23	6	16		
1836	86	21	8	4	1	2
1837	72	12	15	10	1	
1838	70	5	4	3		
1839	73	30	10	15	2	
1840	78	24	4	14	1	
1841	48	28	13	7	2	
1842	92	20	9	3		

TABLE 4—*continued*.

Year.	In Prison.	Committed.	Discharged.	Pardoned.	Removed to Asylum for Insane.	Died.	Escaped.
1843	99	28	17	4			
1844	88	25	19	15		1	
1845	81	14	8	12		2	
1846	74	30	12	22		1	
1847	61	14	12	13		1	
1848	77	42	11	14			1
1849	82	17	9	.2		1	
1850	91	36	10	14	1	2	
1851	92	26	7	11		1	1
1852	111	44	11	11		6	
1853	109	24	9	15		2	
1854	105	28	13	13		6	
1855	97	26	10	17	1	6	
1856	94	32	19	8		3	
1857	86	23	27	9		4	
1858	110	49	14	9			
1859	105	37	22	16	1	3	
1860	110	35	18	10	1	1	
1861	119	42	19	10		4	
1862	112	31	20	12	1	5	
1863	101	22	13	14		5	1
1864	92	22	14	17			
1865	70	9	17	8	1	5	
1866	112	60	7	15		2	1
1867	118	45	11	16		3	2
		1360	656	460	6	88	19

REGISTER OF CONVICTS IN PRISON, MAY, 1867.

NAME.	AGE	WHERE BORN.	WHAT COUNTY CONVICTED IN	FOR WHAT CRIME.	WHEN.	SENTENCE. YRS. MO'S. DAYS.	EXPIRA'T'N OF TERM.
Cornelius Haskell,	24	Warner, N. H.	Merrimack.	Murder.	Sept., 1856.	Life.	Feb., 1875.
Stephen Smith,	45	Bingham, Me.	Strafford.	Burning barn.	Feb., 1860.	15	May, 1890.
Frank S. Wright,	29	Ryegate, Vt.	Grafton.	Murder.	April, 1860.	30 30	April, 1898.
Samuel C. Lamos,	22	Lee, N. H.	Rockingham.	Breaking and stealing.	Aug., "	8	Aug., 1870.
Amasa A. Arlin,	25	Northfield, N. H.	Merrimack.	Burglary.	April, 1861.	10 3	April, 1881.
Charles E. West,	40	Jay, Me.	Carroll.	Burning barn.	May, "	20 2	May, 1870.
Maxim Guyon,	46	St. Nicholas, C. E.	Hillsborough.	Attempt to rob.	Jan., 1862.	9 2	Jan., 1870.
Charles Forbes,	26	Irasburg, Vt.	Merrimack.	Passing counterfeit money.	Feb., "	6 2	Feb., 1868.
Augustus Thorndike,	43	Boston, Mass.	Grafton.	Stealing yoke of oxen.	Aug., "	6	Aug., 1877.
Barnard Page,	60	Weare, N. H.	Grafton.	Manslaughter, 2d degree.	March, 1863.	15	Mar., 1881.
John Brown,	27	Scotland.	Grafton.	Burglary.	Sept., "	18	Sept., 1888.
Brewster Young,	54	Lisbon, N. H.	Rockingham.	Murder second degree.	Oct., "	26 30	Oct., 1868.
Luther J. Austin,	25	Haverhill, Mass.	Hillsborough.	Breaking and stealing.	Feb., 1864.	5 20	Feb., 1882.
Samuel V. B. Bennett,	32	Staffordshire, Eng.	Merrimack.	Murder second degree.	Oct., "	18 5	Oct., 1863.
Hartwell Bonney,	59	Hallowell, Me.	Rockingham.	Passing counterfeit money.	Oct., "	4 3	Oct., 1867.
George A. Wing,	21	Windsor, C. W.	Cheshire.	Stealing horses.	Nov., "	3	Nov., 1871.
John Gray,	50	Ireland.	Sullivan.	Manslaughter.	Feb., 1865.	7	Feb., 1870.
William R. Tenney,	38	Londonderry, Vt.	Rockingham.	Breaking and stealing.	April, "	5	April, 1868.
Michael Hoffman,	30	Nova Scotia	Cheshire.	Stealing rope.	May, "	3	May, 1867.
Henry F. Hamilton,	26	Boston, Mass.	Cheshire.	Breaking and stealing.	" "	2	" 1880.
Sarah E. Webber,	25	Worcester, Mass.	Hillsborough.	Manslaughter.	" "	15 1	" 1880.
Alexander Lavone,	32	Canada East.	Strafford.	Stealing money.	Sept., "	4	Sept., 1869.
John Rowe,	69	Acton, Me.	Strafford.	Breaking and stealing.	" "	5	" 1870.
George Reynolds,	36	Nova Scotia	Strafford.	Breaking and stealing.	" "	5	" 1870.
Samuel Davis,	25	Elliot, Me.	Hillsborough.	Stealing watch.	" "	3	" 1868.
John Gallagher,	15	Providence, R. I.	Strafford.	Highway robbery.	" "	7	" 1872.
Charles E. Pinkham,	25	Farmington, N. H.	Belknap.	Murder.	" "	15	" 1880.
Moses Sifles,	19	Ellingham, N. H.	Strafford.	Stealing horse and carriage.	" "	5	" 1870.
Charles Smith,	18	New York.	Strafford.	Breaking and stealing.	" "	5	" 1870.
Enoch Hayes,	32	Dover, N. H.	Merrimack.	Breaking and stealing.	Oct., "	2	Oct., 1867.
John C. Ward,	17	Bangor, Me.	Merrimack.	Stealing horse.	" "	3	" 1868.
John Snyder,	26	Pennsylvania.	Merrimack.	Stealing horse.	" "	3	" 1868.
Joseph Latouch,	24	Vermont.	Merrimack.	Breaking and stealing.	" "	2	" 1868.
Dennis Crowley,	17	Ireland.	Merrimack.	Breaking and stealing.	" "	2	" 1867.
Neal Nelson,	46	Finland.	Merrimack.	Breaking and stealing.	" "	3	" 1868.
Thomas Wier,	52	Grafton, Vt.	Grafton.	Murder.	" "	30 1	" 1896.

33

Name	Age	Birthplace	County	Crime	Committed	Years	Discharged
James Johnson,	19	England.	Merrimack.	Breaking and stealing.	Oct., 1865.	8	Oct., 1878.
Abby N. Batchelder,	26	Chester, N. H.	Rockingham.	Burning mill.	"	6	" 1871.
Samuel George,	25	Seabrook, N. H.	Rockingham.	Stealing money.	"	3	" 1868.
William Sullivan,	25	Manchester, N. H.	Grafton.	Stealing horse.	Nov., "	6	Nov., 1871.
John Harvey,	23	Warner, N. H.	Hillsborough.	Highway robbery.	"	5	" 1870.
Daniel Sullivan,	16	Manchester, N. H.	Hillsborough.	Stealing money.	Dec., "		Dec., 1870.
Joseph Johnson,	26	England.	Hillsborough.	Breaking and stealing.	Jan., 1866.	3	Jan., 1869.
John Berry,	19	Canada.	Hillsborough.	Breaking and stealing.	"	3	" 1869.
Charles Stewart,	27	Mt. Desert, Me.	Hillsborough.	Stealing horse and buggy.	"	6	" 1872.
Edward Hickey,	27	Boston, Mass.	Hillsborough.	Stealing horse.	"	3	" 1869.
Patrick Foley,	14	Newburyport, Ms.	Hillsborough.	Stealing watch.	"	4	" 1870.
Edward Lawrence,	53	Correy, N. Y.	Strafford.	Forgery.	Feb., "	3	Feb., 1869.
Henry Grant,	27	Dover, N. H.	Strafford.	Breaking and stealing.	"	2	" 1868.
Sidney Nelson,	40	Dublin, N. H.	Cheshire.	Highway robbery.	"	7	" 1873.
Darius L. Lovejoy,	17	Barnstead, N. H.	Cheshire.	Stealing money.	Nov., 1865.	2	Nov., 1867.
Napoleon Drolette,	24	Montreal.	Cheshire.	Burning barn.	"	7	" 1868.
Charles Minor,	28	New-York.	Cheshire.	Stealing money.	"	20	" 1865.
William Nash,	40	Chesterfield, N. H.	Grafton.	Breaking and stealing.	Mar., 1866.	2	Mar., 1872.
Edward G. Dewey,	36	Hanover, N. H.	Hillsborough.	Highway robbery.	"	6	" 1873.
James Welch,	22	Roxbury, Mass.	Hillsborough.	Highway robbery.	"	7	" 1873.
James Nicholson,	22	Scotland.	Hillsborough.	Highway robbery.	"	7	" 1873.
Michael Broderick,	22	Ireland.	Hillsborough.	Highway robbery.	"	7	" 1873.
Timothy Mahanna,	23	Hallowell, Me.	Hillsborough.	Highway robbery.	"	7	" 1873.
John M. Mahanna,	21	Hallowell, Me.	Merrimack.	Stealing coat.	"	7	" 1873.
John Traverse,	47	Louisiana.	Grafton.	Stealing horse and carriage.	April, "	2	April, 1869.
Sylvester G. Closson,	21	Dixfield, Me.	Merrimack.	Stealing watch.	"	5	" 1871.
James Reed,	26	Scotland.	Merrimack.	Rape.	"	3	" 1869.
William H. Horner,	22	Concord, N. H.	Carroll.	Stealing money.	"	10	" 1876.
James McCrillis,	24	Newbury, Vt.	Carroll.	Burning barn.	"	2	" 1868.
Mary Cook,	23	Conway, N. H.	Rockingham.	Stealing coat.	"	7	" 1873.
Alvah L. Bruce,	28	Ohio.	Rockingham.	Breaking and stealing.	"	2	" 1868.
Charles E. Foster,	31	Dover, N. H.	Rockingham.	Highway robbery.	"	5	" 1871.
John Cross,	21	Newbury, Mass.	Rockingham.	Highway robbery.	"	10	" 1876.
Charles N. Clifford,	24	Portsmouth, N. H.	Hillsborough.	Forgery.	"	10	" 1876.
Patrick Shean,	33	Charlestown, Mass.	Hillsborough.	Forgery.	May, "	3	May, 1869.
William English,	48	Salmon-Falls, Vt.	Hillsborough.	Breaking and stealing.	"	5	" 1871.
John A. Gannett,	25	Cambridge, Mass.	Che-hire.	Stealing horse.	"	3	" 1869.
Francis Reed,	29	Antrim, N. H.	Hillsborough.	Stealing horse.	Sept., "	4	Sept., 1870.
David Wood,	25	Jackson, N. Y.	Hillsborough.	Breaking and stealing.	"	2	" 1868.
A. H. W. Emerson,	27	Haverhill, Mass.	Hillsborough.	Stealing horse and buggy.	"	2	" 1868.
John Ross,	21	Scotland.	Hillsborough.	Stealing horse.	"	3	" 1869.
James W. Rollins,	22	South-Berwick, Me.	Strafford.	Breaking and stealing.	"	1	" 1871.
John Murphey,							
William W. Jones,	38	New-Durham,N.H.					

3

REGISTER OF CONVICTS IN PRISON MAY 1, 1867.

(CONTINUED.)

NAME.	AGE.	WHERE BORN.	WHAT COUNTY CONVICTED IN.	FOR WHAT CRIME.	WHEN.	SENTENCE. YRS. MO'S. DAYS.	EXPIRAT'N OF TERM.
George W. Chamberlain,	30	Alton, N. H.	Belknap.	Highway robbery.	Sept., 1866.	15	Sept., 1881.
Charles E. Wiggin,	17	East-Boston, Mass.	Carroll.	Breaking and stealing.	Oct., "	4	Oct., 1870.
George G. Stearns,	44	Billerica.	Rockingham.	Passing counterfeit money.	" "	2 6	1868.
Henry A. Wheeler,	16	Danbury, Vt.	Merrimack.	Attempt to poison.	" "	6 11 16	1872.
Henry Stewart,	17	Ossipee, N. H.	Strafford.	Stealing horse.	" "	5 4 28	1871.
William N. Roberts,	24	Buston, Mass.	Rockingham.	Stealing horse.	" "	3	Oct., 1869.
Deborah Warren,	52	Barnstead, N. H.	Rockingham.	Perjury.	" "	2	1868.
Jeremiah Wiggin,	23	Moultonboro' N. H.	Carroll.	Stealing sheep.	" "	5	1871.
Martin F. Rickard,	21	Pomfret, Vt.	Cheshire.	Stealing horse.	Nov., "	3	Nov., 1869.
John W. Witham,	33	Pittsfield, N. H.	Merrimack.	Passing counterfeit money.	" "	2	1868.
Thomas H. Daley,	28	Ireland.	Grafton.	Stealing horse.	" "	3	1869.
Sumner Hardy,	36	Haverhill, N. H.	Grafton.	Stealing butter.	" "	2	1868.
David Parker,	17	Lisbon.	Grafton.	Stealing.	" "	1	1867.
James Parker,	25	Thetford, Vt.	Grafton.	Stealing.	" "	2	1868.
Henry C. Stevens,	29	Concord, N. H.	Grafton.	Stealing horse.	" "	3	1869.
George Warren,	22	Barnestown, C. E.	Hillsborough.	Forgery.	" "	3 1	1869.
Charles Ross,	20	Boston, Mass.	Hillsborough.	Stealing money.	Jan., 1867.	3	Jan., 1870.
George Inman,	27	Orono, Me.	Sullivan.	Stealing clothes.	" "	2	1869.
Philo Mason,	28	Salmon-Falls, Vt.	Strafford.	Breaking and stealing.	Feb., "	1	Feb., 1868.
Charles Colbath,	24	Porter, Me.	Strafford.	Stealing coat.	" "	2	1869.
James G. York,	25	Dover, N. H.	Grafton.	Forgery.	" "	4	1871.
Rodney Hardy,	19	Piermont, N. H.	Merrimack.	Breaking and stealing.	Mar., "	2	Mar., 1869.
Joseph S. Floyd,	33	Centreville, Me.	Merrimack.	Breaking and stealing.	April, "	5	April, 1872.
Richard Powell,	22	Virginia.	Merrimack.	Rape.	" "	5	1872.
James Garvey,	20	Spikenville Creek, [N. Y.]	Rockingham.	Breaking and stealing.	" "	1	1868.
Peter Kelley,	22	Troy, N. Y.	Cheshire.	Breaking and stealing.	" "	1	1868.
Patrick Ryan,	46	Salem, N. H.	Rockingham.	Breaking and entering.	" "	4	1871.
Alfaretta Boyce,	18	Fitzwilliam, N. H.	Cheshire.	Murder second degree.	" "	7	1874.
John T. Blazo,	21	Bartlett, N. H.	Rockingham.	Breaking and entering.	" "	2	1869.
Joseph B. Staples,	43	North-Berwick, Me.	Rockingham.	Stealing.	" "	3	1870.

REPORT OF THE CHAPLAIN.

To His Excellency the Governor, and the Honorable Council:

GENTLEMEN :—My report of the department of the Prison under my care can be but partial, as I was temporarily appointed to the Chaplaincy in January last.

The opinion has largely prevailed heretofore, that crime should be punished with a severity that would scarcely admit of mercy, and that nearly every claim to humanity is forfeited by a man who should be so unfortunate as to find himself in the uniform of a convict. It is clear that there should be a faithful administration of law and of proper penalty attached thereto; but the age of barbarism has gone by, and the dictates of humanity and religion should now permeate the whole system of human government. While crime should be met with a certainty of punishment, it should be administered in that spirit of kindness which so strongly characterized the teachings of our Saviour. I think, also, the idea prevails more largely than heretofore, that reformation of the criminal is not only desirable, but should be deemed an important result, so far as possible to be attained; and thus, instead of throwing back upon society, from time to time, a mass of moral corruption of which they have been relieved for a season, these men should go forth with strong virtuous impulses and high purposes, to cultivate those excellencies of character that will make them a blessing rather than a curse. Then there are always to be found some—not a few—who are criminals more from accident than malicious wickedness. Many very young men, who have had little or no parental instruction; orphans who, from early childhood have been drifting in society, usually of the worst type, with no good influences ever moving them to right action, should not, surely, be treated with that unyielding severity which should be shown to the more intelligent and hardened criminals. Between twenty and thirty now here are from 15 to 20 years of age, and they mostly belong to the class referred to above, and are objects of pity and commiseration. To awaken some aspirations in these young minds for future good and usefulness, is certainly the spirit of our holy religion.

Of the general management of this institution, it is only proper for me to say, that, from a somewhat careful observation, I see much to approve. While the strictest observance of discipline is enforced by the Warden and his Deputy, every possible attention is paid to the health and comfort of the men. The Warden, by much personal intercourse, has become familiar with each individual character, and takes a deep interest in their moral and religious welfare. He is always present at the morning service, and also in the Sunday School, and an active participant in all that is done. Much of his time on the Sabbath is devoted to visiting the men at their cells, and, in words of kindness, giving them religious counsel and encouragement. His excellent wife has, with praiseworthy patience and sacrifice of personal ease, taught several men to read, who did not know the alphabet when they entered the institution, and is faithful in her attention to the female convicts under her immediate supervision.

The Deputy Warden, Mr. Bean, is ready and energetic in the discharge of his duties, and mindful of the comfort of the men. Immediately after the morning service, on the Sabbath, he visits every cell, pencil and paper in hand, and learns the little wants of every man, and, so far as practicable, supplies them.

I have particularly noticed that harsh language is not

used as a means of enforcing discipline, and it seems to me that the excellent order, every where prevailing, is a practical demonstration of the power of kind words.

RELIGIOUS SERVICES

are observed every Sunday morning at 9 o'clock, in the prison chapel, and all the men are required to be present, unless sick, or excused by the Warden. For their interest and benefit the reading of the "Psalter" has been introduced. They also repeat the "Lord's Prayer" in unison at the close of the morning service. In this way they are allowed to hear the sound of their own voices, and it is to be hoped the truth they read will make a deeper impression upon the mind than when read by another. The singing by the "prison choir," under the direction of Miss Jones, to whom we are much indebted for the interest she has taken in this department, is interesting and creditable. The preaching is plain and brief, designed, if possible, to touch the conscience and lead to a reformation of life. The tearful eye is no slight evidence that these men are not all entirely lost to all good impressions.

THE SUNDAY SCHOOL

is held every Sunday afternoon at 4 o'clock. It being optional with the convicts to attend or not, some more than half are usually present, and manifest much interest in the study of the Bible. Many of them have had but little knowledge of the Scriptures before coming here, but the interest they now manifest, leads us to hope for much good fruit in the future. The classes are taught by gentlemen from the different religious societies in the city, who kindly offer their services for this work.

THE LIBRARY

is largely used by the convicts. For several years — perhaps always, heretofore — the books have been selected by the Chaplain, the men having no access to the library to choose for themselves. A thorough examination of the library has been made, and many books, so worn as to be unfit for use, taken out, and a catalogue of the remainder printed. There are now about nine hundred and fifty volumes, many of them, it is true, give evidence of having been much read, and must soon give place to new ones. Each man is furnished with a tablet upon which he designates several numbers of books desired selected from the catalogue, one of which he is likely to obtain. This mode of changing the books has greatly increased the interest of the men in the library, some who have been here several years finding books they did not know it contained. The limited appropriations, and the increased cost of books, has afforded but small additions for several years. If possibly consistent, it is hoped that at least $200 will be appropriated for the current year.

EDUCATION,

at least in the rudiments of learning, is certainly important, if not indispensable, to virtue and prosperity. It has already been stated that several have been taught to read since they came into the Institution. They manifest a great desire to learn, and, considering the little time devoted to their instruction, are making good progress. Most of the young men referred to above have had but few advantages; and those few have been sadly neglected. They now see the folly of their negligence, and the importance of education, and avail themselves of every opportunity for improvement. Many of them have read more, while here, than in all their lives before, but they are very deficient in all but the simple ability to read. They know but little of the fundamental rules of Arithmetic, and many can not write at all—and many others, but poorly. If these young men can receive instruction in those simple elements of that education so freely offered to the poorest who have their liberty, they certainly will be better prepared to enter again into society, by which they must inevitably be absorbed for good or ill. Little or no education, and bad associations, has left them an easy prey to vice and crime. I take the liberty to suggest that an *evening-school*, taught in the Chapel, would supply a want in this institution, deeply felt by those familiar with the real condition of the convicts. This can be done so as not to interfere in the least with the labor of the convicts; and indeed I believe it will increase their interest in the prosperity of the prison, and make their labor more productive. They will feel that, so far from there being any vindictive spirit mingled with their punishment, that their best interests are regarded, with a purpose to their improvement, and they will be more easily controlled by wholesome discipline, and the more cheerfully perform their allotted tasks. That intelligent labor is the most productive, is a truth so clearly demonstrated by facts, that it needs no argument of mine to prove it. I am satisfied that a fair trial of this suggested improvement would develop that the State has been financially a gainer, while the benefits to society can not easly be estimated. I earnestly hope this matter will recieve proper attention, and if found practicable, some system of instruction will be adopted.

As soon as practicable, after entering upon my duties, and becoming familiar with the character and condition of the men, with the advice of the officers I commenced, on a small scale, the instruction of those who are learning to read. All the opportunities they have heretofore had was what little could be done for them on the Sabbath. With a little instruction nearly every night, they progress quite rapidly,—and manifest a deep interest in what is being done for them, and it is hoped some good will result from this experiment in this hitherto, in this institution at least, untried department of prison discipline.

I am greatly indebted to His Excellency, Governor Smyth, and the officers of the prison, for their ready cooperation in such efforts as I have been able to put forth for the moral and religious improvement of the convicts.

I am, gentlemen,
Very respectfully yours,
S. HOLMAN,
Chaplain of the New-Hampshire State Prison.

REPORT OF THE PHYSICIAN.

To His Excellency the Governor, and Honorable Council:

The sanitary condition of the State Prison, during the year, has been very much as in other years of its history. Chronic diseases have prevailed in this institution as they do in most penitentiaries. Men who have led lives of criminal irregularity, who have grossly outraged the moral and physical powers of life, are here arrested in their course, and subjected to the unrelenting reaction of the heretofore suppressed and disregarded monitor of life's great and best end. They are given up to that degree of hopeless indifference or desperate submission, which renders life burdensome and dispiriting. Consequently, the vital capacity is diminished; the power of resisting the ravages of disease so overwhelmed, that remedies considered as potent and efficient in ordinary cases, in general practice, have not had the satisfactory effect which is generally obtained.

Having had several years' experience in caring for men confined in this prison, I am convinced of the necessity of an entire change in the size and general arrangement of the cells. They are too small, and imperfectly ventilated. When the doors of the cells are thrown open each morning, there is an intolerable odor; a vitiated atmosphere issuing therefrom, which the inmates have breathed during the greater part of the night. They go forth to their labors with a daily increasing sense of general debility; the stronger, bearing and forbearing; the weaker, eventually passing into the hospital, to be medicated and nursed for an indefinite length of time. Attention to the matter of ventilation would result in good to both State and prisoners.

The Warden and other officers of the prison have discharged their duty to the sick with great faithfulness. I am pleased to bear testimony to the kind and unremitting attention of Mrs. Mayo to the sick.

Whole number admitted to the hospital during the year, forty-seven.

DISEASES.

Jaundice,	20	Bilious fever,	1
Diarrhea,	2	Constipation,	4
Colic,	1	Indigestion,	1
Hemorrhoids,	1	Ague,	1
Rheumatism,	1	Hepatitis,	1
Syphilis,	1	Asthma,	1
Typhus fever,	1	Dysuria,	1
General debility,	1	Epilepsy,	2
Hemoptysis,	1	Catarrh,	2
Opthalmia,	1	Carbuncle,	1
Pneumonia,	1		

Deaths, 3.

Richard R. Pattee, typhus fever, died June 26, 1866; George W. Varney, bilious fever, died November 10, 1866; James Tuttle, bilious fever, died January 16, 1867.

A. A. MOULTON,
Prison Physician.

INVENTORY.

The following is a synopsis of the inventory of the personal property in the Prison, belonging to the State, made by the Appraisers, Messrs. Charles A. Hackett, S. W. Buffum, and J. L. Stevens, April 27, 1867, and sworn to by them.

In the *Warden's Office*: Safe, desks and desk furniture, books, arms, office furniture, &c.,	$365.55
In the *Guard Room*: Steam-heater, beds and bedding, and furniture,	115.50
In the *Hospital*: Bedsteads, beds and bedding, furniture, medicines, medical instruments, &c.,	196.45
In the *Cook Room*: Provisions, kitchen furniture of all kinds, counter scales, &c.,	882.83
In the *Prison Cellar*: Beef, pork, potatoes and other vegetables, &c.,	750.25
In the *Store House*: Steel drills and points, iron and steam pipe, hangers, &c.,	116.60
In the *Wash Room*: Soap, soap-grease, pumps, boilers, and washing utensils,	146.00
In the *Tailor's Shop*: Cloth, clothing, tailor's tools, bed-clothing, &c.,	768.85
In the *Blacksmith Shop*: Forge and blacksmith's tools, &c.,	26.00
In the *Engine Room*: Steam Engine and boiler, shafting, force-pump, &c.,	3202.00
In the *Cabinet Shop*: Shafting and pumps,	298.00
In the *Shoe Shop*: Lasts, rolling, skiving, welt and sewing-machines, shoes, 12 cases thick boats, shoemaker's tools, &c.,	1425.30

On the *Prison Wall:* Arms, stoves and funnel, tools, &c., 28.85

In the *Prison Yard:* Hard and mixed wood, tools of various kinds, &c., 540.75

In the *Prison Barn:* Straw, wagons, harnesses, agricultural tools, &c., 250.00

In the *Piggery:* Sawed wood, 26 hogs, shotes and pigs, tools, &c., 593.00

In the *Prison Chapel:* Seraphine, settees, chairs, funnel, &c., 147.50

In the *Prison Hall:* Bedsteads, beds and bedding, cell furniture, steam boiler, fixtures, &c., 1884.85

In the *Warden's Department:* Furniture, beds and bedding, stoves, carpets, &c., 547.50

In the *Female Department:* Beds, bedding, stoves and chamber furniture, 44.00

In the *Deputy Warden's Department:* Water tank, window blinds, &c., 18.50

Total, $12,348.18

REPORTS

OF THE

BOARD OF VISITORS, TRUSTEES,

TREASURER, AND SUPERINTENDENT,

OF THE

NEW-HAMPSHIRE ASYLUM FOR THE INSANE.

JUNE SESSION, 1867.

REPORTS

OF THE

BOARD OF VISITORS, TRUSTEES,

TREASURER, AND SUPERINTENDENT,

OF THE

NEW-HAMPSHIRE ASYLUM FOR THE INSANE.

JUNE SESSION, 1867.

CONCORD:
GEORGE E. JENKS, STATE PRINTER.
1867.

OFFICE OF THE SECRETARY OF STATE,
Concord, New-Hampshire, June 1, 1867.

SIR: By virtue of authority vested in me by chapter 2398, Pamphlet Laws of this State, I hereby authorize you to print three thousand copies of the Reports of the Board of Visitors, Trustees, Treasurer, and Superintendent of the New-Hampshire Asylum for the Insane, for the use of the State.

WALTER HARRIMAN,
Secretary of State.

GEORGE E. JENKS, *State Printer.*

OFFICERS OF THE INSTITUTION.

BOARD OF VISITORS.
(EX-OFFICIO.)

His Excellency, FREDERICK SMYTH, *Governor.*
Hon. HORTON D. WALKER, ⎫
Hon. BENJAMIN J. COLE, ⎪
Hon. ISAAC SPALDING, ⎬ Councilors.
Hon. JOHN H. ELLIOTT, ⎪
Hon. LUTHER B. HOSKINS, ⎭
Hon. DANIEL BARNARD, *President of the Senate.*
Hon. AUSTIN F. PIKE, *Speaker of the House.*

BOARD OF TRUSTEES.

CHARLES BURROUGHS, D. D., Portsmouth, *President.*
JOSEPH B. WALKER, Esq., Concord, *Secretary.*
ISAAC ADAMS, Esq., Sandwich.
WATERMAN SMITH, Esq., Manchester.
GEORGE B. TWITCHELL, M. D., Keene.
WOODBURY MELCHER, Esq., Gilford.
Hon. ISAAC SPALDING, Nashua.
JOHN CONANT, Esq., Jaffrey.
CHARLES W. FLANDERS, D. D., Concord.
CHARLES A. TUFTS, Esq., Dover.
WILLIAM G. PERRY, M. D., Exeter.
Hon. DENISON R. BURNHAM, Plymouth.

J. P. BANCROFT, M. D., *Superintendent and Physician.*
J. P. BROWN, M. D., *Assistant Physician.*
A. A. PORTER, M. D., *Second Assistant.*
Mr. J. C. SHAW, *Steward.*
Miss H. W. MOORE, *Matron.*

VISITING COMMITTEE FOR THE YEAR.

June	1867.	Hon. ISAAC SPALDING.
July	"	Rev. C. W. FLANDERS, d. d.
Aug.	"	WATERMAN SMITH, Esq.
Sept.	"	JOHN CONANT, Esq.
Oct.	"	Hon. CHARLES A. TUFTS.
Nov.	"	ISAAC ADAMS, Esq.
Dec.	"	WOODBURY MELCHER, Esq.
Jan.	1868.	GEO. B. TWITCHELL, m. d.
Feb.	"	JOSEPH B. WALKER, Esq.
March	"	Hon. D. R. BURNHAM.
April	"	WM. G. PERRY, m. d.
May	"	Rev. CHARLES BURROUGHS, d.d.

REPORT OF THE BOARD OF VISITORS.

To the Honorable Senate and House of Representatives:

The Board of Visitors made a careful examination of the condition of the New-Hampshire Asylum for the Insane, and its patients, on the 31st ult.

They were gratified with the order and neatness every where apparent, in and around the institution. Its internal condition affords convincing evidence of careful and systematic management on the part of its officers. Scrupulous cleanliness was apparent every where, in its cellars, its halls, and its rooms. The patients were all of them as comfortable as their several conditions would admit. In short, it gives us pleasure to say that we feel convinced that the affairs of this important institution are managed ably and economically.

The appropriation to aid the indigent patients at the Asylum has been applied from time to time as directed by the Legislature. This timely aid has enabled many to remain in the institution who would have otherwise been deprived of the benefits of its treatment.

Hereafter we understand the Trustees will be able to coöperate with the State in this benevolent purpose; the increase of the permanent fund of the Asylum, by the legacy of the late Moody Kent, Esquire, putting at their disposal an increased income—a part of which they have devoted to the aid of indigent patients.

The new building, for the accommodation of female patients, for which a partial appropriation was made last year, is now in process of erection. It is admirably adapted to the end for which it was intended, and when finished will compare very favorably with the best constructed buildings erected elsewhere for this specific purpose.

FREDERICK SMYTH, *Governor*.

DANIEL BARNARD,
President of the Senate.

AUSTIN F. PIKE,
Speaker of the House of Representatives.

B. J. COLE,
HORTON D. WALKER,
ISAAC SPALDING, } Councilors.
LUTHER B. HOSKINS,
J. H. ELLIOTT,

Concord, June 5, 1867.

REPORT OF THE TRUSTEES.

To the Honorable Legislature of the State of New-Hampshire:

The Trustees of the N. H. Asylum for the Insane respectfully present this, their

TWENTY-SIXTH ANNUAL REPORT.

In reviewing the history of the Asylum for the past year, its Trustees find cause of gratitude to Almighty God for the blessings he has vouchsafed to it, and for the great amount of good he has permitted it to accomplish.

The whole number of patients under treatment, as shown by the accompanying report of the Superintendent, has been three hundred and fifty-three, being twenty-six more than during any previous year. The number of admissions has been one hundred and seventeen; while of those discharged—twenty-four had decidedly improved, and thirty-nine been completely restored—an aggregate of sixty-three, and equal to about fifty-four per cent of the number of admissions. The number under treatment to-day (June 5th) is two hundred and forty-six.

FINANCIAL CONDITION.

A reference to the report of the Treasurer, herewith submitted, will show that the receipts of the Asylum, the past year, principally on account of the board of patients, were ($68,329.11) sixty-eight thousand three hundred and twenty-nine dollars and eleven cents, and that the expenditures have been ($68,284.15) leaving a balance of cash on hand, at the close of the financial year, April 30th, of ($44.96) forty-four dollars and ninety-six cents.

The very high price of most articles of consumption, and of labor, has rendered it a matter of difficulty to sustain the institution upon its current receipts. We are happy, therefore, that we can inform your honorable body that the provident and able management of the Superintendent has, nevertheless, secured this result.

Nearly all of the legacy of the late Moody Kent, Esq., has been received by the Asylum, and set apart as a permanent fund, bearing his name. This will afford an annual income of some nine thousand dollars, a part of which will be used to supplement the annual appropriations made by the State for the benefit of the indigent insane, and a part to procure additional curative appliances, to improve the buildings and grounds, and to secure for the patients many attentions and comforts that its ordinary income does not suffice to furnish.

NEW COTTAGE.

The new cottage, designed for the accommodation of the more excited women, for which a partial appropriation was made by the Legislature at its last session, is in process of erection, and will be ready for occupancy at the close of the present year. The foundations were laid last autumn, and the brick work is fast approaching completion. Contracts have also been concluded with competent parties for the slating and for the wood and iron work, and are being executed from time to time, as the progress of the building requires. The cost of this structure will not vary materially from the estimate submitted last year, and an additional appropriation of a like amount is requisite to finish it. When completed it will increase the usefulness of the Asylum, by the addition of thirty-three new rooms, for a long time greatly needed, and by the removal of very serious inconveniences, which, for years heretofore, have been experienced. We respectfully call your attention to the subject of an additional appropriation which will be necessary to secure completion.

DECEASE OF MEMBERS OF THE BOARD.

During the past year two members of this Board have been removed by death. Hon. Charles H. Peaslee and Hon. John Preston, who were both present at the last meeting of the Trustees, will meet with us no more. Both of those gentlemen were devoted friends of the Asylum, and had long been assiduous in repeated efforts for its welfare. Entertaining for them a high personal regard, we feel constrained, in transmitting to your honorable body this report, to put upon record an assurance not only of our deep regret at their removal, but of our appreciation of their distinguished worth as citizens of the State, and as friends of the unfortunate class whose sad condition it is the constant effort of this institution to ameliorate.

GEN. CHARLES H. PEASLEE.

Gen. Peaslee was born at Gilmanton, on the sixth day of February, 1804. After the usual preparation at the Academy of his native town, he entered Dartmouth College, at which he was graduated in 1824. He chose the profession of law, and prosecuted his legal studies for a time in the office of the late Stephen Moody, Esq., of Gilmanton, and afterward in Philadelphia. In 1829 he settled at Concord, and entered at once upon the active duties of his profession. Here he very soon won the general confidence, and secured to himself a fair share of the legal business of the town.

He had not been long at Concord when he became deeply interested in the condition of the insane of the State, for the amelioration of which no provision had then been made. A large number were living here and there in the different towns, in a condition as deplorable as it was hopeless. While a portion of these were as well cared for as surrounding circumstances would admit, many were kept in out-buildings, some even in cells and cages, while others were confined by chains, and other appliances equally rude. Few efforts for their recovery were attempted, and their friends, in most instances, looked forward to chance or to death as their only hope for the removal of the sad burden thus devolved upon them.

In common with several other philanthrophic gentlemen in different sections of the State, Gen. Peaslee became deeply impressed with the importance of at once making such provisions for the treatment of this unfortunate class as humanity and the true interests of the State demanded. He caused to be published important statistics relative to the number and condition of the insane. He also delivered lectures and made personal appeals to individuals in their behalf, with a view of awakening an enlightened public sentiment upon the subject.

In 1834-5-6-7 he was elected a representative to the Legislature, and was there earnest and unwearied in efforts to induce the State to provide for its insane a suitable asylum. After repeated discouragements and delays, the object sought was attained, and in June, 1840, Gen. Peaslee was appointed one of its trustees. In this office he has been continued by repeated reappointments to the day of his death. No one ever connected with it had the good of the institution more at heart. No one has been more earnest in his efforts to promote its welfare. For more than twenty-five years he has lavished upon it his time, his invaluable counsels, and his heart-felt interest. His sudden removal has taken from this Board one of its two original members, and from the Asylum a most devoted friend.

General Peaslee also took an active part in developing the railway interests of the State. He was one of the originators, and one of the first directors of the Concord Railroad; and the value of his services may be inferred from the fact that he was continued in the Board of Directors from the commencement of the enterprise until the May preceding his death; a period of more than twenty-six years.

To the militia of the State he also rendered important service, and from 1840 to 1848 he held the important position of Adjutant and Quartermaster-General. This office he resigned upon his election to Congress, in the year last mentioned. For six years he represented his District in the National Council with uniform ability, and was there ever industrious, faithful, and assiduously devoted to the important interests entrusted to his charge. Soon after the inauguration of President Pierce he was appointed Collector of the port of Boston, and for the succeeding four years discharged, to general acceptance, the responsible and often difficult duties of that position. Upon retiring from it he removed to Portsmouth, which has since been his residence. While there he gave his attention to his private business, and to the discharge of such public trusts as were devolved upon him. At the beginning of the last autumn he went on a visit to St. Paul, and while there was suddenly attacked with an illness which terminated his life on the eighteenth day of September, at the age of sixty-two years.

HON. JOHN PRESTON.

Some six months after the death of General Peaslee the sad intelligence was received of the death of Mr. Preston. When present at the annual meeting of the Board, one year ago, his health, which for years had been delicate, seemed confirmed, and all heartily rejoiced in the prospect before him of additional years of usefulness. Our anticipations, however, have been disappointed, as a brief illness terminated his life on the fifth day of March last.

Mr. Preston was the son of Dr. John Preston, and was born at New-Ipswich, on the 12th day of April, 1802. When about ten years old an illness, caused by sudden exposure in winter, developed an infirmity of health from which he suffered, at times, very severely, for nearly the whole period of his subsequent life.

He was fitted for College at the New-Ipswich Academy, and entered Harvard University in 1819, at which he was graduated four years later. His classmate, George Ripley, Esq., of the New-York Tribune, says of him, "In college he was distinguished for his successful devotion to study, the rare kindness of his disposition, and his friendly and winning manners."

After graduation he pursued the study of the law, for a time in the office of the late Judge Hubbard, of Boston, and subsequently in the office of George F. Farley, Esq., of New-Ipswich. He began his professional career in Townsend, Massachusetts, where he remained two years, and then removed to New-Ipswich, which was his residence ever after.

The chief business of his life was the practice of his profession, which he followed successfully for more than thirty years. But this did not occupy all of his time. Soon after returning to his native town, he purchased the farm of his grandfather, the late Judge Champney, and in the intervals of professional duties devoted a considerable time to its management and improvement. He was very fond of agriculture, and the State had few more intelligent or successful farmers than Mr. Preston. A friend of his remarks of him, "It was a source of infinite delight to him to walk through his fields and pastures, watching the progress of his crops and his various breeds of cattle." His efforts to promote an intelligent, sound and practical agriculture were earnest and constant, and their influence will remain for generations to come.

Mr. Preston ever stood very high in the estimation of his neighbors who knew him best. Not only did he hold important town offices, but he was repeatedly sent to represent his town and district in each branch of the General Court. Here he always proved himself an able, industrious and efficient legislator; a friend and advocate of virtue and temperance; of liberty, education and benevolence. At all times, both in public and in private, the friends of every good cause felt sure of his sympathy; the advocates of wrong felt equally sure of his conscientious opposition.

In 1856 he was appointed a Trustee of the New-Hampshire Asylum for the Insane. He at once identified himself with its interests, and gave to it freely of his time and his advice, which always proved sound, intelligent, and very valuable. Many a kind wish for this institution had birth in his heart, and developed into earnest efforts to promote its welfare.

In formally communicating to your honorable

body the decease, during the past year, of these two respected members of their Board, the trustees would embrace the occasion to express their sincere and profound regard for these devoted friends of the insane so suddenly and mysteriously called away. They have left an honorable record behind them, and the friends of this unfortunate class of our citizens owe them a lasting debt of gratitude.

In closing this report the Trustees would respectfully refer you, for statements in detail of the condition of the institution to the accompanying report of the Superintendent, which we have the honor herewith to transmit.

CHARLES BURROUGHS, *President.*

GEO. B. TWITCHELL,
ISAAC SPALDING,
JOHN CONANT,
C. W. FLANDERS,
WM. G. PERRY,
D. R. BURNHAM, } *Trustees.*
CHARLES A. TUFTS,
WATERMAN SMITH,
JOSEPH B. WALKER,
ISAAC ADAMS,
WOODBURY MELCHER,

SUPERINTENDENT'S REPORT.

In obedience to the requirement of the Statute, the Superintendent respectfully submits to the Trustees of the New-Hampshire Asylum for the Insane, the

TWENTY-FIFTH ANNUAL REPORT.

On the first day of May, 1866, there were in the Asylum two hundred and thirty-six patients, of whom one hundred and eleven were males, and one hundred and twenty-five were females.

The number of admissions to the first day of May, 1867, was one hundred and seventeen; sixty-three males and fifty-four females.

The whole number of patients under care during the year was three hundred and fifty-three; one hundred and seventy-four males and one hundred and seventy-nine females.

The largest number at any one time was two hundred and fifty-six, and the smallest number was two hundred and twenty-nine. The largest number of males was one hundred and twenty-six, and the smallest one hundred and nine. The largest number of females was one hundred and thirty-one, and the smallest one hundred and fifteen.

The daily average for the whole year has been, for males, one hundred and nineteen and three tenths, and for females one hundred and twenty-two and six tenths, and the total daily average for the year has been two hundred and forty-one and nine tenths.

The largest number at any time exceeds that of last year by sixteen, and that of the year previous by thirty. The general average exceeds that of the preceding year by thirteen, that of 1862 by fifty, and that of 1857 by eighty.

The removals of all descriptions were one hundred and seven; of these ninety—forty-five of each sex—were discharged, and seventeen—seven males and ten females—died.

The number now in the Asylum, May 1st, 1867, is two hundred and forty-six: one hundred and twenty-two males and one hundred and twenty-four females.

The conditions of those discharged were as follows: viz., thirty-nine had recovered, of whom eighteen were males and twenty-one were females; twenty-four—thirteen males and eleven females—were more or less improved, and twenty-seven—fourteen males and thirteen females—were not improved. Eleven of those "improved" were fit for regular and responsible employment and prepared to be useful in their avocations at home, and so far as heard from, all maintain their improvement, and some have since recovered.

Of those called "unimproved," fifteen were taken to other residences, either private or alms-houses, to diminish the expense of support. Seven, in whom there was little hope of improvement, were taken to their homes in such conditions that they could be taken care of by their friends, and two were in advanced stages of bodily disease.

Seventeen of the class "not improved" were persons supported at public expense, and were removed to alms-house—six being taken to one county receptacle.

Fourteen of those discharged "recovered" were persons supported at public expense.

The immediate causes of death in the seventeen who died were as follows: exhaustion, from acute mania, three; exhaustion from long continued mania, four; chronic abscess, structural disease of the brain, general paralysis, marasmus, pulmonary consumption, pneumonia, and epilepsy, each one; the decay of old age, two; and suicide by suspension, one.

In the last case there was a little relaxation of the rigorous watching which had been practiced for many months, on the disappearance of the inclination to self-destruction, and this was long after many opportunities had been passed without any attempt.

Of the persons who died, two were over seventy years of age, and seven were over sixty, and only one died from a disease independent of the mental maladies from which they were suffering.

The principal facts, relating to the persons admitted, may be found in the following tables:

TABLE 1.
Showing the residence of those admitted.

Rockingham,	23	Carroll,	7
Hillsborough,	23	Cheshire,	6
Merrimack,	21	Sullivan,	3
Grafton,	14	Coös,	7
Strafford,	5	From without the State,	4
Belknap,	4		

These last, from without the State, were exceptional cases, whose admission was urged on special grounds, such as having previously recovered here, or other personal consideration, and were admitted with express agreement to leave whenever their presence might interfere with our plans of classification.

TABLE 2.
Showing the ages of those admitted.

From 10 to 20 years old,	3
" 20 " 30 "	31
" 30 " 40 "	21
" 40 " 50 "	17
" 50 " 60 "	28
" 60 " 70 "	12
" 70 " 80 "	4
Over 80,	1

TABLE 3.
Showing the stage of the disease on admission.

The attacks recent in	57	Second or subsequent admission,	41
The disease was chronic in	60		
First admission,	76		

TABLE 4.
Showing the civil state of those admitted.

	Males.	Females.	Total.
Married,	28	27	55
Single,	31	19	50
Widowers,	4		4
Widows,		8	8

Table 5.
Showing the occupation of those admitted.

Farmers,	30	Wool Picker,	1
Common laborers,	2	Paper-makers,	2
Traders,	3	Soldiers,	2
Shoe-makers,	3	Clerk,	1
Students,	2	Fireman,	1
Dentists,	2	Household occupations,	49
Printer,	1	Seamstress,	2
Carpenter,	1	Teacher,	1
Blacksmith,	1	Factory operative,	1
Currier,	1	No particular occupation,	10
Clock-maker,	1		

Table 6.
Showing by whom the persons were committed.

Committed by private individuals,	76
" towns,	87
" county commissioners,	3
" order of court,	1

Table 7.
Showing the form of the disease in those admitted.

Acute mania,	54	Senile Dementia,	4
Chronic "	16	Epilepsy,	3
Melancholia,	16	Hystero mania,	1
Dementia,	21	Mental impairment from	
General Paralysis,	1	paralysis,	1

Table 8.
Showing how long the disease had existed in those committed.

One month or less,	29
From one to two months,	14
" two " three "	9
" three " four "	5
" four " five "	1
" five " six "	5
" six " twelve "	13
Over one year,	40
Not known,	1

Of the forty who had been insane over one year, ten cases were of more than five years' standing, and two over ten years.

TABLE 9.

Statistics of admissions, discharges and deaths, from the opening of the Asylum.

Year.	Admitted.	Disch'd & died.	Recovered.	Partly recov'd.	Unimproved.	Died.	Whole number.	Now in Asylum.
1843	76	29	12	10	6	1	76	47
1844	104	81	37	20	19	5	151	70
1845	88	82	37	17	22	6	158	76
1846	98	76	26	23	16	11	174	98
1847	89	87	38	17	23	9	187	100
1848	92	83	29	20	26	8	192	109
1849	81	76	36	15	11	14	190	114
1850	108	90	45	18	20	7	217	127
1851	88	98	45	25	16	12	215	117
1852	107	106	66	13	16	11	224	118
1853	132	107	65	25	11	8	250	143
1854	141	123	63	24	22	14	284	161
1855	95	91	50	20	9	12	246	155
1856	85	96	66	13	7	10	250	154
1857	97	81	47	15	7	12	251	170
1858	76	77	34	20	5	18	246	169
1859	98	85	31	22	18	14	267	182
1860	85	83	38	16	12	17	267	184
1861	106	94	34	34	10	16	290	196
1862	86	94	42	32	7	13	282	188
1863	101	85	30	32	17	16	289	204
1864	105	92	36	16	17	23	309	217
1865	107	102	42	23	14	22	324	223
1866	104	91	26	28	16	21	327	236
1867	117	107	39	24	27	17	353	246

Whole number ever admitted, 2461

A highly satisfactory state of health has prevailed throughout the year. We have not been visited by any serious sickness; indeed, with the exception of a single case of pneumonia, we have seen no acute disease uncomplicated with that of the mind.

With a larger population in the house than ever before, the mortality has been less than for several years, having been four and eight tenths per cent on the whole number of patients, against six and four tenths for the preceding year, and two per cent less than the average mortality for three years before. We may regard this as a good degree of exemption, when it is considered that in almost all the forms of disease of which mental disorder is the leading symptom, there is greatly reduced vitality, and that in all forms of insanity, the subject is an easy victim to any attack of intercurrent acute disease.

That the character of the season may have had its influence on the health and mortality in the asylum is suggested by the fact that there has been, during the year past, in this whole community, unusual immunity from disease. But I can not doubt that the standard of health is materially affected by the amount of time spent by the patients in active exercise in the open air.

This has been carried further during the last year than ever before, and, in all pleasant weather, a very large majority have passed the largest portion of the day out of doors.

We could not expect, however, under less favorable conditions as to season and the like to enjoy uninterrupted continuance of so high a standard of health, and hence it is gratifying to have near at hand such an increase of rooms in the asylum as to place all our patients in the most satisfactory hygienic conditions, when the cold of winter or the storms of other seasons forbid life in the open air. This we shall be able to do on the completion of the new building now in course of erection. I may here refer to some statements made in my last report showing the necessity of an increase of rooms. It was then stated that the present male wings had accommodations for one hundred and sixteen patients, that the hall on that side occupied by women was needed for men, and that if the rate of increase should continue, the necessity for this room would be urgent before the end of the year.

The facts have proved the correctness of this view, as the average number of men has been one hundred and nineteen, or thirteen more than last year, and three more than all the rooms on the male side of the house.

It was also stated that the number of rooms on the female side of the house was one hundred and two. The daily average of females having been one hundred and twenty-two, there has been an average surplus of twenty; and when the largest number have been present—viz., one hundred and thirty-one, there has been a surplus of twenty-nine, a number sufficient to occupy all but four of the rooms which will be added by the new building. In view of these facts, it is apparent that the movement for this addition was not begun too early, and that a due regard for the health, comfort and proper classification of the patients requires its completion as soon as is consistent with reasonable economy. At the rate of increase for the past year every room will be filled as soon as the building can be made ready for occupancy.

The situation was presented to the last Legislature and they promptly responded by an appropriation of fifteen thousand dollars, which was estimated to be one half the amount required, and sufficient to enable the Trustees to proceed with reasonable dispatch with the construction of the building till the present meeting of the Legislature.

The stone work has all been completed, the bricks purchased, and the the walls are carried up to the third story, and will, in a short time, be ready for the roof. The contracts for the slating of the roof, and for all the carpenter work have been made, and the work is progressing favorably on every part. The appropriation made last year has been exhausted in what has already been done, and an equal amount will be required to complete the work begun, in accordance with the several contracts.

There has been nothing in the history of the past year to distinguish it from the ordinary course of Asylum life.

No new principles have been introduced into the medical or moral treatment of mental disorders, but this, as every successive year, has quietly done its work in extending the practical application and illustrating the kindly and beneficent working of the methods of relief now every where acknowledged and practiced.

Each year does something more than its predecessors to dispel the false and superstitious fancies formerly entertained in regard to insanity, to give it the light of science and experience, and to place *this disease*, in the same relation as others, to scientific examination and remedies. And it would be only modest truth to say, that in no department of medical science and practice, is more substantial progress being made, than in the means and methods of relieving the various forms of mental disorder. As though it was a supernatural visitation, or stroke of implacable fate, insanity was formerly thrown out of the category of natural diseases, to be opposed by rational means, and the work of restoration given over to chance; but the number grows yearly less who would neglect to invoke the aid of science and experience, for the relief of one of the gravest of human maladies, and each year is giving more and more gratifying proofs that this is not less under the control of remedies, than other diseases.

When, as is very often the case, the mental disturbance depends on physical derangements, functional or otherwise, that derangement becomes the object of treatment, and a cure is sought by the removal of the cause, as in diseases in which the mind is not implicated. The peculiarity of the remedial measures is in this, that while the medical treatment (which is not peculiar) is in progress, a combination of influences, not necessary in ordinary diseases, is called for, to put the disturbed mind in an attitude most favorable to relief. To inaugurate and support these influences, is the distinguishing work of an asylum.

Primary among these influences, is safe, healthful, varied, pleasant occupation, for body and mind, filling up the daily life of the patient.

This subject was remarked upon in my last Report, and it is referred to now, only to say that during the past year this branch of effort has been carried much further than ever before, and every advance in this direction has been followed by the most satisfactory results. By all means in our power we have varied and multiplied the forms of occupation, capable of securing the interest of the patient. More of useful labor on the farm and in the garden, as well as in the house, has been performed by those who incline to these forms of occupation. Carriage drives have been a daily exercise in all pleasant weather, and a commodious boat has been in use upon the pond and become a favorite recreation. By a systematic distribution of attendants, there has been a great increase in the practice of walking in the grounds and surrounding country. For in-door purposes, cue alleys and bagatelle tables have been multiplied in the halls, in addition to the games in use before. Although we have not been able to satisfy our wishes, and reach the full measure of usefulness attainable, in the matter of social entertainments, we have at least doubled the number of evenings hitherto occupied in this way, and with increasing interest to all engaged. These evening exercises have consisted of lectures, concerts of vocal and instrumental music, dancing, charades, tableaux, and rhetorical and dramatical exhibitions. They have not only proved an entertainment for the hour, but a healthful stimulus to the mental powers of the convalescent, as well as a real tonic to many minds, long in a state of apparent chronic torpor.

I only add that these things greatly increase the happiness of the patients, during their necessary stay in the Asylum; and this is by no means among the least of the good results. Nor is it true of the recent cases only, and the convalescent, but the chronic, and even demented, who may have little hope of restoration of the lost harmony of their minds, find in these a pleasant interruption of the monotony of life, and no inconsiderable substitute for the pleasures of general society, from which their diseases necessarily separate them.

To estimate the whole force of this fact, it is to be borne in mind that, contrary to the popular notion, insanity *disorders*, oftener than destroys the powers; and that oftentimes, even when the mind may be so far diseased, as to require separation from general society, it still retains its activity, its power to appreciate and enjoy, in many, or even most directions, wholly unimpaired. Hence, much in the way of instruction or entertainment meets an appreciation and a response, not so different from that awakened in the general mind as many imagine. To suppose that the felicitous expression of thought and feeling, eloquence, wit, music, beauty, or whatever instructs, interests or pleases the mind in health, would be wasted on the population of an asylum, is simply to be ignorant of facts. In this light, we find ample encouragement to go on multiplying the means and occasions, properly regulated, not only of affording occupation salutary in a hygienic point of view, but of imparting, meantime, a high degree of rational enjoyment to a portion of our fellow-citizens, than whom none have a stronger claim to our benevolent regard.

The Library, by means of the contributions of visitors, added to the appropriation for its enlargement, has been increased by the addition of nearly two hundred volumes. This is becoming one of the greatest privileges of our patients as well as the household generally, and is a most constant and efficient means of usefulness.

Public worship on the sabbath has been continued through the year with the usual interest and profit, with a congregation as large as our small and unsatisfactory chapel will accommodate, but which might be much increased with a better room for the purpose.

To our regret Rev. J. H. Eames, D. D., who had sustained this service for eight years, in the most useful and satisfactory manner, was obliged, on the first of January, from regard to the state of his health, to discontinue his services with us. Rev. N. Bouton, D. D., has since that time conducted our public worship, and its interest and usefulness continue unabated.

FINANCIAL SITUATION.

When the cost of the necessaries of life was so much increased during the war, it was hoped that at its close, for the relief of that large portion of our patients whose pecuniary resources are small, prices would recede. In this we have as yet been disappointed, but instead, the cost of subsistence has been higher than ever before. In no year has it been so difficult to maintain the Asylum without deterioration in any respect, and yet not transcend, in the charges for support, any price which is practicable for the majority of our patients. This difficulty is shown in the fact, that while, according to the best authorities, the actual cost of supplies has been from ninety to one hundred per cent more than in 1860, the charges have not quite reached seventy-three per cent above the price at that time, and for several years before. But with all care to keep the expense as low as possible, it has still been found a very heavy burden in many instances, and one calling for great personal sacrifice on the part of friends. Indeed, had it not been for the State appropriation, and the income from legacies, a considerable number would have been entirely unable to enjoy the benefit of the Asylum. Under these circumstances, it is with great satisfaction that we anticipate an increase of means to assist the most needy during the coming year, derived from a source not available heretofore.

Eighty-one private patients have received aid from the State appropriation, and seventy-nine persons supported by towns; the several sums to which each one has been entitled having been credited in their board account. The year's income from the Sherman Legacy has been divided among twenty persons, selected with reference to their pecuniary necessities.

The Asylum is out of debt, but with less working capital than would sometimes be convenient in the transaction of its business. Heavy repairs have been demanded in the laundry, during the past year, owing to the decay of some part of the building. The rotten wooden floor has been replaced by one of iron, brick and cement, which will be permanent.

An important improvement in the supply of water has also been completed, which brings to the steam pump, at all times, any quantity, which an unusual drought, or the accident of fire, might render desirable. The two last seasons had shown, that in a very dry time, our fine spring was not sufficient for the increasing demands of the house.

FARM AND GARDEN.

The products of the farm were as follows: hay, 60 tons; straw, 8 tons; corn fodder, 12 tons; oats, 200 bushels; potatoes, 900 bushels; corn in the ear, 850 bushels; beans, 24 bushels; pumpkins, 20 cart loads; milk, 21,740 quarts.

The following were the products of the garden: carrots, 500 bushels; beets, 65 bushels; onions, 81 bushels; string and shell beans, 50 bushels; peas, 30 bushels; cucumbers, 80 bushels; tomatoes, 78 bushels; sweet corn, 40 bushels; lettuce, 14 bushels; turnips, 200 bushels; potatoes, 225 bushels; squash, 8¼ tons; melons, 540 pounds; beets for greens, 30 bushels; radish, 8 bushels; apples, 125 bushels; hops, 3 bushels; cabbage, 1800 heads; currants, 175 pounds; grapes, 112 quarts; strawberries, 100 boxes; cabbage plants, 150.

ACKNOWLEDGMENTS.

We are indebted to our friends for the following highly esteemed favors, which we take pleasure in publicly acknowledging: To the Nashua Quartette Club, for a delightful serenade; to visitors to the Asylum, for contributions for the library to the amount of $200; to Rev. J. H. Eames, D. D., for the remainder of his valuable course of lectures on travels in the East; to Rev. E. A. Lawrence, D. D., for two very excellent lectures on Rome; to Hon. Daniel Clark, Hon. E. H. Rollins, and Hon. Geo. G. Fogg, for valuable books and congressional documents; to the Concord Brigade Band and the Concord Orchestra Club, for evening entertainments of instrumental music; to Miss Emma Elliott, for valuable musical assistance on many occasions; to B. B. Davis, Esq., with his juvenile choir, for a pleasant concert of vocal music; to Col. David A. Warde, for a fine lot of bulbous plants; to the proprietors of the following newspapers, for their regular issues gratuitously: the N. H. Statesman, the N. H. Patriot, the Independent Democrat, the Concord Daily Monitor, the Nashua Gazette, Morning Star, the N. H. Sentinel, the Coös Republican, the Laconia Democrat, the N. H. Gazette, the Wolfborough News, and the Boston Daily Evening Traveller; to the proprietors of the several Concord newspapers for numerous exchange papers. Our good friend, Miss D. L. Dix, has added to the many former evidences of her kind interest, two beautiful colored photographs of monuments, erected by our soldiers in the field, to their fallen comrades.

Mr. A. G. Chadwick, who, at your last annual meeting, filled the place of apothecary, left the Asylum in July to complete his medical studies. While attending lectures at Hanover, he contracted typhoid fever, and after a short illness died at the residence of his father, in Boscawen, before reaching the profession of his choice and hopes. Albert A. Porter, M. D., has, for nearly a year, held the office of second assistant physician. No other changes of officers have occurred.

It gives me great satisfaction to express, at this time, my sense of the value of the services of my associates in office, who have ever cordially, promptly, and efficiently, seconded all my plans for the prosperity and welfare of the Asylum. Among many employees, undertaking peculiar and oftentimes difficult and trying duties, it is too much to expect that all would prove adapted to the calling. Those who fail to promise usefulness are encouraged to discontinue their services, while the best encouragements at our command are extended to those who succeed; and it is with sincere pleasure that I state that generally the different places are filled by faithful and competent persons, whose services contribute in no small degree to the good condition of the Asylum.

In closing, I desire to renew my thanks for the respect, sympathy, and judicious support, which I have uniformly received from you, gentlemen of the Board of Trustees, as also to record my respect for the memory of those Trustees, whose large sympathies had always made them most devoted friends of the insane, but whose cheering presence at your annual meetings we miss to-day, for the first time in many years.

Aided by your counsel, and trusting in a kind Providence for protection, we enter another year, hoping that its history will show a larger record of usefulness than any which has preceded it.

J. P. BANCROFT.

N. H. ASYLUM, MAY 1, 1867.

AUDITOR'S REPORT.

N. H. ASYLUM FOR THE INSANE,
Concord, June 4, 1867.

I have examined six hundred and sixty one bills, covering the last year's accounts of the Asylum, and have found them all correct, agreeing with the books of the Institution, and also with the private accounts kept by the Superintendent. I find the accounts satisfactorily vouched.

The receipts for the Institution for the past year, commencing May 1, 1866, and closing April 30, 1867, were $68,329 11
Expenditures for the same time,   68,284 14

Balance in favor of the Institution, $44 97

Faithfully submitted,

D. R. BURNHAM, AUDITOR.

TREASURER'S REPORT.

To the Trustees of the N. H. Asylum for the Insane:

From the first day of May, 1866, to the 30th day of April, 1867, inclusive, the receipts have been as follows: namely,

Cash balance on hand from old account,	$94 00
" received for board of private patients,	28,872 99
" " " " Town "	15,443 10
" " " " County "	10,631 53
" " of State Treasurer for support of insane convicts,	988 24
Cash received of State Treasurer, appropriation for indigent insane,	6,000 00
Cash received of State Treasurer, two years' appropriation for Asylum Library,	200 00
Cash received of State Treasurer, interest from Kimball legacy,	219 21
Cash received as income from legacies,	2,301 95
" for stock and articles sold,	1,987 65
" for land sold, Chandler estate,	91 19
Cash borrowed from Merrimack County Bank,	1,499 25
	$68,329 11

EXPENDITURES.

For provisions and supplies,	$26,813 37
salaries and wages,	14,192 71
furniture, utensils, mttreasses, bedding, &c.,	3,248 22
repairs, alterations and improvements,	6,397 07
clothing furnished, and charged in account to patients,	2,812 95
postage, freight, express, &c.,	593 67
fuel,	6,043 02
Trustees' expenses,	269 11
stationery, printing, books, &c.,	352 23
stock and farming implements,	2,260 55
gas,	1,218 98
burial expenses, charged in accounts,	249 05
medicines,	494 59
tax on lands (Chandler estate),	12 20
insurance on buildings,	243 87
improvements of the grounds,	343 65

For carriages,	331 70
cash refunded on account of over-payment,	275 41
books, and book-case for library,	265 56
miscellaneous articles,	332 74
cash paid Merrimack County Bank (note and interest),	1,533 50
Whole amount expended,	$68,284 15
Balance on hand, and carried to new account,	44 96
	$68,329 11

J. P. BANCROFT, Treasurer.

Concord, May 1, 1867.

CONCERNING ADMISSIONS.

Those wishing the admission of a person to the Asylum should make application to the Superintendent previous to bringing the patient, unless the urgency of the case precludes it.

On application, full information as to terms, conditions, etc., and the necessary papers, will be furnished.

With the application, a brief statement of the case should be given.

Some person should accompany the patient who can give a correct history of the case, if possible.

On no account should deception be practiced. The necessity of the step, and the arrangements having first been settled, the patient should be honestly informed of what is to take place.

FORM OF BEQUEST.

I give, devise, and bequeath, to the New-Hampshire Asylum for the Insane, the sum of   , to constitute a permanent fund, the income of which shall be devoted to the charitable purposes of said asylum.

THIRTEENTH

ANNUAL REPORT OF THE DIRECTORS

OF THE

Insane Asylum of California.

1865.

SACRAMENTO:
O. M. CLAYES, STATE PRINTER.
1866.

THIRTEENTH ANNUAL REPORT OF THE DIRECTORS

OF THE

Insane Asylum of California.

1865.

O. M. CLAYES............STATE PRINTER.

Officers of the Asylum.

RESIDENT OFFICERS.

G. A. SHURTLEFF, M. D., Resident Physician.   ASA CLARK, M. D., Assistant Physician.

DIRECTORS.

AUSTIN SPERRY, President.   E. S. HOLDEN, Vice-President.

T. R. ANTHONY,   J. G. GASMANN,   R. B. PARKER,   WM. M. BAGGS.

MEDICAL VISITORS.

J. P. WHITNEY, M. D., Chairman ....San Francisco.
LORENZO HUBBARD, M. D...Marysville.
JOHN F. MORSE, M. D., Secretary ....San Francisco.

R. HAPPERSETT, Treasurer.

REPORT.

To His Excellency,
      FRED'K F. LOW,
            Governor of the State of California:

The undersigned, Directors of the Insane Asylum of California, respectfully submit herewith their annual report, showing the progress and condition of the institution under their care.

For information in regard to the financial condition of the institution we respectfully refer your excellency to the report of the Treasurer, which is annexed to this report and constitutes a part thereof.

From said report it appears that the entire receipts in the General Fund, for the year ending October first, eighteen hundred and sixty-five, including a balance of twelve thousand four hundred and forty-five dollars and sixty-seven cents, ($12,445 67,) on hand at date of last report, amount to one hundred and twenty-five thousand and fifty-one dollars and fifty-six cents, ($125,051 56,) and the disbursements to one hundred and twenty-one thousand four hundred and forty-five dollars and five cents, ($121,445 05,) leaving a balance in that fund of three thousand six hundred and six dollars and fifty one cents, ($3,606 51.) The deficiency for the fiscal year ending June thirtieth, eighteen hundred and sixty-four, was four thousand nine hundred and four dollars and fifty-seven cents, ($4,904 57,) which has been paid out of the present year's appropriation. But for this fact no deficiency would now exist, although one is anticipated before the expiration of the present fiscal year, as you will see by the Treasurer's estimate. It will be observed that the disbursements for interest have been but trifling during the past year compared with those of previous years; and the estimated deficiency for the two years, ending June thirtieth, eighteen hundred and sixty-six, eight thousand four hundred and fifty-five dollars and seventeen cents, ($8,455 17,) notwithstanding the exorbitant prices of almost all articles purchased for the institution during most of this period, shows that the institution has virtually lived within its income. The fact that the contract bills have been paid promptly when due, and other purchases have been made for cash for the most of the year past, has given the institution a first class credit in the commercial world, and enabled the Directors to obtain supplies at the lowest market rates. It is to be hoped that it will not be necessary to impair this credit in the future, nor to resort to the ruinous system of discounting the State warrants to sustain it.

In the Improvement Fund the receipts have been sixty-six thousand six hundred and one dollars and fifty-three cents, ($66,601 53,) and the disbursements fifty-seven thousand seven hundred and ninety-seven dollars and seventy-two cents, ($57,797 72,) leaving a balance of eight thousand eight hundred and three dollars and sixty-one cents ($8,803 61) to the credit of the fund. The balance unexpended, after deducting bills unpaid, is stated to be seven thousand one hundred and fifty-nine dollars and eighty-seven cents, ($7,159 87.)

It gives us pleasure to call your excellency's attention to the new edifice erected on the Asylum grounds from the proceeds of this fund.

By reference to the report of this Board for the year eighteen hundred and sixty-three, it will be seen that the Board were compelled by the crowded condition of the old buildings, "to make some additions to the Asylum previous to the commencement of the new building provided for" by the "Act concerning the Insane Asylum of California, and to levy a tax therefor, approved April twenty-fifth, eighteen hundred and sixty-three."

This system of improvements being completed, as far as immediate necessities required, the Board directed their attention to the matter of carrying out what they conceived to be the grand design of the Legislature in providing in said Act for a fund "to be expended in the erection of additional buildings, yards, and other improvements in connection with the present buildings."

The purpose of the Legislature in this matter is to be gathered from the history of the projected improvements. We begin with the following proposal made by the Resident Physician in his report for the year eighteen hundred and sixty-one: "The most pressing want of the institution," says the Resident Physician in said report, "is additional room. We have enough at present for about two hundred and fifty patients, while there are under treatment four hundred and thirty-four. This necessity can be best met, perhaps, by the erection of a separate female department, for the location of which there is no lack of beautiful places on the Asylum property. The most eligible, however, and which, while convenient to the medical and other offices, would add more, perhaps, than any other to the present imposing appearance of the institution, is immediately in a line with the present building, about as far north as this is south of the Resident Physician's dwelling. Such an improvement should be made with the view of affording accommodation for one hundred and seventy-five or two hundred patients."—(Ninth Annual Report, p. 25.)

With this suggestion of the Resident Physician before them, the committees of the two branches of the Legislature visited the institution; and after a full examination of the grounds and buildings, being fully advised of the deficiencies then existing, the Senate committee, in their report to the Senate in eighteen hundred and sixty-three, say:

"For the remedy of these deficiencies, your committee recommend the purchase of two blocks of land, one in front, the other in the rear of the present buildings, and the erection of a building containing suitable accommodations for two hundred patients, and that the female patients should all be removed into that building; also the erection of a suitable fence, either of wood or of brick, as the Trustees may deem best, around the whole farm, now containing one hundred acres of as good farming land, probably, as can be found in the State."

The Assembly committee, in their report, after quoting *verbatim* the foregoing, say:

"The above extract from the report of the Senate committee we most heartily indorse, assuring your honorable body that its every word is true."

As upon these reports the Senate and Assembly acted in providing for the levying of a special "tax of five cents upon each hundred dollars value of taxable property" in the State, and that the money collected thereby should "be expended in the erection of additional buildings, yards, and other improvements, in connection with the present buildings, and in the purchase for the State of two blocks of ground adjacent to the Insane Asylum," the intention of the Legislature, in the Act in question, is, in the opinion of the Board, clear and unmistakable, that a distinct and separate building should be erected, from the proceeds of said tax, on the Asylum grounds, for the accommodation of the female patients, and that they "should all be removed into that building;" and that said building, so erected and so occupied, should be under the care and management of the same officers, on the Asylum grounds, *connected* by the same regime and interest with the other buildings, and forming with them a congeries of buildings and appliances, constituting, collectively, the "Insane Asylum of California."

But the Board of Directors, before fully determining their course of action in this matter, asked the opinion and advice of the Board of Medical Visitors, and received from them a communication under date of May eleventh, eighteen hundred and sixty-three, in which they say:

"In obedience to our promise before we left you, we hereby communicate our views upon the subject of the necessary improvements which you are expected to make in the structure and capacity of the institution in your management. We presume that there can be no disagreement as to the propriety of repudiating the present building as a principal structure to which additions should be erected and made to conform.

"You seem to manifest the only policy in this respect which could commend itself to our minds—to make the present edifice answer all demands until the most thorough and patient steps could be taken to design, locate, and build a new structure, so wholly and eminently adapted as to make it a source of unparalleled humanity and pride. We do not think that even the present want of room should enforce any precipitate measures that would make perpetual badly adapted means for the future care of the insane. We feel confident that any patchwork or extension of the present building would end in failure and mortification."

Confirmed in their views by the advice and opinions of the Medical Board thus ably expressed, the Board of Directors proceeded to locate and build the structure now completed. Before the work had made much progress, however, your excellency's attention was called to the matter, and your counsel sought in the premises. Your excellency kindly visited the institution, and after fully advising yourself of the facts, submitted them, with the law under which the Board were acting, to the Attorney-General of the State for his opinion. His views are given at length, and are doubtless now on file in your excellency's office. We will take the liberty of quoting a passage or two from a copy in our hands. He says:

"That the object to be attained in the construction of this, as of all statutes, is to discover the intention of the Legislature; and to do this, that the whole statute is to be taken together, and the meaning to be gathered from the context; that the words are to be taken in their plain and obvious ordinary and familiar signification; that such interpretation is to be given as will advance the remedy and suppress the mischief; that we are to see that all the parts harmonize with each other and with the general object of the whole; that we are to look at the whole and every part, to the subject matter, to the effects and consequences, to the reason and spirit of the law, in order to effectuate the purpose of the lawgiver, are cardinal rules of legal construction, and it is needless to refer to authority to support them.

"The statute is a compendious whole, and upon reading it, it seems to embrace parts of many prior statutes. But from its general context it shows it is not the establishment, however, of a new Asylum—the inauguration of an entirely new system—but rather an extension of the old Asylum, and a remodelling of the prior system. It was simply to make the present institution approach more nearly an Insane Asylum; not to create and build up a new institution in Santa Cruz County, or in any other part of San Joaquin County—not the inauguration of *another*, but the amelioration of the *existing* Asylum.

"Under the rules before laid down, I do not consider that the words just quoted require the 'additional buildings' to be constructed in *actual contact* with the present buildings for many reasons.

"The word 'connection' does not necessarily, if usually, mean immediate contact, either in common parlance or legal contemplation, and in this case, where such construction would lead to absurdity or manifest and serious inconvenience and evil, and fail in a great measure in accomplishing the obvious intent of the Legislature to alleviate the sufferings of the most unfortunate class of our citizens, it is not to be entertained, and I therefore dismiss such an interpretation.

"The Board doubtless may, they are not bound to, build in adjoining proximity. But in the erection of this new building, are the Board constructing an 'additional' one, in the sense used by the statute—one in such close dependence upon the principal building as the word 'connection' implies? Because the Board may go one foot or fifty from the old building, they cannot therefore go into a neighboring county. They may go a reasonable distance (and what is reasonable must depend upon the facts of each particular case) upon the Asylum grounds to erect the new buildings, always keeping in view the end aimed at, viz: the amelioration of the condition of the present Asylum.

"And the Board are permitted to exercise a judicious, not an arbitrary discretion, a wise and prudent judgment, in acting under and within the powers conferred on them.

"But here I may say, assuming that in other respects the Board are acting prudently and within their powers, the mere fact that the present building is on such a plan as that it may constitute a part of a new Asylum, if the Legislature at some future time so will that such new Asylum shall be erected, to my mind is no objection, but rather a recommendation.

"From the facts (assuming them to be such) and from your verbal explanations to me of the position of the new building, its distance from the old, its probable requirements, expense, the advantages, curative and others, likely to be effected by its erection, and generally of the considerations intimated in the above queries, and similar ones suggested by them, I conclude that this new structure is but a part and extension of the present Asylum buildings.

"It only remains for me to add, that in view of the above, and that so long as the Board follows such a course, as a matter of law, it is my opinion that they are acting within the scope of the powers conferred upon them by the Act, and should not be interfered with.

"Truly and respectfully,

(Signed:) "J. G. McCULLOUGH,
"Attorney General."

In your excellency's communication of June twenty-seventh, eighteen hundred and sixty-four, having reference to the foregoing, you are pleased to say:

"In the haste with which I wrote the note inclosing the opinion of the Attorney-General, I perhaps did not say explicitly that I concurred in his opinion, yet sending it as I did, 'as a reply to your communication,' my opinions I thought would be readily understood.

"The Attorney-General is the law adviser of the Executive Department, and in all ordinary cases I am quite content to be guided by his opinions on the legal questions on which I am called upon to act.

"Truly yours,

(Signed:) "F. F. LOW."

The Board being now fully satisfied of the correctness of their views, and propriety of their action in the matter in question, proceeded with their work, and as before stated, have recently brought the same to completion.

The new building, as your excellency is aware, is somewhat further north of the Resident Physician's dwelling than the old building is south, and somewhat to the westward of a line with the old building, the highest ground being at the point chosen.

The objects attained by this improvement, thus located, in general, are:

First—The removal of the female patients from the noise and confusion of the hitherto crowded male department, quietness being especially desirable for the female wards, it being also desirable that the sexes should not be in the sound of each other's voices.

Second—Better ventilation for the new building, and the retaining of all of the ventilation of the old building, much of which a new structure in contact with it would have cut off.

Third—Protection against fire. As the danger from this source is imminent, from the incendiary disposition of many of the patients, the building having been on fire several times already, and as a conflagration is possible, however great the precautions used to prevent it, it would be sheer madness to so construct the buildings that if one is consumed all will be consumed, with the terrible exposure of life consequent thereon—dangers which immediate contact of all the buildings would imply.

Fourth—That good building ground was obtained in the location, and the means of observing the rules of architectural science. The city street on the south of the old building, and the slough or watercourse on the north, with numerous outhouses in the rear, rendered it absolutely impossible to locate a new building of suitable size in contact with the old building, while, if this were possible, architectural science would revolt at the idea of such an unsymmetrical and uncouth assemblage of structures as would thus be produced.

We have spoken more at length on this subject, as much has been said in condemnation of the action of the Board in this matter.

Mr. Henry Winslow, the superintendent of construction of the new building, whose fidelity, skill, and economy in the conduct of his work are worthy of especial commendation, has kindly furnished the following detailed description of the new building. He says:

"The addition, built and finished the past season, to the Insane Asylum, is a part, or about one-fifth, of a plan drawn by G. F. Bryant, of Boston, under the direction of Dr. Luther V. Bell, formerly Resident Physician of the McLean Asylum of Massachusetts.

"A brief description is as follows:

"The entire length from east to west is one hundred and fifty feet, in a quadrangular form, the east end being four stories high above the basement, thirty-five feet wide by sixty-two feet long; and containing twenty-four rooms, ten feet by twelve feet, for patients, with four bath rooms, four wash rooms, four water closets, and four sink rooms, with China closets for each.

"A hall in each story, twelve feet by sixty feet, with entries and stairways leading from basement to attic.

"The west end is thirty-three feet by forty-two feet, and four stories high, containing reception rooms, Matron's room, sewing room, attendants' rooms, associated and domestic rooms, with halls, stairways, and closets.

"The centre, connecting the two, is ninety-one feet six inches by thirty-seven feet, and three stories high. It also contains forty rooms for patients; three halls, ninety-one feet long by twelve feet wide, each containing a bay window about twenty feet square; three dining-rooms, three bath rooms, three wash rooms, and three water closets; three China closets, and dumb waiters leading from basement to all the dining-rooms. It also has the attic finished and well ventilated, accommodating twenty beds.

"The basement, a part of which is used for cooking purposes, being furnished with modern improvements.

"The warming of the whole building is done by steam, the coils being placed in the basement.

"Two iron tanks for water are placed in the central attic, which have a capacity for about six thousand gallons.

"Hot and cold water are distributed throughout the building.

"The entire building is piped, and lighted with gas.

"The south and west fronts are finely finished with oil mastic.

"The roof covering, gutters, and cornice are of heavy galvanized iron.

"The whole number of rooms, exclusive of attics, is one hundred and twenty-six, and they are at present occupied by one hundred and twenty-five patients.

"It contains one hundred and eighty-seven windows, all of which are strongly guarded by an outside iron sash.

"An engine and pump house has been built, thirty feet by forty-five feet, one and one-half stories high. It contains one of Worthington's duplex pumps, capable of raising ten thousand gallons of water seventy feet high, with fifteen pounds steam pressure, per hour. It also has a large room for ironing clothes, and four chambers for lodging.

"Also a brick shaft, ten feet square at its base and seventy-five feet high, for the purpose of ventilating the water closets in the building and carrying off the smoke from the boilers.

"The entire cost of the building, thus far, exclusive of furnishing, is sixty-six thousand eight hundred and eighty-five dollars and thirty-four cents ($66,885 34.)"

We beg leave to report the following changes as having taken place in the Board of Directors during the past year: On the ——— day of ———, eighteen hundred and sixty-five, Judge H. B. Underhill tendered his resignation, on account of the decision of the Supreme Court in the Sanderson and State Library case, and Mr. William M. Baggs was elected in his place.

On the first day of August, Dr. G. A. Shurtleff tendered his resignation, he having on that day been elected to the office of Resident Physician of the Asylum, and Mr. R. R. Parker was elected a Director in his place.

The Board would respectfully call your excellency's attention to the law of eighteen hundred and sixty-three, in reference to the election of Resident and Assistant Physicians. Section six of said law provides that:

"The Board of Directors and Board of Medical Visitors shall elect, in joint ballot, one Resident Physician, who shall hold his office for a term of four years, and until his successor shall be elected and qualified." (Statutes 1863, p. 460.)

Section eight provides that:

"There shall be one Assistant Physician, who shall be elected at the same time and manner as the Resident Physician." (Statutes 1863, p. 461.)

Section nine provides that:

"The first election for Resident and Assistant Physicians, under this Act, shall take place at a joint meeting of the Directors and Medical Visitors, to be holden at the time of the stated meetings of these two bodies next preceding the expiration of the term of office of the present incumbents, the twentieth day of April A. D. eighteen hundred and sixty-five." (Statutes 1863, p. 462.)

At the time of the stated meeting of the two Boards, as provided by the by-laws, in April last, there not being a quorum of both Boards present, the joint meeting was adjourned to a specified time, and at that time, for the same cause, adjourned again, and so on from time to time till the first day of August last, on which day all the members of both Boards being present, an election was held in joint meeting, which resulted in the election of Dr. G. A. Shurtleff, Resident Physician, and Dr. A. Clark, Assistant Physician, both of whom have performed their duties thus far with such distinguished ability and success, as to justly deserve the highest meed of praise.

We would call your excellency's special attention to the able, elaborate, and complete report of the Resident Physician, hereunto annexed, and forming a part of this report—showing not only the present condition of the institution, but giving the results of its workings from its establishment in eighteen hundred and fifty-one to the present time. It will be noticed as a matter of just pride, while it proves the utter falsity of the charges so often and so flippantly made—that but few cures are here effected—that the percentage of cures in this institution from the year eighteen hundred and fifty-one, when it was established, to the present time, is more than fifty-one per cent of the entire number of cases admitted. The value of this fact will be more apparent when it is considered that in England, of sixteen thousand five hundred and sixteen cases treated, only thirty-five per cent recovered; while in France, of three thousand nine hundred and thirty-eight cases treated, about fifty per cent recovered; and in the United States the percentage of cures in all the Asylums, the reports of which through a period of years have been received, with one exception, is considerably less than in the Asylum of California—the single exception being the Central Asylum of Ohio, in which the percentage of cures through a series of years is fifty-two per cent.

We would call your excellency's attention also to Table Fifth, in the Appendix to the report of the Resident Physician, showing the estimated value of the Insane Asylum property—amounting in the aggregate to the very respectable sum of three hundred and twelve thousand one hundred and thirty-three dollars.

It will be also seen from the tables in said Appendix that a net profit of over five thousand dollars has been derived from the farm during the past year. The advantage to the patients who are allowed to work there cannot be estimated.

It gives us pleasure to speak in terms of unqualified approbation of the employés of the institution, one and all. They have been watchful, faithful, and prudent, as is evinced by the cleanliness of the patients and wards, and the air of comfort and neatness which pervades all departments, as well as the comparative quietness and good order everywhere manifest.

We would take occasion here to recommend a continuance of the special tax for improvements. We think it advisable to provide for the erection of another portion of the edifice, a part of which, according to the original plan, has just been completed. Though this part is perfect and complete of itself, and could be made by some crowding to accommodate all the female patients now in the institution, we do not think it advisable to mar the harmony and comfort of the present arrangement by congregating more in the new building than it was designed to accommodate—a condition of things which the constant increase of patients seems to foreshadow.

We would also recommend a small increase of the amount of appropriation for the current expenses of the institution, say one hundred and ten thousand dollars, instead of one hundred thousand, as during the last two years.

In conclusion, we would state that the Directors have noticed, at different times, attacks in the public prints upon the institution and its officers, with charges of improper management, mostly vague and indefinite, but we have not felt called upon to enter upon any newspaper controversy in reference to these matters. Conscious of an honest purpose to perform our duties faithfully, we desire that all our acts should be open to the public, and therefore earnestly request that the proper committees shall be appointed and the most thorough scrutiny exercised in investigating the affairs of the institution and the actions of the Board.

And especially do we desire that the wants of the unfortunate and afflicted human beings who are thrown upon the charities of the State, as here dispensed, shall be duly appreciated, and that the most humane and liberal provision shall be made for their treatment and care.

AUSTIN SPERRY,
E. S. HOLDEN,
T. R. ANTHONY,
J. G. GASMANN,
R. R. PARKER,
WM. M. BAGGS.

TREASURER'S REPORT.

REPORT.

STOCKTON, October 1st, 1864.

To the Board of Directors of the Insane Asylum of California:

GENTLEMEN—The by-laws of the institution require the Treasurer to submit an annual report up to the first day of October of each year, of the transactions of his office for the preceding year; and although, as you are aware, I only assumed the duties of the office on the first day of May last, I have deemed it proper to submit a report for the whole term, such as I am enabled to compile from the books in my possession. According to said books, on the first day of October, eighteen hundred and sixty-three, there was a cash balance of twenty-eight hundred and thirty-eight dollars and fifty-three cents, ($2,838 53.) This, it appears, belonged to the "Improvement Fund," (as we have designated the fund derived from the tax of five per cent levied by the Legislature for the erection of additional buildings and other improvements at the State Insane Asylum,) together with the sum of one thousand eight hundred and fifty-two dollars and seventy-two cents, ($1,852 72,) which had been drawn from that fund for the use of the General Fund, making a balance to the credit of the Improvement Fund of four thousand six hundred and ninety-one dollars and twenty-five cents, ($4,691 25.)

The following is a statement of the receipts and disbursements of the

IMPROVEMENT FUND.

	RECEIPTS.	
Oct. 1, 1863	By balance as above...................................	$4,691 25
Dec. 29, 1863	By amount received from State Treasurer.....	24,300 00
Jan. 29, 1864	By amount received from State Treasurer.....	7,800 00
Mar. 11, 1864	By amount received from State Treasurer.....	6,833 32
June 7, 1864	By amount received for premium on currency draft...	29 50
June 17, 1864	By amount received from State Treasurer.....	18,000 00
June 17, 1864	By amount received from premium on gold remitted East..	162 32
	Carried forward.............................	$61,816 39

	Brought forward......	$61,816 39
Sept. 27, 1864	By amount received from State Treasurer.....	2,151 35
	Total receipts......	$63,967 74

DISBURSEMENTS.

To bills paid as per vouchers, from October 1, 1863, to October 1, 1864......	$64,042 32
Leaving balance overdrawn......	$74 58

The bills audited against this fund, contracted prior to this date, amount to eleven thousand seven hundred and sixty-nine dollars and twenty-eight cents, ($11,769 28,) including above balance.

The following is a statement of the receipts and disbursements of the

GENERAL FUND.

RECEIPTS.

Oct. 8, 1863	By Controller's warrant......	$12,218 09
Oct. 15, 1863	By amount from Resident Physician collected from patients......	5 00
Oct. 21, 1863	By balance of estimate for December, 1862, accounted for by J. M. Douglass......	1,820 69
Oct. 31, 1863	By am't for brick from Improvement Fund..	205 20
Nov. 1, 1863	By balance of estimate, January, 1863, accounted for by J. M. Douglass......	2,057 26
Nov. 7, 1863	By Controller's warrant......	10,154 06
Nov. 16, 1863	By balance of estimate of March, 1863, from J. M. Douglass......	1,521 20
Nov. 24, 1863	By balance of estimate for February, 1863, from J. M. Douglass......	1,607 21
Nov. 24, 1863	By balance of estimate of April, 1863, from Fitzgerald......	1,685 04
Nov. 10, 1863	By amount from Resident Physician from patients......	258 39
Dec. 7, 1863	By Controller's warrant......	11,000 00
Dec. 11, 1863	By amount from Resident Physician from patients......	283 08
Jan. 11, 1864	By Controller's warrant......	9,409 28
Jan. 11, 1864	By amount from Resident Physician from patients......	503 50
Feb. 8, 1864	By amount from J. V. Leffler for brick......	11 00
Feb. 11, 1864	By amount from Resident Physician from patients......	197 50
Feb. 16, 1864	By amount from Sperry for brick......	88 00
Feb. 20, 1864	By amount from J. Diedrich for same......	5 50
	Carried forward	$52,930 00

	Brought forward............................	$52,930 00
Feb. 22, 1864	By amount loaned by W. C. Ralston............	6,800 00
Mar. 9, 1864	By amount from patients........................	19 00
Mar. 11, 1864	By Controller's warrant...........................	7,096 10
Mar. 12, 1864	By amount received from sale of brick.........	55 00
Apr. 27, 1864	By amount borrowed on warrant of $8,000...	6,400 00
May 11, 1864	By am't borrowed on warrant of $24,412 70..	20,020 00
May 11, 1864	By amount from Resident Physician from patients in March................................	242 83
	By amount from same source in April.........	184 33
	By amount from Steward for sales of sundry articles..	347 27
	By amount from Wm. Saunders for brick.....	5 50
	By amount from P. L. Shoaff for old engine..	100 00
June 7, 1864	By amount borrowed on warrant of $8,000...	6,400 00
June 9, 1864	By amount from Resident Physician from patients...	515 45
June 30, 1864	By amount borrowed on warrant of $8,000...	6,400 00
July 1, 1864	By amount from Ainsworth for brick..........	315 50
July 15, 1864	By amount from Resident Physician............	85 00
July 28, 1864	By amount from W. C. Ralston—bal. warrant	1,200 00
Aug. 16, 1864	By amount from Hale & Newell for forfeiture of contract...	300 00
Aug. 29, 1864	By amount from Fund Commissioners for balance of warrant..................................	4,392 70
Aug. 29, 1864	By amount from Fund Commissioners for balance of warrant..................................	1,600 00
July 14, 1864	By amount borrowed on warrant................	6,700 00
Aug. 9, 1864	By amount from Resident Physician from patients...	45 00
Aug. 26, 1864	By amount borrowed on warrant................	6,700 00
Sept. 9, 1864	By amount from Resident Physician from patients...	206 00
Sept. 14, 1864	By amount borrowed on warrant................	6,000 00
	By amount transferred from Improvement Fund for bills paid from this fund prior to 1st October, 1863...................................	5,801 02
	Total receipts.................................	$140,960 70
	DISBURSEMENTS.	
	To amount of bills paid as per vouchers on file...	128,530 03
	Leaving a balance of............................	$12,430 67

The above disbursements include the sum of one thousand eight hundred and fifty-two dollars and twenty-two cents refunded to the Improvement Fund, and seventeen thousand five hundred and seventy-six dollars and two cents paid interest and discount on Controller's warrants.

Since the last annual report, it has been ascertained that there was a deficiency in the appropriation for the fiscal year ending June thirtieth, eighteen hundred and sixty-three, of eight thousand one hundred and ninety-one dollars and fifty-six cents, which was carried forward and made a charge upon the appropriation for the fiscal year which closed on the thirtieth of June last. At this time it is impossible to ascertain the exact deficiency for that year, because some warrants that have been hypothecated will not be paid for some time. It is my opinion, however, that the deficiency, if any, will be small.

Up to the date of this report, warrants have been pledged on loans to the amount of..	$40,999 99
The sums borrowed at different times amount to...............	32,200 00
Balance in favor of Asylum...	$8,799 99

From which interest is to be deducted when the warrants shall have been paid.

The bills contracted against the General Fund up to this date, and remaining unpaid, amount to	$19,297 15
Less cash on hand as reported.....................................	12,430 67
Deficiency for first three months of present fiscal year...	$6,866 48

Should the warrants which have been hypothecated be paid within a short time, it is reasonable to suppose that the deficiency will be small. I am induced to believe, from information received, that after the first of January next, the institution will be no longer under the necessity of borrowing money, but that its affairs will be conducted on a *cash* basis.

RECAPITULATION.

Oct. 1, 1864	Balance in General Fund...........................		$12,430 67
	Balance in fund belonging to patients..........		582 81
	Balance for payment of small accounts not called for...		88 09
			$13,101 57
	Less Improvement Fund overdrawn............		74 58
	Balance in Treasury.................................		$13,026 99

All of which is respectfully submitted.

R. HAPPERSETT,
Treasurer.

OFFICE OF TREASURER OF THE INSANE ASYLUM,
Stockton, October 1st, 1865.

To the Board of Directors of the Insane Asylum of California:

GENTLEMEN:—In pursuance of the duties of my office, I herewith submit my report as Treasurer for the year commencing October first, eighteen hundred and sixty-four, and ending October first, eighteen hundred and sixty-five.

GENERAL FUND.

	RECEIPTS.	
Oct. 1, 1864	Balance in Treasury, as per report...............	$12,430 67
	Add clerical error..	15 00
	Correct balance.............................	$12,445 67
Oct. 3, 1864	Amount received for brick.........................	400 00
Dec. 10, 1864	Amount of Contingent Fund paid over by Resident Physician.............................	100 00
Feb. 13, 1865	Amount of fund belonging to patients, transferred..	582 81
March 8, 1865	Amount received from sale of cattle............	185 00
July 1, 1865	Amount received from sale of bags, &c.........	20 17
Aug. 1, 1865	Amount received from sale of calves............	46 95
Sept. 1, 1865	Amount received from sale of horses............	260 00
	Amount of balances on warrants hypothecated prior to October 1, 1864...............	8,799 99
	Amount of warrants drawn from State Treasury, from October 1, 1864, to October 1, 1865, inclusive.................................	99,999 97
	Amount received from patients, from October 1, 1864, to October 1, 1865................	2,211 00
	Total receipts...............................	$125,051 56
	DISBURSEMENTS.	
	Bills paid, as per vouchers on file, from October 1, 1864, to October 1, 1865...............	$121,445 05
	Leaving balance in General Fund of......	$3,606 51

Since my last annual report, the account of the appropriation for the fiscal year ending June thirtieth, eighteen hundred and sixty-four, has been closed, the warrants issued thereon having been paid, and the loans for which they were hypothecated settled, with interest thereon. The deficiency for that year has been ascertained to be four thousand nine hundred and four dollars and fifty-seven cents, ($4,904 57,) which has been paid out of the appropriation for the succeeding fiscal year.

The interest accrued on loans and accounts contracted previous to the first of October, eighteen hundred and sixty-four, amounts to eleven hundred and fifty-one dollars and forty-one cents, ($1,151 41.) The whole amount paid since that time is two hundred and seven dollars and sixty-seven cents, ($207 67.)

The following statement will exhibit the entire expenditure for the year ending this date:

Amount disbursed during the year, as per foregoing statement..		$121,445 05
Bills contracted prior to October 1st, 1865, and unpaid......		7,966 25
Total..		$129,411 30
Deduct:		
Bills unpaid October 1st, 1864, as per report..	$19,297 15	
Deficiency for previous year.......................	4,904 57	
		$24,201 72
Actual expenditure for twelve months..........................		$105,209 58

If to this be added bills rejected by the Board, because not purchased in conformity with the by-laws, which amount to two hundred and fifty-seven dollars and thirty-two cents, ($257 32,) the total expenditure reaches the sum of one hundred and five thousand four hundred and sixty-six dollars and ninety cents, ($105,466 90,) being an average of eight thousand seven hundred and eighty-eight dollars and ninety-one cents ($8,788 91) per month.

Estimating the expenditure for the remainder of the fiscal year—nine months—at nine thousand five hundred dollars ($9,500) per month, which, in view of the rapid increase of patients, and the exorbitant price of almost every article required, is not extravagant, the following estimate will exhibit the probable deficiency for that period:

Expenses for nine months, from October 1, 1865, to June 30, 1866, inclusive, at $9,500 per month......................		$85,500 00
Bills unpaid this date..		7,966 25
Total..		$93,466 25
Deduct:		
Balance of appropriation...........................	$75,000 00	
Cash in Treasury....................................	3,606 51	
Board of patients, say.............................	1,500 00	
		$80,106 51
Estimated deficiency...		$13,359 74

This includes the deficiency of four thousand nine hundred and four dollars and fifty-seven cents ($4,904 57) for the fiscal year ending June thirtieth, eighteen hundred and sixty-four, so that the actual deficiency created during the two years ending June thirtieth, eighteen hundred and sixty-six, will be but eight thousand four hundred and fifty-five dollars and seventeen cents, ($8,455 17,) provided the foregoing estimate proves correct.

IMPROVEMENT FUND.

RECEIPTS.	
Amount drawn from State Treasury from October 1, 1864, to October 1, 1865	$66,281 53
Premium on gold	320 00
Total	$66,601 53
DISBURSEMENTS.	
Amount paid, as per vouchers on file, from October 1, 1864, to date, including balance of $7,458 overdrawn at date of last report	$57,797 72
Balance in Improvement Fund	$8,803 61

Bills have been contracted, payable from this fund, to the amount of one thousand six hundred and forty-three dollars and seventy-four cents, (1,643 74,) which leaves a surplus unexpended of seven thousand one hundred and fifty-nine dollars and eighty-seven cents, ($7,159 87.)

The following is a statement of the balances in the Treasury belonging to the different funds:

General Fund	$3,606 51
Improvement Fund	8,803 61
Special Fund, for payment of certain accounts	88 09
Total amount in Treasury	$12,498 21

All of which is respectfully submitted by your obedient servant,

R. HAPPERSETT, Treasurer.

REPORTS
OF
VISITING PHYSICIANS.

MAJORITY REPORT.

To his Excellency, Governor F. F. Low:

DEAR SIR:—We regret that circumstances have caused us to delay our report to an unreasonable degree. At our last official visit to the Asylum we were told of matters affecting so seriously the welfare of that institution, that, with the promise of Doctor Hubbard (our colleague) to furnish us documentary confirmation of their truthfulness, we concluded to wait until he should communicate with us. But as we have received no word from him, we have concluded to submit our report and have any undeveloped questions injurious to the Asylum to be investigated by the Legislature.

In so far as the undersigned have been officially related to the Insane Asylum of the State, we have endeavored to do the best we could to promote the best interests of the State and to protect the great charity with which we were connected without any expressed or implied desire on our part.

None lament more sincerely than ourselves, that there should have been anything developed in our official relations to the Asylum which was calculated to distrust the administration of Asylum affairs, or in any way to connect our names with acts and duties which had, as we believed, been unnecessarily rendered unpleasant; but that such things were developed, entailing upon us disagreeable duties, is now too well known to require mention in this report.

On April sixth, eighteen hundred and sixty-five, when the unhappy affairs of the Asylum were being generally discussed, and our own motives and acts animadverted upon by the Board of Directors, we published the following letter in the San Francisco Evening Bulletin:

THE INSANE ASYLUM QUESTION.

CARD FROM DRS. WHITNEY AND MORSE.

SAN FRANCISCO, April 6th, 1865.

Editor Bulletin:—The undersigned, physicians of the Medical Board of Visitors to the State Insane Asylum, would respectfully request you to publish the following statement:

The official relations we sustain to the above institution was not sought or desired by us, nor even known until weeks after our election. We accepted the same only after being urgently requested by the present Superintendent, to aid him in making the charity worthy of the cause of humanity and the pride of the State. We fulfilled the duties incurred to the best of our ability, and watched with the greatest interest the efforts made to amend the many defects of the institution. Until after our April visit, a year ago, nothing could have been more cheering than the progressive improvement manifesting itself.

From that time, however, we have seen enough to convince us that the enactment organizing and governing the institution has been misconstrued and applied in such a way as to arrest improvement, to injure the charity in its already imperfect accommodation, and to inflict embarrassment and injustice upon the Superintendent. Indeed, we feel convinced that the law as it is now construed and administered, would vitiate, if not destroy, the chief office of the Insane Asylum, and subject such a charity and State institution to the capricious and almost unchecked control of local interests. Our opposition is not against the City of Stockton. We do not believe that the official acts of the present Board of Directors, if well understood, would be justified by the citizens of that place.

At our April visit referred to, one of the Directors, in the presence of several other members of the Board, appealing to the three Medical Visitors, made the following request: "The Board of Directors desire you, gentlemen, in connection with your sanitary duties, to examine well the building and grounds of the Asylum, and give us your advice as to what you think would be the best use we could make of the funds appropriated by the State. We assure you that in doing so you will confer a favor upon us, and your advice will receive a liberal consideration in our deliberations and plans."

We performed the duty as requested, and said to them that, in our opinion, considering the urgent and immediate demand for more room, and the small sum of money appropriated, the best plan would be to erect inside buildings which would require no architectural embellishment, which would be quickly and cheaply built, and which would yield the largest accommodations to the crowded patients, referring them to the very economical structures which had already been erected. When we gave this advice we had been informed by the highest authorities, through whom the appropriation had been made, that the funds so set aside by the State were for the purpose of providing the most immediate relief to the crowded and inadequate accommodations of the Asylum— that this was the avowed and distinct understanding under which the appropriation had been obtained. Not only did this information come to us through many senators and representatives, but Dr. Hubbard, our colleague, who was a member of the succeeding legislative session, at which this subject was elaborately discussed, attested to the truth of these representations in respect to the object of the funds.

Our advice was asked for, and we gave it. Whatever consideration it may have received is unimportant. The Directors certainly ignored it, and commenced as soon as possible the construction of an isolated building, so far from the others as to necessitate the establishment and maintenance of two kitchens, to largely increase the number of employés, at the same time that it will not afford more than one half the room that the same money would have provided in four months if applied as advised, and yet this addition of the Directors cannot be finished probably before next June. In the superintendency of this building the Directors have taken the right from the executive and qualified officers of the Asylum, and conferred it upon an individual who has not been in the State more than four or five months.

In respect to the present Superintendent, we need only say, that up to the time of our visit, a year ago, there was no language too extravagant to convey the high estimate in which he was held by the Board of Directors, and that we have seen no change in this officer's capacity or conduct, except in so far as the Board has embarrassed and disturbed him by withholding their favor and encouragement. We believe that, disagreeable as it may be, it is our duty to vindicate, not Dr. Tilden, but the important office of Superintendent, from the evil effects of what we consider to be misconstrued law and perverted authority. We do not belive in the soundness or justice of the official acts of the Board of Directors. The course we are pursuing, whilst suggested by eminent counsel, has but one object, and that is, humanity.

JAMES P. WHITNEY, M. D.,
JOHN F. MORSE, M. D.

P. S.—With the foregoing statement we believe our colleague, Dr. Hubbard, would unhesitatingly concur could we see him.

W. and M.

The course of conduct referred to in the conclusion of that card was, on our part, a refusal to go into a Joint Convention for the election of a Superintendent, Resident and Visiting Physicians of the Asylum, at the time appointed by law. In that card we have referred to the general causes that led us to take the step we did, but they are by no means the controlling considerations which induced us to determine upon such a measure.

We knew and dreaded the onus of any dereliction in violation of duty, but when we felt ourselves urged to such a step as a sacrificial protection to every interest which we believed to be suffering, we thought it our duty to incur the responsibility and accept the penalty.

In addition to the general reasons assigned in the printed card, we were informed by the Superintendent, Dr. Tilden, and by the Steward, Mr. Arents, that the most essential requirements of the Asylum, in connection with the supplies of the institution, were being disregarded by the Board of Directors to the positive injury of the supplies and pecuniary interests of the State.

Upon our demanding positive illustration of such facts, we were told of a specific contract for potatoes, in which a bond had been originally demanded and given, we believe of one thousand dollars, and that subsequently, after a rise in potatoes of some three or four hundred per cent, the contractor had been permitted to withdraw said bond, or it had been destroyed, and to execute and file in its place a bond of three hundred dollars, which was at once forfeited, the same contractor continuing to furnish the material at the advanced valuation, and himself asserting to the Superintendent or Steward that he had made a large sum of money by the transaction.

Of the merits or accuracy of these charges, we had no means of informing ourselves; but coming to us from such sources, in connection with our official relations to the institution, and associated with what we were informed from high legislative authority was, on the part of the Board of Directors, a direct violation of the intentions of the State in its appropriation for an expansion of Asylum accommodations, we were induced to believe that any act by which the State would be impelled to make a thorough investigation of the affairs of the institution would be just, and philosophically if not legally right.

In our card we expressed the opinion that the new building would not be completed and ready for occupation before June, eighteen hundred and sixty-five. As an evidence of our intention of keeping within bounds of prudence, we may now mention the fact that it was not opened for hospital purposes until the last of September.

Let any one examine the statute organizing and managing the affairs of the Asylum, and nothing will appear more conclusive than the defects of that enactment requiring revision and amendment. As it is now organized, the institution is placed in the arbitrary control of six men, and all of them located in the town which is chiefly interested in furnishing supplies. We say, in their arbitrary control, for the only check upon them is through the Superintendent, and in electing that officer they constitute six interested to the three disinterested votes.

In the present system of organizing that charity, the Superintendent and Board of Visiting Physicians are as nothing against any policy which the ruling six have adopted. With the authority as now possessed by the Board of Directors, exclusively of Stockton, there is no man in the world who could exercise the function of Superintendent and Physician of such an institution, unless it were entirely congenial for the Managing Board to have him in the place. He must, indeed, become the mere creature of their will, or he runs the risk of being made so uncomfortable in his position that most men would either succumb or indignantly resign their commission.

The Board need not commit any act of aggression upon the Superintendent; they have only to cease doing many things which habit and inspiring civility had been rendering, and they can easily make the place a burden to any man of spirit or ability. Locality, interest, and association, make the testimony or charges of six as the report of one man, yet the countercharge of the one man is always against six men individually and collectively.

That the evils to which we have referred as possible, and even probable under the present organization of the Asylum, have been manifested in the workings of the State Insane Asylum during the last two years, we think will be conclusively shown whenever the affairs of that institution are properly investigated. Upon this question we may be mistaken, and an investigation may clearly demonstrate that Dr. Tilden has been the principal cause of all the evils which have arisen to embarrass or obstruct the progressive improvement of that charity; but we do not believe anything of the kind will be established; and if it were it would not remove the defects of the law, which will be apparent upon examination.

After the authority at the Asylum had been concentrated, by forced ejectment of Dr. Tilden, in the hands of the Board of Directors and Dr. Clark, we consented to attend a convention which was appointed by these officers. At that convention we saw a complete illustration of the shocking defects of the Asylum enactments to which we have referred. We saw the same unanimous six, whom the Superintendent had publicly charged with the most unjust treatment towards him, who had accepted and cautiously maintained the parties and institution after the Superintendent had been riotously ejected; we saw the same six, with more strength than sagacity, elect one of their own Board, a Stockton man, to the chief executive office of the institution, thus adding another officer and the only conservative check which the State retained, to the already arbitrary local majority.

Now, out of ten officers of that institution, in whose hands are vested the entire interests of the State, who exercise the whole moral, scientific, and financial control of the institution, seven of them are the interested residents of Stockton, and the other three are but semi-annual visitors, with not one vestige of power except by the way of suggestion, and those suggestions liable to the same contemptuous treatment which was shown to our recommendations in respect to the improvements of the Asylum in April, eighteen hundred and sixty-four.

We do not say anything personally or professionally against the fitness of Dr. Shurtleff, whom the Board elected as Superintendent and Resident Physician; on the contrary, we believe he was eminently the best man who could have been selected from Stockton, and quite possibly as good a man for such a place as we have in the State, aside from his connections with the Board of Directors with Asylum affairs that are to be investigated, and which have been demonstrated to be already under an unsound, injudicious, local control.

At that visit, and at our last visit, we saw nothing in the Asylum which exhibited any feeling of administrative ability, except in the retention in most important places of parties who had cautioned the public against believing more than one statement out of two which they had made, and which were in direct antagonism, and in the restoration of an individual as Matron whom we believe to have been properly discharged for incompetency and insubordination.

Having said thus much about our connection with that institution in the past, we will close our report by submitting the following considerations:

We must substantially reiterate the opinion given in our report for eighteen hundred and sixty-three to your predecessor in the gubernatorial chair, and state that in the location of this institution, the principles which should guide in such matters seem to have been almost entirely ignored, and in a State containing the most perfect sites in all their topographical and hygienic relations to the amelioration or cure of insanity, one has been selected which is almost entirely destitute of the characteristics which should be sought for.

Common sense should have suggested and common humanity should have dictated the selection of a site for such an institution that was elevated, salubrious, and well watered, as well as fertile and easy of access. The insane should not have their blood poisoned either by marsh malaria or emanations from their own excretions; nor should their minds be wearied through the senses by a dull monotony. But they require and profit by the purest air and the most picturesque scenery that can be furnished.

We cannot believe that insanity can ever be very successfully treated at an institution situated on a vast plain of adobe soil, no part of which is sufficiently elevated to admit of complete natural drainage; not often fanned by any breeze that has not swept over more than forty miles of marsh land, alternately exposed to the rays of a burning sun, and covered with mixture of salt and fresh water, as the tide ebbs and flows in the slough which forms the water front of the City of Stockton; thus furnishing, according to all authorities, a most fruitful source of one of the most lethal causes of bodily and mental disease.

In a well located and managed institution seventy-five per cent of cases of insanity are cured in less than one year, and only twenty-five per cent left on the chronic list, mostly incurable, and destined to remain on an average fifteen years in the institution. The tables show that in the institution at Stockton, only about forty per cent has ever been cured, leaving sixty per cent in the Asylum as fixtures for a term of years. It will make a wide difference to the State whether seventy-five or only forty of every one hundred are cured and restored to usefulness and their families, and only twenty-five left as fixtures for life, or only forty cured and sixty die, or become worse than useless to themselves—sore trials of affliction to friends and families, and a tax upon the State.

With two hundred annual admissions, which is below the average, what a frightful difference would it make in the tables whether one hundred and twenty or only eighty were annually restored to self control, and the comforts of home and family, or these figures reversed, and the larger number lost to their friends, and taxable for years to the State, and only the smaller number restored.

In our opinion a larger difference than this depends upon the location, construction, organization, and management of such Asylums or Hospitals as the State may provide for this most unfortunate class of her citizens. We use the plural number here because it has been amply proved by the most enlightened experience that the number of insane should never exceed three hundred in one institution, and that even as this number is nearly reached, the statistics begin to show the impropriety of further increase.

We would therefore respectfully recommend that a thorough inquiry be made by competent commissioners appointed by the Legislature—proper sites chosen, and a proper organization effected in accordance with the recommendations of the Association of Medical Superintendents of American Institutions for the Insane, or other investigators of these subjects who have devoted their energies thereto.

Sense and experience unitedly point to the propriety of committing financial questions to financiers, and medical questions to medical men.

J. P. WHITNEY, M. D.
JOHN F. MORSE, M. D.

MINORITY REPORT.

MARYSVILLE, November 1, 1865.

To His Excellency, F. F. Low, Governor of the State of California:

DEAR SIR:—The time has again arrived when it becomes the duty of the Board of Medical Visitors to report to your excellency their proceedings since their last report, and the management and present condition of the institution with which they have been connected.

The fact that two reports are furnished is no evidence that the members of the Board do not agree in regard to the practical operations of the Asylum. In this particular, I am happy to say, the Board have, as I believe have always been, a unit. But, unfortunately, a difference of opinion did exist between members in regard to their powers and duties in the matter of franchise.

The law provides that on the first Tuesday of April, eighteen hundred and sixty-five, the Board of Medical Visitors and Directors of the Asylum should meet in Joint Convention, for the purpose of electing a Resident and an Assistant Physician.

Notice having been served on the members of each Board, the terms of officers having expired, and the law being explicit, that the " election shall take place," it seemed there could be no avoiding the conclusion. Nevertheless, my colleagues saw matters in a different light, and refused to meet the Directors in convention, which convened as required by law, and adjourned from time to time, on account of the want of a quorum in the Medical Board. After a number of months delay and litigation, the convention was organized and performed its legitimate functions.

While these proceedings were pending, the Asylum necessarily suffered in many respects. It was a house divided against itself. An Insane Asylum is near enough a Bedlam at best; but what can be expected when insubordination reigns among officers from the highest to the lowest?

The terms of office of the incumbents had expired. An election was necessary under the law; and if that had not been prevented at the proper time, much, if not all, of the unfortunate proceedings that took place at the Asylum would have been avoided. The result was to delay the election; and of course the incumbents remained lawfully in charge of the institution.

Up to this period the Directors had cautiously kept within the bounds prescribed by the strictest letter of the statute, and under the advice of wise counsel were on the point of closing the contest quietly, in a way that must have given satisfaction to the public, if not to the parties concerned. Just at this instant an evil spirit seemed to prevail, and in an unguarded moment the Directors yielded to counsels we deem most pernicious, which resulted in a high-handed infraction of law, such as has seldom been witnessed in any community. The Superintendent, lawfully in power by State authority and the Act ratified by the signature of the Governor, ejected from his solemn trust by violent hands, having no authority or right save that of force!

We would gladly have passed the last paragraph without remark, but, in justice to all parties concerned, as well as the public, we are compelled to say this much—besides, the act is fraught with too much danger as a precedent to be allowed to pass without proper criticism.

Finally the convention took place, which resulted in the election of Dr. G. A. Shurtleff, of Stockton, as Resident Physician, and Dr. Clark, former incumbent, Assistant Physician. From this moment things have progressed with much harmony.

While we would by no means detract from the merit of the former Superintendent, we can but regard the election of Dr. Shurtleff as most fortunate for the institution at the present juncture. Besides much experience, he takes with him professional and business tact; these, with his high moral reputation, secure for him not only the confidence of the public, but the confidence and respect of the employés and inmates of the institution.

Already, chaos has given place to order; insubordination to perfect obedience. In saying this for the institution under present management, we are not pretending to account for the confusion that prevailed there a few months ago. Unfortunately, the officers could not agree; and, as always happens in such cases, the disputation spread among the attendants; and even the patients shared in the general spirit of disaffection. What among the general officers alone would have resulted in no injury or discomfort to the patients, when in the hands and brains of attendants who were governed altogether by passion, became serious, and, it is charged, even "fatal" in one or two instances.

That patients, in the absence of the Superintendent and Physicians were harshly treated, there is no doubt, and moreover, the evidence is conclusive, as charged, that a young woman brought to the Asylum on the sixth of September, eighteen hundred and sixty-four, was taken by two female attendants, and forced, against her will, into a cold bath, from which she was taken senseless, "dying or dead." The testimony is, that she was "forced into a cold bath, and her head held under water until she was dead or dying." And, again, it is charged, that a certain male patient was maltreated by one of the attendants by "blows, kicks, and stamps," insomuch that he died. On post mortem examination, the body was found horribly mutilated—limbs broken and skull crushed in a shocking manner. It is proper to state that it is believed that most of the wounds were posthumous. Here the dark chapter closes as far as we have knowledge. What a scrutinizing examination might develop we have no means of knowing.

In dwelling on these circumstances, perhaps we have diverged somewhat from our proper line of duty. Nevertheless, the facts are patent, and if avoided altogether, we should at least render ourselves obnoxious to the charge of entertaining a desire to cover what, above all things else, should be made public. And while, as I believe, the members of the Visiting Board are of one mind in regard to the present able management of the Asylum, they are equally as unanimous in their desire that the public should be as perfectly informed in regard to the past, as to what is to be the future management of this public charity, to which they subscribe so liberally and cheerfully.

The Medical Visitors have no power in this connection beyond reporting facts relating to the "sanitary condition and medical management of the Asylum;" hence they have no means of ascertaining who, if any one, is particularly in fault, except so far as they can draw conclusions from the circumstances developed without positive evidence.

We have no idea that any of the principal officers were aware that cruelty was being practiced on the unfortunate inmates by attendants at the time, nor that it would have been permitted had they known to what extent such abuses were carried.

If there is culpability, it exists because it was not known what was taking place every day in an institution of so much magnitude.

This again, however, was the result of the unfortunate difficulty into which the Asylum had fallen. So general was the defection, that officers from the highest to the lowest participated.

To avoid like difficulties hereafter, the law providing for the election of officers should be amended or repealed altogether and returned to the Legislature. Under the existing, laws two members of one Board, or three of the other, may prevent an election indefinitely.

ASYLUM BUILDINGS.

Since our last report some improvements have been made to the old buildings. An entire new story has been added to one of the wings, affording sleeping accommodations for some forty or more patients, and the old ground cells attached to the main yard, heretofore dark and damp, without ventilation, have had windows opened into each on both sides of the hall, rendering them perfectly comfortable. It was the discomfort exhibited in this part of the establishment that properly gave the institution the character of a prison; happily, the dingy walls and rusty gratings have disappeared, and light, airy rooms have taken their places. The heretofore dreary yard, also, occupied by some three or four hundred patients, has been nicely graded, and the centre portion roofed. From this is partitioned a reading room, where may be found some of the State papers; comfortable seats and tables are here arranged, and in the morning most of them occupied by patients anxious to learn the news of the day. No doubt if the attention of journalists was called to the fact, this room would be more liberally supplied with papers. It is an interesting fact, that quite a large portion of the inmates exhibit a taste for reading and inquiry.

THE NEW BUILDING.

This is located some six hundred yards to the north of the old Asylum, and perhaps four hundred yards north of the Resident Physician's house. A difference of opinion seemed to exist in the minds of the Medical Board and Directors in regard to the location of this building. It was the opinion of the Medical Board, so expressed, at least, at their semi-annual meeting in April, eighteen hundred and sixty-four, that whatever expenditures of money were made for improvements between that time and the meeting of the next Legislature, ought to be applied, as contemplated by the Legislature which had just adjourned, in erecting wings or rooms directly attached to the old Asylum, so as not to duplicate its internal operations in any essential particular. But, contrary to their expectations, a new edifice was commenced. and the first wing—or about one fifth of the whole—is now completed.

Without desiring to condemn or approve the proceeding, we have given the plain statement for information, with the knowledge that the Directors are willing to assume all responsibility, and to abide the verdict of the coming Legislature.

It is evident, however, that if Stockton is to remain the site of the *mother* institution of the State, the Directors have expended money more judiciously than to have patched the old building, which, notwithstanding, would soon be inadequate, and necessarily give place to other buildings, erected on a more enlarged and improved plan.

The wing is, as we before stated, about one fifth of what is to be the complete structure, and is of a quadrangular form, one hundred and fifty feet in extreme length from east to west.

The west end is four stories high above the basement, and is forty-two feet in length from north to south, and thirty-three feet in width from east to west, containing a suite of rooms for the use of the Matron, a sewing room, attendants' rooms, reception rooms, a suite of rooms used for common purposes, and a suite denominated domestic rooms, with accommodating hall, stairways, and closets.

The east end, being also four stories high, is thirty-five feet by sixty-two feet, containing twenty-four rooms, ten feet by twelve feet, for patients. with four bath rooms, four wash rooms, four sink rooms, with closets to each. There is also a hall in each story, twelve feet by sixty feet. with entrances and staircases leading from basement to attic.

The centre building is ninety-one feet six inches by thirty-seven feet, and only three stories above the basement. This also contains forty rooms for patients; three halls, ninety-one feet long by twelve feet wide, each containing a bay window about twenty feet square; three dining rooms, three bath rooms, three wash rooms, three water closets, three China closets, and a dumb waiter leading from the basement to all the dining rooms.

The attic has been provided with much care, being well furnished to accommodate twenty beds.

The basement is mostly used for cooking purposes, and is furnished with all modern improvements, not only for cooking, but for warming the whole establishment, which is done by steam, through coils artistically arranged through the basement.

The tanks for water are placed in the centre of the attic, and will contain about six thousand gallons. Cold and hot water are distributed throughout the building.

The entire establishment is lighted by gas from the city gas works.

The fronts are finely finished with oil mastic; the roof covering, gutters, and cornice, are of heavy galvanized iron, and the whole fabric composed of the firmest material, and finished in the most substantial manner.

The whole number of rooms, exclusive of attic, is one hundred and twenty-six, and at present are occupied by one hundred and twenty-five female patients. The windows are guarded by an outside iron sash, and are about one hundred and eighty in number.

The vaults are ventilated, and all offensive steam and gases from the boilers are carried off through pipes leading to a brick shaft, erected some two hundred feet from the main building, and seventy-five feet in height.

The entire cost of the structure and its appendages is sixty-six thousand eight hundred and eighty-five dollars and thirty-four cents.

This building is certainly very well adapted to the purposes intended, and is about the first step yet taken towards a curative institution. Another wing of the same, of much larger dimensions, is now imperatively demanded for the milder and better class of males. Expense cannot be taken into account. The Asylum is a public charity, intended to benefit those committed to it. A *cure* is the first object; and second, to afford relief beyond what can be received in private, or by mere imprisonment.

The herding of three or four hundred patients in a common yard, with indiscriminate association, affected as they are with insanity in every degree, can scarcely be regarded as a curative measure, nor can we reasonably expect that any will be benefited. It is a natural law of mind, as well as physics, that the weak yield to the strong; hence it is with the insane—the mild to the turbulent; and when closely associated, all to assimilate with those whose hallucinations are most confirmed and violent.

Strange as it may appear, the only accommodation afforded in the present institution, except the yard and reading room mentioned, are for eating, sleeping, and confinement. And even with late improvements, nothing beyond these is contemplated. Means for varied amusements are important, but altogether absent here. No provisions are made for religious service; no wards are especially set apart for convalescents; and no separate apartments are provided for the sick. We can but believe that a humane Legislature will not be tardy in furnishing the means for these especial objects.

We may be permitted to repeat, that for the accommodation of the present inmates, another wing is required immediately. In this no calculation is made for the increase during the next two years.

The annual increase of insane persons in this State, since the adoption of the present Asylum system, has been a fraction over fifty. But with our increased population, and the inadequate means of treatment, we may calculate that the annual increase during the next two years will be something above those figures. Hence it will devolve upon the Legislature to provide fully one third more accommodations than are now at command.

The five cent tax, levied in eighteen hundred and sixty-three, for building purposes, has in three years been just sufficient to make necessary repairs about the old Asylum buildings, and erect and furnish the wing above mentioned, which is now occupied by one hundred and twenty-five patients—twenty-five less than the increase for the three years occupied in collecting the money. Therefore the tax continued will only maintain the institution in its present crowded and unsatisfactory condition.

Without ample room and appliances, the Asylum can never rise to a curative point. And until adequate accommodations, such as shall be completely adapted to the wants of the State and humanity, the annual increase of permanent patients and a corresponding increase of expenses, will remain a settled feature of the institution.

The above facts indicate that economy as well as humanity demands a change in the Asylum policy. In round terms, with a view of attempting to establish a curative institution, as much more room as is now occupied could, with great propriety, be immediately provided, either at Stockton or on some other site selected.

But even with such improvements, the institution would not then equal those of the Eastern States.

It is estimated, by those quite competent to judge, that a new Asylum could be constructed and put in condition for the accommodation of about three hundred patients, as they are provided for in Eastern institutions, for three hundred and fifty thousand dollars. With such a provision, no additional expenditure would be required, probably, for the next six years to come, and perhaps indefinitely, as then the annual increase of cures would nearly if not quite equal the present increase of insane.

The question has been raised, and doubtless will be again, as to the proper place of locating future buildings. Those who have the best opportunity to judge correctly, give it as their opinion that " three or four hundred patients are as many as can be cared for to the best advantage in one institution." Again, it is urged that a branch Asylum for the insane, as a matter of convenience to the northern part of the State, is peremptorily demanded, such institution to be located somewhere north of Sacramento. Others insist that the site should be selected on tide water, about the Bay of San Francisco, as being more accessible to all parts of the State, and combining more requisite conveniences, such as " altitude, picturesque scenery, fertility of soil, natural drainage, and ample water facilities," than any other point.

We have before suggested that Marysville afforded all requisite natural advantages, and was the place above all others that accommodated the whole of the northern counties in the State, except the coast tier, which could reach this point just as easy as Stockton. The inconvenience and expense of transporting patients from Marysville to Stockton is among the strong arguments in favor of locating a branch at the last named place, this being the general starting point.

Buildings for the care of one hundred and fifty of the mild class of incurables could be provided at Marysville at a small present expense, and before other patients from the northern section of the State could accumulate to any extent, suitable buildings could be erected on proper grounds.

In a former report we referred to the class of persons confined at the Asylum. Notwithstanding the law of eighteen hundred and sixty-four, a large number of imbeciles and epileptics still remain there that should be provided for in county poor houses or hospitals. The tax for the maintenance of the poor is among the heavy items of public expenditures in the State, yet there is no law on the statute books economizing and equalizing the burden. Proper poor laws would relieve the State from the care of a very large percentage of persons who now find their way into the State charities.

In this connection we may speak of the present government of the Asylum. If no change is contemplated in the locations of buildings, to avoid a repetition of the occurrences of the last convention for the election of Physicians, the quorum of the Joint Convention of Medical Visitors and Directors should be fixed by law at a majority of the two Boards, without reference to representation of either.

If a branch institution should be organized, very naturally two Boards of Trustees would be provided; both should act in conjunction in the location and construction of buildings for either Asylum, and also in the Joint Conventions.

The Medical Board could very properly have an oversight of the two, and their powers should be enlarged, and in any event, their duties more specifically defined.

There seems to be an objection to the locating of all the Directors in one place. Very likely it would give better satisfaction if three were residents of Stockton, and two taken from the State at large. This would, in a measure, do away with the prejudice against permitting private and local interests governing too much public institutions.

The following table exhibits the operations of the Asylum during the current year:

From September 1, 1864, to September 30, 1865.	Males.	Females.	Total.
Number of patients September 1, 1864	441	140	581
Admitted during the year, September 3, 1864, to October 1, 1865	191	77	268
Total number under treatment during the year	632	217	849
Discharged cured	69	24	93
Discharged improved	5	6	11
Discharged unimproved	3	1	4
Number died	66	16	82
Number escaped			27
Total discharged, died, and escaped			217
Leaving in the Asylum, September 30, 1865			632
Increase during the year			51

In closing this report, so impressed are we with the importance of the subject, that we venture, for the second or third time, to call attention to the absolute necessity of abundant room in the successful treatment of the insane. It should never be forgotten that a *cure* is the object of the charity. Wards of the size of ours, in which are crowded from eighty to a hundred patients, in eastern institutions are occupied by fifteen or twenty. When a certain amount of room is found to be essential, it is provided. Patients are properly classed and allotted to their suite of rooms, and on no account are innovations permitted. So it should be here. Every consideration sacred to Christian benevolence, moral obligations, and humanity, demands that a high and open handed liberality be bestowed upon this noble charity.

With the highest considerations of esteem for yourself, the above is respectfully submitted.

LORENZO HUBBARD,
Member Board of Medical Visitors of Insane Asylum, Cal.

THIRTEENTH ANNUAL REPORT

(Fifteenth, including the Insane Department of the General Hospital,)

OF THE

RESIDENT PHYSICIAN

OF THE

Insane Asylum of California.

1865.

REPORT.

To the Directors of the Insane Asylum of California:

GENTLEMEN:—In compliance with the seventh section of an Act of the Legislature concerning the Insane Asylum of California, approved April twenty-fifth, eighteen hundred and sixty-three, the annual report of the Resident Physician of said institution is respectfully submitted.

On the first day of August, of the present year, I was, by a joint meeting of your Board and the Board of Medical Visitors, elected Resident Physician; and on the fifth day of the same month I entered upon the discharge of the duties of the office.

You are therefore aware that it is only during the brief period of two months that I have occupied my present official connection with the institution.

With no other special knowledge or experience than that acquired in so short a time, one would meet with discouraging embarrassments in even presenting from the records "the principal facts and results" connected with the annual transactions of an institution ranking among the largest of the kind on the western hemisphere; while an attempt to occupy your attention with a report thereon, embracing views and deductions of his own, would be a futile and graceless exhibition of inordinate vanity.

I trust, however, that a connection with the Asylum in another capacity, prolonged from an ever cherished interest in its welfare and success, will shield me from the appearance of immodest pretension, should I even venture to comment upon some of the statistical facts and results herein exhibited.

The following table shows the number of patients at the commencement of the year, the admissions, discharges, recoveries, deaths, and elopements, and the number remaining October first, eighteen hundred and sixty-five:

From September 30, 1864, to October 1, 1865.	Males.	Females.	Total.
Number of patients September 30, 1864............	441	140	581
Number of patients admitted........................	190	78	268
Number of patients under treatment...............	631	218	849
Number of patients discharged cured...............	69	24	93
Number of patients discharged improved..........	5	6	11
Number of patients discharged unimproved.......	3	1	4
Number of patients died	66	16	82
Number of patients eloped.........................	26	1	27
Number of patients discharged, died, and eloped....	169	48	217
Number of patients remaining October 1, 1865......	462	170	632

It will be observed that the increase of patients during the year is fifty-one—a large addition compared with the previous year, when the number was two less at the close than at the beginning of the year. But it will also be seen by reference to the report of eighteen hundred and sixty-four, that the number of admissions has been forty-nine more during this year than last, which, in a great measure, accounts for the comparatively large increase.

The percentage of recoveries to the admissions is about thirty-four and seventy one-hundredths, which, though not as great by nearly twenty per cent as the average of cures in previous years, is yet by no means a small or discreditable rate for a single year, viewed in comparison with the curative results obtained in other institutions of the kind; in which, also, it will be observed, wide variations occasionally occur.

The number of deaths, by a remarkable coincidence, is exactly the same as during the preceding year—it being eighty-two. But the whole number of inmates being greater, the percentage of deaths on the number treated, and on the number resident, is not as large as last year.

A comparison of the results of the past year, as exhibited in the foregoing table, with those of previous years and other similar institutions, may be of interest, and afford desirable information. For this purpose we will give a brief history of

INSANITY, AND THE RESULTS OF ITS TREATMENT IN CALIFORNIA.

Hardly had the acquisition of California to the United States, and the discovery of the precious metals, put in motion upon this coast the enterprise of modern civilization, before insanity began to be developed. Nor is this a matter of wonder, when we consider the peculiar manner in which our State was peopled, and the peculiar influences which operated upon its early inhabitants. Suddenly crowded together from all parts of the world, in a fierce and selfish struggle for wealth and position, with energies quickened by new hopes, and anon paralyzed by overwhelming disappointments; restless, unsettled, and improvident, at once relieved from the steadying cares and deprived of the composing influences of home; to-day surfeiting upon the profuse luxuries of unfostered wealth, and to-morrow pining over the privations of unresisted want; enjoying a liberty expanded to licentiousness, and often yielding to the impulses of passions pampered by vice, and severed from the moral restraints of society, the early settlers of California laid the foundation and contributed much to the present vast accumulation of mental disorders.

During the year eighteen hundred and fifty, there were fourteen insane persons sent to the Station House in San Francisco. It is estimated that the whole number of insane of that year amounted to twenty-two. Some of these received care and medical treatment in the Marine Hospital at San Francisco, and others were temporarily secured in prisons. In eighteen hundred and fifty-one, the State Hospitals at Sacramento and Stockton afforded accommodations for the insane. During this year the Hospital at Sacramento received thirty-four, and the one at Stockton thirteen, making the whole number forty-seven.*

In eighteen hundred and fifty-two, the Legislature ordered all the insane persons of the State to be sent to Stockton, and placed in the State Hospital; and accordingly, one hundred and twenty-four were this year admitted into what was termed the Insane Department of the General Hospital. Thus were brought together all the insane of the State, at the early period of eighteen hundred and fifty-two, in the place where they have ever since been maintained and treated. Some of the very individuals who were received at that time, now more than thirteen years ago, are still inmates of the Asylum. In the following year, eighteen hundred and fifty-three, the Legislature abolished the State Hospital at Stockton, and created in its place the *Insane Asylum of California*. As soon as practicable thereafter, the patients in the Hospital Department were removed, and the institution devoted exclusively, as it has been ever since, to the care of the insane. Appropriate buildings were erected, which have since been added to from time to time, to meet the rapidly increasing wants of the institution, until it has reached a capacity affording crowded accommodations for and containing about six hundred and fifty beds; the late necessity of having to nightly prepare temporary beds on the floor having been just overcome by the occupancy of the new building.

Extending back more than fourteen years, when the thirteen homeless and forlorn pioneers of insanity were confined temporarily in a little wooden building, on the corner of El Dorado and Market streets, receiving their scanty supply of air and light through small auger holes cut in closely boarded windows, the following tables will show the result of the treatment of insanity in California from its incipiency in the Insane Department of the State Hospital in eighteen hundred and fifty-one, to October first, eighteen hundred and sixty-five.

The first table shows the number of admissions, the number of recoveries, and the number of deaths annually, the number in the Asylum at the close of each year, and the annual increase of patients. The second table exhibits the whole number treated, the percentage of recoveries to the admissions, the percentage of deaths on the number treated, and the percentage of deaths on the number resident:

---

* Superintendent's Report, 1855.

YEAR.	Admissions.	Recoveries.	Deaths.	Number resident at close of each year	Increase.	Decrease.
1851	13	6	1	6	6	
1852	124	50	10	62	56	
1853	160	108	12	103	41	
1854	202	150	21	134	31	
1855	214	168	18	162	28	
1856	210	126		172	10	
1857	206	81	28	188	16	
1858	244	112	32	273	85	
1859	276	112	49	370	97	
1860	248	123	54	417	47	
1861	198	154	33	416		1
1862	301	127	65	499	83	
1863	252	105	47	583	84	
1864	219	101	82	581		2
1865	268	93	82	632	51	
Totals	3,135	1,616	534		635	3

YEAR.	Whole number treated	Per cent of recoveries to admission	Per cent of deaths on Number treated	Per cent of deaths on Number resident
1851	13	46.15	7.69	16.67
1852	130	40.32	7.69	16.13
1853	222	67.50	5.40	11.65
1854	305	74.00	6.89	15.67
1855	348	78.50	5.20	11.11
1856	382	60.00		
1857	378	39.32	7.33	14.89
1858	432	45.90	7.41	11.72
1859	549	40.58	8.91	13.24
1860	618	49.59	8.73	12.95
1861	615	77.77	5.86	7.93
1862	717	42.19	9.06	11.02
1863	751	41.67	6.26	8.06
1864	802	46.12	10.22	14.11
1865	849	34.70	9.66	12.97

These general statistics of the institution, deduced and compiled from the annual reports of its several Superintendents, afford the tangible and incontestible proofs of its success, and cannot fail to be satisfactory and most gratifying to the humanity and State pride of our citizens. They exhibit the Insane Asylum of California, in its curative results, in an extremely favorable comparison with the most successful institutions of the kind in the world. With no adequate preparation or conveniences on the start to render its ministrations of charity "twice blessed," with its columns of admissions already advanced and fast progressing while yet the foundation walls of the contemplated buildings were unlaid, of the three thousand one hundred and thirty-five patients received, one thousand six hundred and sixteen—more than fifty-one per cent—have been discharged cured.

In order the more fully to appreciate the curative success of the Asylum, it will be necessary to consider as ascertained by the proportion of recoveries in others, and by conclusions of reliable authors on the subject

THE CURABILITY OF INSANITY.

Esquirol, in his investigations, obtained the results of the treatment of sixteen thousand five hundred and sixteen cases, admitted into the leading hospitals for the insane in England, and three thousand nine hundred and thirty eight cases received into the principal Asylums of France. Of the former number, five thousand eight hundred and nineteen, or thirty-five per cent of the number admitted, recovered, while of the latter, one thousand nine hundred and ninety-two, or fifty per cent of the number admitted, recovered. These were treated to a conclusion, which is not the case with the admissions noted in our tables, as they embrace the patients received up to the very day of their date, who, consequently, have had no time for restoration. In Germany and Prussia the cures were much more rare than in England and France. Having presented these statistics, this corypheus of authors upon insanity says: "From the reports made in different establishments or hospitals for the insane, we conclude, first, that the absolute cures of the insane are about one third; second, that the number of cures varies from a fourth to a half. This difference depends upon the peculiar circumstances of locality, maladies, and treatment." *

Dr. Thurman gives the results of treatment in more than fifty Asylums—English, French, American, Scotch, Irish, and German—showing the ratio of recoveries to the number of admissions in each, and exhibiting a range of twenty-six to forty-nine per cent. † Bucknell and Tuke, adding the results of their own investigations to these tables, say: "The conclusions to which an examination of these statistics leads us may be thus stated in the words of the above writer, namely: 'that as regards the recoveries in Asylums which have been established during any considerable period, a proportion of much less than forty per cent of the admissions is, under ordinary circumstances, to be regarded as a low proportion, and one much exceeding forty-five per cent as a high proportion.'" ‡

An examination of the reports of some of the principal Asylums of our own country will not change the high position to which the Insane Asylum of California is entitled among them as a curative institution.

---

* Esquirol on Insanity, p. 61. † Statistics of Insanity, p. 106.
‡ Bucknell and Tuke on Insanity, p. 261.

INSANE ASYLUMS.	Admissions.	Cures.	Percentage of cures to admissions.
Maine Insane Hospital, Augusta, for 21 years.....	2,398	989	41
Central Asylum, Ohio, for 24 years................	3,857	2,000	52
State Hospital, Worcester, Mass., for 25 years....	4,641	2,551	45
Retreat for the Insane, Hartford, Conn., for 41 yrs.	4,378	2.060	47
State Lunatic Asylum, N. J., for 14 years.........	2,076	841	40
State Lunatic Asylum, Utica, N. Y., for 21 years.	7,235	2,823	39
Average of five Asylums, Pennsylvania, 1860.....			40
Eastern Lunatic Asylum, Kentucky, for 38 years.	2,571	968	37
State Hospital, Taunton, Mass., (Rep. 1860) 6 yrs.	1,258	497	39
Insane Asylum of California, commencement in 1851 in General Hospital, to October 1st, 1865, 14 years..	3,135	1,616	51

It is unnecessary to pursue these comparisons further, gratifying as they must be to the philanthropist, whose sympathies are with the unfortunate, or to the political economist, who justly looks for a commensurate return for the public munificence which so early commenced, and has ever since so liberally sustained this costly charity.

PROPORTION OF RELAPSES OR RE-ATTACKS.

In connection with the ratio of cures, and to obtain a full and comprehensive view of the beneficial results obtained from the operations of the Asylum, we will also consider the proportion of relapses or re-attacks; or, in other words, the comparative effectiveness of the reported cures. A relapse, in the proper use of the term, is a remanifestation of the disease while the recovery is incomplete—a rekindling of the apparently extinguished fire from a concealed spark. A re-attack is a recurrence of the disease subsequently to complete recovery.

The situation of the Insane Asylum of California is such as to insure the return to its own wards of a large proportion of the patients who have once been discharged as recovered, and have afterwards suffered a relapse, or re-attack of their malady.

What proportion of cases re-admitted into the institution have been returned with a relapse of the original attack in consequence of the imperfection of the cure, and what proportion from re-attacks after complete recovery, we have not the means of knowing. But the re-admissions, of course, include both forms of renewed eruption, and in my judgment, they do not bear a large proportion to the number dismissed as cured.

It is reasonable to suppose, basing the statement upon the observations of the scientific and experienced, that twenty per cent of all who have been once insane and have recovered, will, sooner or later, be re-afflicted with their former misfortune. If the predisposition did not already exist, the first attack establishes it; and if it did exist, it is increased by the disease having been once developed.

This institution has discharged as recovered during the last fourteen years, one thousand six hundred and sixteen patients. It has now in its wards six hundred and thirty-two. Of this number about seventy-five are persons who had been previously in the Asylum and discharged as cured. This is less than five per cent of the whole number discharged as recovered. This proportion, in an institution which, from its extreme isolation from any other of the kind, would be peculiarly liable to have its imperfect or impaired work returned, is not large.

More than fifty per cent of the patients dismissed cured from the Glasgow Royal Asylum in eighteen hundred and sixty-two had been previously insane. Some of the number had been twice discharged during the year. "One female patient who had been admitted twice during the year, had been in the Asylum above thirty times; and one male patient who was also twice admitted, had been seven times in the Asylum. One gentleman had been above twelve times an inmate of the Asylum." *

MORTALITY.

The following table will show the number and cause of death, nativity, age, sex, length of residence in the Asylum, and duration of insanity, of all who have died during the past year.

Months.	Number.	CAUSE OF DEATH.	NATIVITY.	AGE.	SEX.		RESIDENCE IN THE ASYLUM.			DURATION OF INSANITY.	
				Years.	Male.	Female.	Years.	Months.	Days.	Years.	Months.
1864.											
Oct......	1	General paralysis............	Italy.........	36	1	......	1	4	......	1	10
	2	Inflammation of bowels......	Ireland......	36	......	1	......	2	13	......	......
	3	Marasmus..................	Mexico......	28	1	......	......	9	......	......	10
	4	Softening of the brain......	Ohio.........	......	......	1	......	......	2	......	2
Nov....	1	General paralysis............	Poland......	33	1	......	......	......	5	......	4
	2	Acute mania.................	China........	......	......	1	......	......	21	......	......
	3	Consumption................	Kentucky..	32	1	......	2	3	......	8	......
	4	General paralysis............	France......	46	1	......	......	8	......	......	......
Dec,....	1	Softening of the brain......	Germany...	46	......	1	1	2	......	1	3
	2	Acute mania.................	Holland.....	......	......	1	......	1	2	......	1	3
	3	Softening of the brain......	Pennsylv'a	44	......	1	......	......	3	......	......
	4	Acute mania.................	New York..	......	......	1	......	......	......	1	......
	5	Softening of the brain......	France......	31	1	......	1	7	......	......	......
	6	Consumption................	Tennessee..	42	1	......	7	8	......	......	......
	7	Consumption................	Illinois......	38	......	1	......	......	8	8	8
	8	Inanition.....................	Ireland......	31	1	......	......	......	10	1	5
1865.											
Jan.....	1	Softening of the brain......	Ireland......	30	1	......	......	......	11	......	......
	2	Softening of the brain......	New York..	47	1	......	......	1	22	......	......
	3	Softening of the brain......	Ireland......	......	......	1	......	2	11	......	......
	4	Consumption................	....	......	......	1	......	6	7	......	......
Feb.....	1	Acute mania.................	Belgium.....	......	......	1	......	......	25	......	1
	2	Chronic diarrhœa...........	China........	42	1	......	1	9	......	1	11
	3	Consumption................	Arkansas...	......	......	1	......	2	10	......	......

* Report of Glasgow Asylum for 1863.

Months	Number	CAUSE OF DEATH.	NATIVITY.	AGE. Years.	SEX. Male.	SEX. Female.	RESIDENCE IN THE ASYLUM. Years.	RESIDENCE IN THE ASYLUM. Months.	RESIDENCE IN THE ASYLUM. Days.	DURATION OF INSANITY. Years.	DURATION OF INSANITY. Months.
Feb	4	Softening of the brain	Virginia	38	1		1	7		3	5
	5	Softening of the brain	Prussia	45	1			4		1	10
	6	Consumption		36	1		6				
	7	Consumption	China	54	1			5			
	8	Consumption	Ireland	44	1		4	11			
	9	Acute mania	Pennsylv'a	40		1			3		14
	10	Consumption	America		1						
	11	Epilepsy	Australia	18	1		1	10		3	10
Mar	1	Marasmus	Spain	34	1		6	11		7	
	2	Consumption	Mexico	27		1	3	8		7	
	3	Consumption	Ireland	28	1		3	11		4	1
	4	Epilepsy	Pac. Ocean	15	1		4	6		11	6
	5	Consumption	U. S.			1	2	2		10	2
	6	Scrofula	Jamaica	30	1		5	6			
	7	Marasmus	Italy	33		1		7		11	7
	8	Epilepsy	Kentucky	44	1			2	9	8	
	9	Acute mania			1		3	3			
	10	Consumption	Ireland	35		1	4	2		4	2
April	1	Consumption	China	37	1		1	11			
	2	Consumption	New Jersey	40	1		6	5			
	3	Softening of the brain	England			1	1	5		1	11
	4	Consumption	China			1	3	4			
	5	Softening of the brain	Vermont	32	1			6			8
	6	Marasmus	Scotland	26	1		4	3			
	7	Softening of the brain	Germany	51	1		1	9		3	9
May	1	Dropsy	N. Hamp	35	1			3			
	2	Softening of the brain	Kentucky	35	1			1	11		
	3	Softening of the brain	Illinois	23	1			2			3
	4	Softening of the brain	Pennsylv'a	41	1		3	7			
	5	Softening of the brain	Mass	36	1			6			7
	6	Marasmus	China		1		1				
	7	Consumption	Tennessee	39	1		3	2		6	
	8	Marasmus	Ireland	36	1		5	9		5	11
	9	Consumption	Ireland	32	1		5	8			
June	1	Suicide	New York	44	1			2	20		5
	2	Wound in the larynx*	England	40		1		1	14		3
	3	Consumption	Ireland	47	1		7			7	
	4	Chronic disease of the brain	Scotland	39		1	3	1			
	5	Congestion of bowels	Ireland	47	1			8			
	6	Consumption	Washingt'n	30	1		4	3		4	4
	7	Erysipelas	Germany	42	1			1	26	1	2
July	1	Softening of the brain	France			1	1	11			
	2	Softening of the brain	Maryland	46	1			11			
	3	Acute mania	Maine	43	1			1	19		8
	4	Acute mania	China	41	1			1	10		
	5	Acute mania	China	50	1			1	4		3
	6	Softening of the brain	Pennsylv'a	68	1			10		3	10
	7	Acute mania	Germany	29		1		1	5		2
	8	Softening of the brain	France	52	1		2	1		2	2
	9	Consumption		23	1		2	4		2	5
Aug	1	Apoplexy	Ireland	31	1		3	5		3	8
	2	Exhaustion f'm acute mania	C. America	24		1			26		1
	3	Consumption			1		8				
	4	Puerperal fever	Missouri	19		1			1		
Sept	1	Epilepsy	Ireland		1		2	3		5	3
	2	Exhaustion f'm acute mania	America	43	1			1			
	3	Inflammation of the brain	Illinois	31	1		6			7	6
	4	Scirrhus of stomach	Chili		1			7			8
	5	Consumption	France	41	1		5	11			

* This wound was received in attempting suicide before admission to the Asylum, and death was caused by stricture of the larynx after the wound closed.

Notwithstanding the inmates have enjoyed a remarkable immunity from all physical diseases except such as were the recognized cause or the obvious result of their respective mental disorders, the ratio of mortality is large compared with that of a majority of Asylums for the insane. It is not, however, large when we take into consideration those modifying circumstances which are never overlooked by the statistician in collating his figures and stating his conclusions. "The mortality must be more considerable when we have to treat every form of insanity. * * It is one to six or eight."*

One to eight, on the number resident, is about the ratio of mortality in this Asylum during the past year. The cases sent here comprise every conceivable variety of mental unsoundness. The changeless idiot, the apparently well but hapless victim of jealousy, the helpless paralytic, and even the cold and pulseless moribund, in the inaudible delerium of approaching death, are sent and admitted to this institution. . We are informed of a recent case in which death intervened between the order of commitment and the departure of the public conveyance which was to take the patient on the same or the next day. More than one hundred miles away the corpse lay, just committed to the Insane Asylum at Stockton. Providence mercifully sent the worn-out traveller to a more undisturbed repose. Many come from city and county hospitals where the silent ravages of chronic organic disease have at length dethroned the mind. Nearly all the inmates of our Asylum are supported by charity. Many of them are homeless, and some friendless. We have no almshouses and but few charitable institutions of any kind. Consequently the fifty per cent of incurables, or at least a majority of them, remain here even after they become harmless; and in the course of nature must sooner or later die. Many of them annually die of those diseases to which the insane are peculiarly liable. One of the chief of these is consumption. Twenty eight per cent of the deaths of the past year are attributed to this disease. In the Asylum at Taunton, Massachusetts, thirty per cent of the deaths for seven years were from consumption. A still more deplorable and equally prolific cause of death as well as of mental alienation is general paralysis. The second ward of our Asylum presents the melancholly examples of this revolting and fatal form of insanity. It is noted in the tabular statement and on the records as softening of the brain. "The duration of the disease extends from one to three, and in solitary cases, from five to six years. It almost invariably terminates in death."†

The great number of cases of this form of insanity found in our Asylum is a verification of the following observations of the author above quoted: "The male sex is more predisposed to this form of paralysis than the female." * * * Those ranks of society "in which there is much room for the play of ambition, and where there is great temptation to debauchery, are peculiarly prone to it. Venereal excesses and intemperance frequently give rise to the affection." Nearly three fourths of the inmates of this Asylum are males; and in what country has there been more room for the play of ambition, or greater temptation to debauchery and intemperance, than in California?

Twenty-eight per cent of the deaths were from general paralysis.

With the exception of twelve deaths from acute mania, six from marasmus, and four from epilepsy, there were only solitary instances of deaths from other causes.

---

* Esquirol, pp. 65 and 66. † Romberg on Diseases of Nervous System.

GENERAL HEALTH.

As has already been observed, the patients have been blessed with their usual remarkable exemption from the ordinary acute diseases. Aside from the common and unavoidable complications of insanity, sickness has been almost unknown in the wards of the Asylum. It might be supposed that an institution so crowded as this has been for years past, would have been visited by some of those frightful endemics which occasionally decimate the passengers of crowded ships, spread terror through the camps of great armies, and drive from large cities their panic-stricken inhabitants. In the first place, as one reason for the invariable general healthfulness of the institution, its wards, the inmates, and their clothes, are kept scrupulously clean. There is no indulgence or relaxation respecting this rule. In the second place, much less room is required for the preservation of health in an institution of this kind, in the climate of California, than would be necessary in that of the Eastern States. So mild and equable is its temperature, that the patients literally live out of doors during the daytime, the whole year round. In the yards or airing courts are large roofs, erected to protect them from the heat of the sun in summer and from rain in winter; and there such as are not trusted to saunter about the pleasure grounds spend their time. A large room or hall, used as a reading room, and warmed by a fire when necessary, to which the patients at all times have free ingress and egress, is also situated in the central part of the main yard. And during night and day, summer and winter, the windows of the Asylum are let down from the top, admitting a constant circulation of fresh air, of grateful temperature, through the wards.

The climate of our State is known to be, even in the hottest weather, remarkably exempt from that sultry, pestiferous heat existing between the trade winds in the low latitudes, and experienced more or less in the East, in the night as intensely as in the daytime, during the season termed dog days, as well as occasionally in other parts of the summer. On the other hand, in the rigorous climate of the Eastern States, the physical comfort of the patients requires them to be housed most of the time during nearly six months of the year, and that their rooms be closed during the hours of sleep against the inclemency of the external atmosphere. For these reasons, though much more room is desirable, the inmates of our Asylum have endured, with apparent impunity, the scanty supply of room afforded them. Much relief, however, is now obtained from our former crowded state by the recent occupation by the female patients of the

NEW BUILDING.

All the female patients recently occupying the north wing of the old Asylum building, and about one third of those in the two small one story brick buildings in the northeast yard, have been transferred to the new building. Thus we have about one hundred and twenty-five patients in the new structure, and about forty-three remaining in the above named detached accompaniments of the old.

This valuable improvement, in its capacity and means of comfort and security, as well as in all other respects, fully answers our expectations. It is but the section of a perfect and more extensive plan of building, but it is sufficiently complete and independent in itself to possess the capacity and conveniences, so far as its present use is concerned, that the same part would afford in union with the whole. It may thus be added to without derangement of architectural design, or remain as it is without waste of expenditure. It contains seven wards, admirably arranged for the classification of patients—an important curative necessity, of which we have been heretofore nearly destitute. Before this change we only had three wards for one hundred and sixty-eight female patients, whereas we now have eight. All the apparatus for warming, lighting, cooking, bathing, supplying water, and conveying food, operate in an entirely satisfactory and successful manner. The culinary department is in the basement; and all the work therein is performed by a man and his wife, with the aid of patients, at an expense of sixty-five dollars per month. The kitchen is accessible from the wards by inside stairways. This gives the inmates some of the essential accommodations of a *home*. The duty of procuring hot tea or gruel, or other necessaries of the kind, for the sick or newly arrived and exhausted patient, is made easy and agreeable. You are aware of the annoying inconveniences, to the females, of the old kitchen in this respect. It is situated in the very thoroughfare of the male patients and employés, and was more or less monopolized by the wants or surrounded by the presence of the four hundred and sixty-four male inmates.

By the erection of this building the crowded condition of the male department is relieved as much as that of the females.

It gives to the use of the males the entire old Asylum building, the north wing and its two yards, one at the end and one in the rear, in addition to the part before occupied. The yard containing the one story brick building before named, is another and separate inclosure.

This leaves to the males two of the largest and best wards in the institution, containing one hundred beds. About seventy-five of the male patients have heretofore been compelled to sleep in temporary beds made upon the floors of the corridors. These are now all provided for, leaving about twenty-five spare beds for future use.

I feel it my duty, out of consideration for the unknown and countless friends of the great multitude of unfortunates under our charge, and in view of past events, to say one word in regard to the

TREATMENT OF THE PATIENTS BY THE ATTENDANTS.

We have taken great pains to inculcate the maxim that an insane person is not responsible for his conduct; that he neither directs the performance nor appreciates the character of his own acts; that he is as unanswerable for them as an infant whose nascent mind is not yet endowed with the attributes of reason and volition; and that hence he is to be regarded as incapable of provoking, in the rational mind, the spirit of anger and retaliation.

The feelings of the insane, too, are often actually sensitive to the slightest acts of rudeness or discourtesy, or to any apparent lack of respect or want of consideration exhibited by others in their intercourse with them. And anything that offends an insane person unnecessarily, whether it be the injury, physical or mental, of personal abuse, or the irritations and disturbances of a rude and imperious manner on the part of his attendants, serves to unnecessarily augment his mental disorder and retard or destroy the restorative influences.

It is hardly necessary to say that the attendants are not allowed in any manner to assault the persons of the patients, or to exercise over them any penal or vindictive treatment. They are required to treat them with invariable kindness and respect, using only such restraint as is necessary to prevent self-injury or the injury of each other, and exercising only such compulsion as is required to procure the performance of the necessary daily routine of life. Mechanical restraint is used only under the direction of the medical attendants, except the simplest kind on the hands, to prevent the destruction of clothing. Those barbarous appliances known by the general term of *irons* are not allowed in the institution. There is not a handcuff, or shackle, or chain, or any species of that kind of prison furniture, fit only to be used on criminals, to be found in or belonging to the Insane Asylum of California. Our present attendants are attentive and kind in their treatment of the patients, and observant of the principles and restrictions indicated in the foregoing observations.

We would tender to the editors and proprietors of the following papers our cordial thanks for their valuable literary favors. Their contributions are a source of great enjoyment and benefit to the patients:

San Francisco Daily Evening Bulletin;
San Francisco Daily American Flag;
San Francisco Golden Era;
San Francisco Spirit of the Times;
San Francisco Monitor;
San Francisco Abend Post (German;)
Courier de San Francisco;
Sacramento Daily Bee;
Stockton Daily Independent;
Stockton Daily Evening Herald;
Alpine Chronicle;
Virginia Daily Union;
Le Voz de Mejico;
New York Sunday Atlas;
New York Sun;
New York Dispatch;
New York Irish American;
New York Leader;
Brooklyn Daily Eagle;
The Boston Nation.

We would also respectfully solicit similar favors from others.

In conclusion, I gratefully acknowledge the recent manifestation of your confidence, relying upon your aid in the discharge of the sacred and responsible duties it has imposed. I would invite an ever active vigilance and scrutinous care over the interests of this institution. It is one of vast importance, both in the expenditure it incurs and the good it bestows. It is the first and only public asylum for the insane on this coast. It has opened its doors to a newly inhabited country, far exceeding in area the New England and Middle States combined. It has had its day of small beginnings, and its hours of darkness and of good and of evil report. It is now one of the largest institutions of its kind in our land. It contains the unfortunate representatives of more than forty counties of our own State, and receives on the most liberal terms the afflicted applicants of other States. Its columns of cures are the proud trophies of its success. Its impartial blessings, as the silent rays of a genial sun, have been diffusing themselves unheard throughout the State, lighting up the dark and reason-bereft soul, and warming into joy the forlorn and woe-stricken heart. G. A. SHURTLEFF,
Resident Physician.

Insane Asylum of California,
Stockton, October 20, 1865.

APPENDIX.

TABLE A.

Showing the counties from which two hundred and sixty-eight patients were admitted.

Counties.	Males.	Females.	Total.
Alameda	2	2	4
Amador	1		1
Butte	3	1	4
Calaveras	1	2	3
Contra Costa	2		2
Colusa	1		1
El Dorado	11	1	12
Humboldt	2		2
Los Angeles	3		3
Mariposa	2		2
Mendocino		3	3
Monterey	1		1
Napa	1	2	3
Nevada	7	2	9
Placer	3		3
Sacramento	21	6	27
San Francisco	76	34	110
San Joaquin	15	8	23
San Mateo	1		1
Santa Clara	9	5	14
Santa Cruz	1	1	2
Shasta	2	2	4
Sierra	1	2	3
Solano		1	1
Sonoma	7	2	9
Stanislaus		1	1
Sutter	2		2
State Prison	4		4
Tuolumne	5	1	6
Yolo	3		3
Yuba	2	1	3
State of Nevada	1	1	2
Totals	190	78	268

TABLE B.

Showing the nativity of two hundred and sixty-eight patients.

UNITED STATES.

Nativity.	Males.	Females.	Total.
New Hampshire	3		3
Massachusetts	7	1	8
Vermont	5		5
Tennessee	2	2	4
Ohio	3	3	6
New York	12	4	16
Illinois	7	1	8
Connecticut	2	1	3
Missouri	4	4	8
Kentucky	4	2	6
Maine	5		5
Pennsylvania	6	2	8
South Carolina	1		1
California	2		2
New Jersey	2	1	3
Indiana	4		4
Louisiana	1		1
North Carolina		2	2
Georgia	1		1
United States	2	2	4
Maryland	2		2
Virginia	2		2
Michigan	1		1
Totals, United States	78	25	103
Unknown	7		7
Totals	85	25	110

Table B—Continued.

FOREIGN COUNTRIES.

Nativity.	Males.	Females.	Total.
England...........................	9	5	14
Finland............................	1	....	1
Poland.............................	1	2	3
Ireland............................	42	21	63
Prussia............................	6	3	9
Canada	3	1	4
China..............................	7	2	9
Chili...............................	3	1	4
France.............................	4	1	5
New Brunswick.................	1	....	1
Flores Islands....................	1	....	1
Scotland...........................	2	2	4
Sweden............................	3	....	3
Germany..........................	11	7	18
Belgium...........................	....	1	1
Bavaria............................	....	2	2
Spain...............................	1	....	1
Switzerland.......................	3	....	3
West Indies.......................	1	1	2
Australia..........................	....	1	1
Mexico.............................	1	....	1
New Zealand.....................	1	....	1
Norway............................	2	....	2
Equador...........................	1	....	1
Denmark..........................	....	1	1
Central America.................	....	1	1
Algiers.............................	1	....	1
Manilla............................	....	1	1
Totals........................	105	53	158

RECAPITULATION.

TABLE C.

Showing the ages at which insanity first appeared in two hundred and sixty-eight patients.

Ages.	Male.	Female.	Total.
Between 10 and 15 years...	1	1	2
Between 15 and 20 years...	2	6	8
Between 20 and 25 years...	18	9	27
Between 25 and 30 years...	29	14	43
Between 30 and 35 years...	34	15	49
Between 35 and 40 years...	30	15	45
Between 40 and 45 years...	15	7	22
Between 45 and 50 years...	16	2	18
Between 50 and 60 years...	6	2	8
Between 60 and 70 years...		1	1
Unknown...	39	6	45
Totals...	190	78	268

TABLE D.

Showing the ages of two hundred and sixty-eight patients at the time of their admission.

Ages.	Male.	Female.	Total.
Between 15 and 20 years...	2	4	6
Between 20 and 25 years...	15	9	24
Between 25 and 30 years...	25	14	39
Between 30 and 35 years...	40	19	59
Between 35 and 40 years...	36	12	48
Between 40 and 45 years...	29	11	40
Between 45 and 50 years...	18	2	20
Between 50 and 60 years...	14	4	18
Between 60 and 70 years...	1	2	3
Unknown...	10	1	11
Totals...	190	78	268

TABLE E.

Showing the supposed cause of insanity in two hundred and sixty-eight patients, as stated in commitments.

Cause.	Male.	Female.	Total.
Religion	8	8	16
Typhoid fever	2	1	3
Disappointment in love	6	3	9
Pecuniary trouble	11	2	13
Masturbation	33	1	34
Hereditary	3	2	5
Intemperance	6	2	8
Mental trouble	1		1
Epilepsy	2	1	3
Exposure	1	1	2
Change of life		3	3
Absence of husband		1	1
Disease of brain	1		1
Loss of husband		2	2
Spiritualism	2	1	3
Domestic trouble	6	2	8
Arrested on a criminal charge	1		1
Suppressed menstruation		7	7
Excitement		3	3
Fall from a horse	1		1
Injury on the head	4		4
Disease of the encephalon	1		1
Syphilis	1		1
Jealousy		2	2
Parturition		3	3
Meningial irritation	1		1
Illness		3	3
Softening of the brain	2		2
Quinine given to the mother while nursing		1	1
Cerebral congestion	1		1
Poverty	1		1
Sun stroke	1		1
Hemorrhage		1	1
Puerperal fever		1	1
Loss of children		2	2
Unknown	94	25	119
Totals	190	78	268

TABLE F.

Showing the Mental Condition of two hundred and sixty-eight patients at the time of their admission.

Form of Disease.	Male.	Female.	Total.
Mania	80	46	126
Monomania	12	8	20
Melancholia	25	7	32
Dementia	73	17	90
Totals	190	78	268

TABLE G.

Showing the Civil Condition of two hundred and sixty-eight patients at the time of their admission.

Civil Condition.	Male.	Female.	Total.
Married	43	54	97
Single	129	16	145
Widows		6	6
Widowers	3		3
Unknown	15	2	17
Totals	190	78	268

TABLE FIRST.

Showing the Steward's Account of articles consumed in the Insane Asylum, including the Expense of the Office, Resident Physician's House, Assistant Physician's House, Repairs, and Passage of Discharged Patients, from October first, eighteen hundred and sixty-four, to May first, eighteen hundred and sixty-five; also, the Steward's Account from May first, eighteen hundred and sixty-five, to October first, eighteen hundred and sixty-five, showing all the Expenses of the Asylum.

Articles to May First.	Value.
Flour	$7,519 78
Meat	4,721 24
Potatoes	1,603 80
Butter	899 99
Tea	1,104 33
Coffee	1,371 49
Sugar	1,515 76
Pork	30 55
Lard	174 60
Beans	843 50
Rice	437 55
Dried fruit	145 21
Fruit	16 10
Eggs	18 04
Soup	246 96
Fish	171 86
Syrup	431 01
Salt	93 50
Oil	119 70
Candles	5 70
Small groceries	159 56
Tobacco	372 42
Drugs	579 48
Liquors	361 36
Hardware	86 20
Dry goods	741 17
Clothing	2,244 10
Shoes	766 40
Hats and caps	217 25
Bedding	1,211 86
Blankets	1,316 50
Crockery	138 62
Corn meal	269 00
Pumping	1,395 67
Tinware	327 90
Fuel	1,411 32
Cheese	5 30

TABLE FIRST—Continued.

Articles to May First.	Value.
Dairy	1,744 88
Stable	948 88
Garden	1,720 26
Laundry	953 96
Gas	757 10
Cracked Wheat	256 30
Pay Roll	15,037 47
Miscellaneous	1,256 30
	$55,249 43
Office	1,273 40
Resident Physician	1,532 32
Assistant Physician	549 46
Repairs and extraordinary expenses	2,985 92
Discharged patients	37 00
Total to May first	$61,628 53

STEWARD'S ACCOUNT,

Showing all the Expenses of the Asylum from May 1, 1865, to October 1, 1865.

Articles.	Value.
Flour	$4,293 24
Meat	2,736 35
Sugar	1,393 24
Tea	923 96
Syrup	450 98
Potatoes	1,428 14
Butter	1,488 93
Coffee	1,053 90
Lard	205 00
Pork	88 89
Fish	253 50
Eggs	78 35
Beans	73 38
Rice and cracked wheat	664 90
Corn meal and middlings	453 41
Fruit	130 55
Vegetables	18 21
Salt	61 34
Vinegar	87 72
Small groceries	143 59
Soap and potash	361 45

TABLE FIRST—Continued.

Articles.	Value.
Drugs	$436 28
Liquors	326 31
Tobacco	266 52
Dry goods	1,283 33
Clothing	1,686 83
Shoes	564 41
Blankets	505 00
Crockery	188 01
Hardware	462 87
Hay	1,078 28
Grain and feed	450 48
Tools and seed	159 75
Lumber	124 02
Building material	58 25
Brooms and brushes	193 10
Stationery and blanks	147 48
Oil and gas	282 27
Paints and glass	99 63
Fuel	1,744 14
Discharged patients	242 60
Returning escapes	69 00
House rent	245 00
Pay roll and wages	18,679 49
Miscellaneous	902 47
Total from May 1 to October 1	$41,579 55
Total to May 1, 1865	61,628 53
Total expenditure for the year ending Sept. 30, 1865	$103,203 08

TABLE SECOND.

Showing the cost of the different departments from May 1, to October 1, 1865.

Departments.	Cost.
Kitchen and dining room	$12,730 11
Male department	8,422 94
Female department	4,485 39
Bakery	4,644 81
Laundry and engine	1,966 67
Farm, garden, and dairy	2,774 93
Drugs	1,005 46
Office	915 44
Resident Physician (from August 1st)	525 83
Assistant Physician	730 90
Repairs	666 09
Miscellaneous	2,710 98
Total	$41,579 55

TABLE THIRD.

Averages.

MONTHS.	Average number of patients on hand daily.	Average daily expense.	Average cost per capita per day.	Average cost per capita per month.	Cost per patient per month for boots and shoes.	Cost per patient per month for clothing.
October	585	$265 68	$ 45	$14 08	$ 18	$ 37
November	592	291 97	49	14 80	15	92
December	596	274 54	46	14 28	23	1 13
January	610	277 31	45	14 09	16	98
February	613	308 19	50	14 08	20	62
March	618	318 73	51	15 99	26	67
April	619	300 20	48	14 56	9	26
May	627	309 96	49	15 32	22	1 01
June	637	287 25	45	13 52	20	70
July	639	251 12	40	12 18	13	58
August	626	251 47	40	12 45	20	68
September	628	255 44	42	12 38	15	64
Yearly averages	616	$282 66	$ 46	$13 98	$ 18	$ 71

TABLE FOURTH

Products of the Farm, Garden, and Dairy.

Cabbage, pounds	65,218
Tomatoes, pounds	17,418
Turnips, pounds	88,299
Carrots, pounds	5,492
Squash, pounds	10,844
Beets, pounds	65,035
Onions, pounds	4,704
Beans, pounds	7,602
Cucumbers, dozen	612
Melons	5,561
Peas, pounds	2,851
Other vegetables, pounds	2,678
Other vegetables, bunches	5,852
Peaches, pounds	5,843
Grapes, pounds	2,440
Pears, pounds	356
Other fruits, pounds	936
Milk, gallons	8,403
Meat and lard, pounds	11,327
Eggs, dozen	123
Chickens	9
Cattle and calves, number of head sold	15

Value of products for the year	$12,364 48
Cost of farm, garden, and dairy	7,232 05
Profit	$5,132 43

TABLE FIFTH.

Estimated value of the Insane Asylum property.

One hundred and eighteen acres of land, buildings, furniture, and steam engines.	$300,000
Provisions, clothing, shoes, hats, tinware, hardware, etc.	1,809
Wood	1,038
Carpenters' tools, and lumber	229
Horses	400
Wagons	580
Harness	175
Hogs and pigs	1,103
Dairy stock, (cattle)	1,080
Garden and farm tools	600
Hay	879
Fruit trees and vines	3,500
Nursery stock	740
Total	$312,133

REPORT OF THE DIRECTORS

OF THE

INSANE ASYLUM OF CALIFORNIA,

FOR

THE YEAR 1864.

REPORT.

Stockton, October 1st, 1864.

To His Excellency, F. F. Low, Governor of the State of California:

The undersigned, Directors of the Insane Asylum of California, respectfully submit the following report for the year ending October first, eighteen hundred and sixty-four.

By reference to the annual report of the Treasurer, which is hereto annexed, you will find that at the commencement of the year, October first, eighteen hundred and sixty-three, there was no money in the General Fund at that date, but that the sum of eighteen hundred and fifty-two dollars and seventy-two cents ($1,852 72) was due from this fund to the Improvement Fund. The total receipts from all sources, the details of which will be found in said report, amount to one hundred and forty thousand nine hundred and sixty dollars and seventy cents, ($140,960 70,) and the disbursements to one hundred and twenty-eight thousand five hundred and thirty dollars and three cents, ($128,530 03,) leaving a cash balance in the General Fund of twelve thousand four hundred and thirty dollars and sixty-seven cents, ($12,430 67,) against which bills have been audited to the amount of nineteen thousand two hundred and ninety-seven dollars and fifteen cents, ($19,297 15,) leaving a deficiency of six thousand eight hundred and sixty-six dollars and forty-eight cents. It is quite probable that when the warrants which have been hypothecated on loans shall have been paid, a sum nearly sufficient to meet this deficiency will revert to the institution. The balance to the credit of the Improvement Fund on the first October, eighteen hundred and sixty-three, was four thousand six hundred and ninety-one dollars and twenty-five cents, ($4,691 25,) since which time there has been received at different times, from the State Treasury, the sum of fifty-nine thousand two hundred and seventy-six dollars and forty-nine cents, ($59,276 49,) making a total of sixty-three thousand nine hundred and sixty-seven dollars and seventy-four cents, ($63,967 74.) The disbursements amount to sixty-four thousand and forty-two dollars and thirty-two cents, ($64,042 32,) leaving this fund overdrawn seventy-four dollars and fifty-eight cents, ($74 58.) Bills unpaid amount to eleven thousand seven hundred and sixty-nine dollars and twenty-eight cents, ($11,769 28,) which shows the total expenditure to be seventy-five thousand seven hundred and thirty-seven dollars and two cents, ($75,737 02.)

The following exhibits the condition of the Asylum, as to the patients under care and treatment therein:

Number of patients, October 1st, 1863	583	
Number of patients admitted during the year	219	
Whole number treated during the year		802
Whole number discharged during the year	127	
Whole number escaped during the year	12	
Whole number died during the year	82	
Whole number in Asylum, October 1st, 1864	581	
Whole number accounted for		802
Number discharged cured during the year	101	
Number discharged convalescent during the year	19	
Number discharged unimproved during the year	6	
Number discharged not insane when received	1	
Whole number discharged as above		127
Percentage of recoveries to admissions		46
Percentage of deaths on average number resident		14
Percentage of deaths on whole number treated		10

In compliance with the Act of the Legislature, approved April twenty-fifth, eighteen hundred and sixty-three, an additional building is in process of erection, and except the inside work, nearly finished. It is constructed of brick, with galvanized iron roof. The gutters and cornice are also made of the last named material. It contains one hundred and eleven rooms, (exclusive of basement, halls, and attics,) which are divided as follows:

Single rooms	55
Associated rooms	9
Dining rooms	6
Attendants' room	6
Matron's room	1
Reception room	1
Bath rooms	7
Water closets	7
Corridors	7
Sewing room	1
Sleeping rooms for domestics, with closets	5
Crockery rooms	6

The basement will contain the heating apparatus, and will also be used for the distribution of food to the dumb-waiters, and other domestic purposes. It is estimated that the entire structure will cost about seventy thousand dollars, and that about one hundred patients may be accommodated therein.

The undersigned at this time purposely refrain from making any suggestions or recommendations for legislative action, inasmuch as they will again report to your excellency before the meeting of the Legislature, when the subject will be more elaborately treated.

The report of the Superintendent is also herewith submitted.

G. A. SHURTLEFF,
AUSTIN SPERRY,
T. R. ANTHONY,
H. B. UNDERHILL,
E. S. HOLDEN,
J. G. GASMANN,
Directors.

REPORT

OF THE

RESIDENT PHYSICIAN

FOR

1864.

REPORT.

INSANE ASYLUM, October 1st, 1864.

To the Directors of the Insane Asylum of California:

GENTLEMEN:—At the date of the last annual report, (October twentieth, eighteen hundred and sixty-three,) there were five hundred and eighty-three patients in the Asylum—four hundred and fifty-one males, and one hundred and thirty-two females.

Since that time, two hundred and nineteen have been received—one hundred and fifty-three males, and sixty-six females. Under management during the year, eight hundred and two.

One hundred and twenty-seven were, during the same period, discharged—eighty-six males, and forty-one females; of whom one was not insane. One hundred and one had recovered, nineteen were convalescent, and six unimproved.

Eighty-two died—males, sixty-eight, and females, fourteen. Twelve escaped—all males. Whole number discharged, died, and eloped, two hundred and twenty-one; leaving at this date five hundred and eighty-one—four hundred and forty-one males, and one hundred and forty females. Decrease for the year, two.

The materials and stock on hand are valued as follows:

Provisions, clothing, hats, shoes, hardware, tinware, etc....	85,091 77
Lumber, bricks, wood, etc...	2,695 50
Horses, cattle, hogs, hay, grain, vegetables, etc...............	15,014 65
Total...	$22,801 92

For further "facts and results" respecting the patients, and for full information in relation to the "several departments of labor and expense," with which I have been in any way connected, see tabular statements herewith submitted.

W. P. TILDEN,
Resident Physician.

APPENDIX.

TABLE A.
Deaths.

Months	Numbers	NATIVITY	AGE	SEX Males	SEX Females	RESIDENCE IN ASYLUM Years	RESIDENCE IN ASYLUM Months	DURATION OF INSANITY Years	DURATION OF INSANITY Months	CAUSE OF INSANITY (Taken from Commitments.)	CLASS OF INSANITY	CAUSE OF DEATH
1863.												
Oct....	1	Ireland	22		1	3	3	3	7	Domestic trouble	Dementia	Consumption.
	2	New York	60		1		1	4		Spiritualism	Imbecility	Softening of brain.
	3	Connecticut	33	1		3	6	3	7	Disappointment in love	Dementia	Marasmus.
	4	Ireland	29	1			9		10	Unknown	Melancholia	Consumption.
Nov...	1	Connecticut	29		1		1		2	Religion	Chronic mania	Inflammation of stomach and bowels.
	2	Unknown	38	1		4	9	unk'n.	unk'n.	Unknown	Imbecility	Psoas abscess.
	3	France	47	1			1	unk'n.	unk'n.	Unknown	Imbecility	Consumption.
	4	Illinois	18	1			1		1	Unknown	Acute mania	Exhaustion.
	5	Sweden	30	1		1	3	2	3	Epilepsy	Monomania	Dropsy.
	6	Missouri	28	1		4	4	6	4	Unknown	Periodical mania	Epilepsy.
Dec....	1	Wirtemberg	17		1		1		3	Suppressed menses	Acute mania	Exhaustion.
	2	Virginia	61	1			7	1	3	Family trouble	Imbecility	Paralysis.
	3	Ireland	30	1		1	8	3	8	Intemperance	Chronic mania	Consumption.
	4	France	40	1		4	9	4	10	Unknown	Dementia	Secondary syphilis.
	5	Massachusetts	64	1		2	6	5		Unknown	Dementia	Paralysis.
	6	South Carolina	41	1		5	7	9		Masturbation	Imbecility	Typhoid pneumonia.
	7	Hindostan	31	1		1	6	3	4	Unknown	Imbecility	Consumption.
	8	Ireland	29	1			4	1	6	Unknown	Imbecility	Marasmus.
	9	Massachusetts	55	1			3		9	Intemperance	Dementia	Softening of brain.
	10	Ireland	36	1			1		2	Intemperance	Chronic mania	Apoplexy.
	11	Maine	39	1		2	11	3		Intemperance	Dementia	Softening of brain.

TABLE A—Continued.

Months	Numbers	NATIVITY	AGE	SEX Males	SEX Females	RESIDENCE IN ASYLUM Years	RESIDENCE IN ASYLUM Months	DURATION OF INSANITY Years	DURATION OF INSANITY Months	CAUSE OF INSANITY (Taken from Commitments.)	CLASS OF INSANITY	CAUSE OF DEATH
1864. Jan...	1	China	38	1			4		5	Unknown	Chronic mania	Paralysis.
	2	Equator	25	1		5	6	5	7	Unknown	Chronic mania	Consumption.
	3	New York	12		1	2	3	12		Dentition	Idiocy	Epilepsy.
	4	Pennsylvania	49	1	1	1	4	8	4	Unknown	Dementia	Marasmus.
	5	Illinois	35	1			4		5	Unknown	Melancholia	Marasmus.
	6	Wales	33	1			1	unk'n		Unknown	Acute mania	Exhaustion.
	7	Massachusetts	30		1		5	unk'n	6	Domestic trouble	Dementia	Consumption.
	8	Unknown	unk'n	1		unk'n	unk'n	unk'n	unk'n	Injury on head	Imbecility	Marasmus.
	9	Ireland	27	1			9	unk'n	unk'n	Excessive joy	Acute mania	Exhaustion.
	10	Chili	24	1			3	unk'n	unk'n	Unknown	Melancholia	Consumption.
	11	Scotland	31	1			7	unk u.	4	Unknown	Melancholia	Apoplexy.
Feb...	1	France	47	1		1	3	4	5	Injury on head	Imbecility	Softening of brain.
	2	Rhode Island	32	1		4	2	unk'n	unk'n	Unknown	Imbecility	Softening of brain.
	3	England	64	1		2		unk'n	unk'n	Domestic trouble	Acute mania	Consumption.
	4	Denmark	41	1			6		10	Unknown	Imbecility	Softening of brain.
	5	Canada	37	1		3	2	4	2	Masturbation	Imbecility	Softening of brain.
	6	Hanover	32	1			3	1	3	Domestic trouble	Monomania	Softening of brain.
	7	Ireland	30	1		1	11	2		Religious excitement	Chronic mania	Consumption.
	8	Ireland	31	1		4	4	unk'n	unk'n	Unknown	Melancholia	Hypertrophy of heart.
Mar...	1	New York	40	1			1		2	Spiritualism	Acute mania	Exhaustion.
	2	Tennessee	40	1			1		7	Unknown	Chronic mania	Hypertrophy of heart.
	3	Unknown	26	1			5		7	Masturbation	Melancholia	Softening of brain.
	4	Tennessee	34	1		1	10	2	3	Secondary syphilis	Dementia	Softening of brain.
April.	1	Ohio	29	1			6	unk'n	unk'n	Unknown	Chronic mania	Consumption.
	2	Germany	59	1			1	1	1	Unknown	Acute mania	Exhaustion.
	3	Unknown	unk'n	1			1	unk'n	unk'n	Unknown	Chronic mania	Consumption.
	3	California	24	1		2	1	unk'n	unk'n	Unknown	Melancholia	Consumption.

84

85

Month			Nativity	Age						Supposed Cause	Form of Insanity	Cause of Death
May....	4		England	40	1				1	Injury to scalp and skull	Delirium	Erysipelas.
	1		Chili	25	1				6	Unknown	Dementia	Softening of brain.
	2		Switzerland	39	1		3		3	Unknown	Imbecility	Consumption.
	3		Massachusetts	38	1		2		8	Unknown	Imbecility	Softening of brain.
	4		Ireland	27	1		7	unk'n.	1	Unknown	Imbecility	Consumption.
	5		N. S. Wales	52	1		4	4	4	Unknown	Melancholia	Consumption.
	6		France	unk'n.	1			6	4	Exposure	Chronic mania	Consumption.
June...	1		France	41	1		5	6	10	Unknown	Dementia	Marasmus.
	2		Pennsylvania	51	1		1	4	9	Unknown	Chronic mania	Softening of brain.
	3		England	unk'n.	1		1	unk'n.		Unknown	Dementia	Softening of brain.
	4		Unknown	56	1		1	3	4	Unknown	Imbecility	Consumption.
	5		Germany	36	1		6		4	Unknown	Chronic mania	Exhaustion.
July....	1		Germany	unk'n.		1		unk'n.	4	Domestic trouble	Acute mania	Consumption.
	2		China	unk'n.	1			unk'n.	1	Unknown	Melancholia	Apoplexy.
	3		Ireland	20	1		1	8	6	Intemperance	Delirium	Consumption.
	4		Missouri	unk'n.	1		2	unk'n.	1	Unknown	Dementia	Apoplexy.
	5		Ohio	unk'n.	1			unk'n.	6	Unknown	Acute mania	Typhoid fever.
	6		Unknown	34	1	1		unk'n.	1	Typhoid fever	Delirium	Typhoid fever.
Aug...	1		District Columbia	50	1			1	1	Masturbation	Delirium	Inflammation of brain.
	2		New Hampshire	57	1		1	1	4	Pecuniary trouble	Chronic mania	Softening of brain.
	3		China	unk'n.	1			unk'n.	1	Unknown	Dementia	Consumption.
	4		France	38	1			2	11	Destitution	Imbecility	Consumption.
	5		Germany	26	1			1	10	Apoplexy	Dementia	Paralysis.
	6		Pennsylvania	43	1			7	1	Pecuniary trouble	Imbecility	Softening of brain.
	7		China	unk'n.				3	2	Unknown	Melancholia	Consumption.
	8		Ireland	unk'n.	1		1	7	5	Pneumonia	Chronic mania	Consumption.
	9		Unknown	unk'n.	1			unk'n.	11	Unknown	Dementia	Softening of brain.
	10		Germany	56	1		5	7	1	Pecuniary trouble	Chronic mania	Tabes Mesenterica.
Sept....	1		England	26	1			1	6	Unknown	Chronic mania	Apoplexy.
	2		England	30	1		2	unk'n.	6	Pecuniary trouble	Dementia	Consumption.
	3		California	20				unk'n.	4	Unknown	Melancholia	General debility.
	4		Ireland	39	1		4	6	9	Unknown	Melancholia	Consumption.
	5		Scotland	22	1			unk'n.	6	Masturbation	Dementia	Consumption.

TABLE B.

Counties from which admitted.

Counties.	Males.	Females.	Total.
Alameda...	2	....	2
Amador...	2	1	3
Butte...	1	....	1
Calaveras...	1	1	2
Contra Costa...	....	1	1
Del Norte...	1	....	1
El Dorado...	3	4	7
Fresno...	1	....	1
Los Angeles...	1	....	1
Mariposa...	1	1	2
Napa...	1	....	1
Nevada...	....	3	3
Plumas...	1	....	1
Placer...	11	....	11
San Francisco...	55	35	90
Sacramento...	23	9	32
Siskiyou...	3	....	3
Santa Clara...	4	2	6
San Joaquin...	6	5	11
Solano...	5	....	5
Sierra...	2	....	2
San Bernardino...	1	....	1
Sonoma...	....	1	1
Sutter...	1	....	1
San Mateo...	4	....	4
Shasta...	1	....	1
State Prison...	1	....	1
Tuolumne...	11	2	13
Tehama...	2	....	2
Trinity...	1	....	1
Yolo...	2	....	2
Yuba...	5	1	6
Totals...	153	66	219

TABLE C.

UNITED STATES.

Nativity.	Males.	Females.	Total.
California.............................		2	2
Missouri................................	5		5
Maine..................................	3	2	5
Illinois................................	4	2	6
New York..............................	11	3	14
Massachusetts.........................	5		5
Virginia...............................	3		3
Delaware..............................	1		1
Iowa...................................	1	1	2
Rhode Island..........................	1		1
Connecticut...........................	1		1
Michigan..............................		1	1
Georgia...............................	1		1
Maryland..............................	3		3
Ohio...................................	1		1
Kentucky..............................	1		1
Texas..................................	1		1
Pennsylvania..........................	3		3
New Hampshire........................	2		2
District of Columbia..................	1		1
Vermont...............................	1	1	2
Indiana................................		1	1
Tennessee.............................	2		2
Totals............................	51	13	64

TABLE C—Continued.

FOREIGN COUNTRIES.

Nativity.	Males.	Females.	Total.
Ireland	38	28	66
France	7	3	10
Germany	16	7	23
England	13	3	16
China	8		8
Chili	2	2	4
Italy	2	1	3
Prussia	3	3	6
Mexico	3	2	5
Wales	3		3
Poland	1		1
Canada		1	1
Scotland	1		1
Nova Scotia		1	1
British Columbia	1		1
West Indies	1		1
Saxony	1		1
Sweden	1		1
Switzerland	1		1
Totals	102	51	153
Unknown		2	2
Totals	102	53	155

RECAPITULATION.

Nativity.	Males.	Females.	Total.
United States	51	13	64
Foreign countries	102	51	153
Unknown		2	2
Totals	153	66	219

TABLE D.

Age at which insanity first appeared.

Age.	Males.	Females.	Total.
Between 5 and 10 years............	....	3	3
Between 10 and 15 years............	....	....	....
Between 15 and 20 years............	6	4	10
Between 20 and 25 years............	9	8	17
Between 25 and 30 years............	23	9	32
Between 30 and 35 years............	25	13	38
Between 35 and 40 years............	15	8	23
Between 40 and 45 years............	15	4	19
Between 45 and 50 years............	14	2	16
Between 50 and 60 years............	6	3	9
Between 60 and 70 years............	2	....	2
Unknown............	38	12	50
Totals............	153	66	219

TABLE E.

Age at the time of admission.

Age.	Males.	Females.	Total.
Between 10 and 15 years............	....	2	2
Between 15 and 20 years............	6	4	10
Between 20 and 25 years............	10	8	18
Between 25 and 30 years............	23	7	30
Between 30 and 35 years............	27	13	40
Between 35 and 40 years............	19	12	31
Between 40 and 45 years............	18	4	22
Between 45 and 50 years............	17	2	19
Between 50 and 60 years............	9	2	11
Between 60 and 70 years............	2	3	5
Between 70 and 80 years............	....	....	....
Unknown	22	9	31
Totals............	153	66	219

TABLE F.

Class.

Class.	Males.	Females.	Total.
Acute mania	45	22	67
Chronic mania	20	9	29
Monomania	18	2	20
Melancholia	17	7	24
Dementia	27	9	36
Delirium	9	2	11
Imbecility	15	9	24
Idiocy		3	3
Not insane	2	3	5
Totals	153	66	219

TABLE G.

Civil Condition.

Civil Condition.	Males.	Females.	Total.
Married	28	34	62
Single	105	22	127
Widows		5	5
Widowers	5		5
Unknown	15	5	20
Totals	153	66	219

TABLE II.

Occupation.

Occupation.	Males.	Females.	Total.
Miners	34		34
Printer	1		1
Carpenters	2		2
Laborers	25		25
Farmers	15		15
Housewives		26	26
Servants	2	10	12
Bricklayers	2		2
Merchants	5	1	6
Milliner		1	1
Lithographers	2		2
Teachers	2	1	3
Soldiers	3		3
Seamen	7		7
Contractor	1		1
Mechanics	2		2
Tailors	4		4
Tanner	1		1
Sailmaker	1		1
Teamsters	2		2
Laundresses		4	4
Cook	1		1
Butchers	3		3
Druggists	2		2
Engraver	1		1
Barber	1		1
Clerks	3		3
Fisherman	1		1
Draymen	2		2
Painter	1		1
Dressmaker		1	1
Miller	1		1
Civil engineer	1		1
Lawyer	1		1
Engineer	1		1
Cooper	1		1
Assayer	1		1
Porter	1		1
Shoemaker	1		1
Blacksmiths	2		2
Broom-maker	1		1
Unknown	16	22	38
Totals	153	66	219

TABLE I.

Supposed cause, taken from commitments.

Supposed cause.	Males.	Females.	Total.
Disappointment in love	3	5	8
Injury on the head	4	1	5
Masturbation	32		32
Paralysis	3		3
Spiritualism	3	1	4
Turn in life		1	1
Religious excitement	10	1	11
Inflammation of brain	2	1	3
Intemperance	13	3	16
Uterine derangement		4	4
Domestic trouble	6	10	16
Suppressed menses		4	4
Epilepsy	5		5
Pecuniary trouble	6	2	8
General bad health	2	2	4
Puerperal fever		3	3
Destitution	2		2
Amenorrhœa		1	1
Gestation		4	4
Hereditary	4		4
Pneumonia		1	1
Congestive fever	1		1
Spermatorrhœa	1		1
Typhoid fever	1	1	2
Unknown	55	21	76
Totals	153	66	219

TABLE FIRST.

Steward's Account of articles consumed in the Insane Asylum of California, and Cost of same, including the Pay Roll, from October 19th, 1863, to October 1st, 1864.

MONTHS.	Flour	Meat	Potatoes	Butter	Tea	Coffee	Sugar	Ham and Bacon	Lard	Beans and Peas	Rice
1863.											
October	$222 52	$205 11	$67 53	$70 06	$50 60	$82 50	$74 59	$6 60	$10 20	$3 84	$6 21
November	519 14	436 61	249 14	188 54	124 80	165 00	193 11	8 50	30 50	1 08	29 39
December	551 25	494 06	262 02	215 84	155 77	226 87	197 16	10 12	33 88		45 46
1864.											
January	536 61	520 70	274 90	144 87	162 00	231 01	195 52	9 17	35 20	12 24	30 00
February	502 89	429 34	229 56	150 88	152 00	191 64	182 91	5 70	22 40	30 48	28 23
March	554 12	386 43	215 04	110 49	163 60	192 48	179 10	11 77		40 20	29 78
April	515 17	420 46	184 77	184 26	139 25	240 57	176 23	19 80	16 00	31 55	25 60
May	750 29	400 62	159 69	130 91	164 48	179 30	215 51	27 80	25 76	40 46	36 32
June	810 21	376 75	186 10	143 36	154 60	174 00	215 99	15 50	33 60	51 06	25 52
July	860 47	382 74	403 87	181 74	162 63	222 75	220 35	31 11	28 80	55 50	43 50
August	911 22	417 95	321 88	164 66	159 38	175 60	205 53	6 82	33 60	34 55	34 00
September	896 96	395 16	222 85	160 39	156 53	237 50	192 88	8 69	24 00		37 15
Totals	$7,611 45	$4,875 93	$2,777 75	$1,852 00	$1,765 64	$2,318 42	$2,248 88	$161 58	$293 94	$300 96	$371 18

TABLE FIRST—Continued.

Steward's Account of articles consumed in the Insane Asylum of California, and Cost of same, including the Pay Roll, from October 19th, 1863, to October 1st, 1864.

MONTHS.	Dried Fruit	Vegetables and Fruit	Eggs	Soap	Fish	Syrup	Salt	Lights	Small Groceries	Tobacco	Drugs
1863.											
October	$22 89			$25 45	$7 50	$17 37	$6 02	$183 55	$10 35	$31 50	$30 31
November	12 07	$3 79	$3 18	28 39	17 40	33 75	11 66	217 96	27 81	68 06	72 01
December	73 94		11 67	37 01	31 73	35 11	12 36	164 73	24 91	71 02	42 10
1864.											
January	8 66		13 85	17 51	31 49	32 97	13 88	136 17	24 63	82 16	46 96
February	50 16	4 68	5 09	7 59	31 02	32 50	14 67	106 94	35 22	62 91	58 75
March	03 87		26 28	21 63	37 12	35 65	14 02	82 00	31 08	58 67	60 99
April	57 73	5 50	6 13	19 06	37 65	34 30	11 76	56 28	35 06	71 79	88 50
May	40 12	1 62	20 54	19 12	22 40	42 76	9 93	39 80	30 07	64 28	78 26
June	51 12		9 85	12 46	36 00	44 85	10 47	39 67	26 52	63 29	104 25
July	16 72	16 00	4 05	27 92	42 54	43 05	9 12	47 81	26 55	75 95	70 92
August	18 12	1 25	7 75	21 03	33 55	37 40	9 33	43 85	12 92	57 75	95 21
September	3 96		7 27	16 29	44 21	48 85	8 66	78 28	25 61	53 32	77 00
Totals	$129 36	$32 84	$117 66	$253 52	$272 61	$438 56	$132 48	$1,197 07	$310 73	$760 70	$834 26

TABLE FIRST—Continued.

Steward's Account of articles consumed in the Insane Asylum of California, and Cost of same, including the Pay Roll, from October 19th, 1863, to October 1st, 1864.

MONTHS.	Liquors	Hardware	Dry Goods	Clothing	Boots and Shoes	Hats and Caps	Beds and Bedding	Blankets	Crockery	Corn Meal	Milk
1863.											
October	$5 56	$2 50	$100 42	$292 50	$159 25	$36 00	$94 00	$498 50	$ 40	$13 13	$34 40
November	9 99	64 18	241 49	1,383 88	126 62	37 50	236 00	37 00	37 85	27 03	77 20
December	35 62	16 22	160 31	2,948 00	233 00	186 00	708 40	972 35	113 26	28 50	133 60
1864.											
January	41 24	1 25	223 34	100 63	57 75	5 50	696 29	608 75	35 64	32 72	132 40
February	45 51	2 44	102 83	51 09	99 50	13 00	111 11	52 50	21 13	31 67	34 40
March	46 72	29 48	20 20	294 82	88 12	16 25	117 68	5 00	30 44	27 33	
April	41 33	2 33	115 38	197 42	140 88	4 34	304 67		32 19	25 90	
May	221 75	10 73	35 53	123 55	79 25	19 75	229 49		38 54	33 77	
June	16 00	87	66 00	68 38	142 50	23 00	89 46		24 51	31 50	
July	40 75	6 00	113 12	144 22	88 00	25 50	131 64	7 50	29 62	31 12	
August	45 13	5 92	96 78	98 52	105 26	25 25	85 20		32 18	23 63	
September	35 07	21 37	92 48	65 45	108 05	14 25	157 37		37 51	28 00	
Totals	$587 72	$163 29	$1,310 88	$5,768 46	$1,428 18	$406 34	$2,961 40	$2,181 60	$433 27	$334 90	$412 00

Table First—Continued.

Steward's Account of articles consumed in the Insane Asylum of California, and Cost of same, including the Pay Roll, from October 19th, 1863, to October 1st, 1864.

MONTHS.	Pumping	Tinware	Fuel	Cheese	Dairy	Stable	Garden	Laundry	Cracked Wheat	Miscellaneous	Pay Roll
1863.											
October	$62 68	$18 30	$18 70		$142 83	$58 71	$46 65	$46 41	$9 00	$55 39	$342 86
November	121 78	30 88	170 99		202 08	160 55	173 50	130 97	18 00	105 39	2,177 33
December	111 20	55 00	245 09		185 27	135 44	219 53	136 81	18 00	161 76	2,262 41
1864.											
January	179 70	76 17	213 75		309 80	88 80	344 94	155 27	18 00	104 16	2,300 47
February	256 25	22 87	158 18		331 39	119 62	412 95	136 76	13 50	57 94	2,269 54
March	183 20	138 01	127 60	$3 42	157 12	144 68	219 45	163 11	13 50	141 28	2,210 77
April	156 30	27 50	71 25		193 81	101 41	235 48	151 89	18 00	139 97	2,378 66
May	171 60	4 75	71 25		302 53	101 23	228 45	131 39	29 35	164 51	2,350 00
June	159 60	31 50	59 85	3 80	199 91	186 50	317 51	139 50	34 50	118 27	2,335 65
July	158 05	25 13	57 00		300 10	130 10	221 70	133 74	40 93	170 03	2,345 00
August	212 55	17 25	54 51		244 36	127 51	226 95	139 69	32 97	136 10	2,355 00
September	141 70	39 50	40 88		287 62	157 87	226 03	162 89	29 82	77 56	2,355 00
Totals	$1,914 61	$186 86	$1,319 05	$7 22	$2,855 82	$1,515 51	$2,873 14	$1,618 43	$275 57	$1,432 35	$26,182 69

96

TABLE FIRST—Continued.

RECAPITULATION.

Months.	Totals.
1863.	
October	$3,713 57
November	7,977 70
December	11,762 81
1864.	
January	8,278 54
February	6,693 24
March	6,463 08
April	6,744 93
May	6,844 55
June	6,023 38
July	7,188 02
August	6,918 46
September	6,808 53
Total	$86,016 81

TABLE SECOND.

MONTHS.	OFFICE EXPENSES.						PASSAGE MONEY PAID DISCHARGED PATIENTS.				
	Pay Roll	Post Office	Stationery	Fuel	Miscellaneous	Total	San Francisco—Steamer	Sacramento—Stage	Sonora—Stage	Other Routes	Total
1863.											
October.........	$63 84	....	$1 50	$2 85	$23 00	$91 19	$12 00	$5 00	$10 50	....	$27 50
November......	165 00	$14 00	8 00	....	85 48	272 48	....	10 00	....	$11 50	51 50
December......	165 00	5 00	1 95	11 40	75 18	258 53	21 00	....	....	5 00	26 00
1864.											
January.........	165 00	3 00	1 20	14 25	40 91	224 36	14 00	....	....	46 00	60 00
February........	165 00	20 00	16 00	11 40	25 14	237 54	14 00	5 00	....	5 00	24 00
March............	155 00	6 50	....	5 70	41 87	209 07	7 00	....	....	32 50	39 50
April.............	155 00	14 32	....	....	22 78	192 10	14 00	....	....	7 50	21 50
May..............	155 00	....	1 25	....	23 55	179 80	14 00	10 00	....	5 00	29 00
June..............	155 00	....	....	....	20 75	175 75	14 00	....	....	5 00	19 00
July...............	155 00	3 25	11 12	....	23 36	192 73	42 00	20 00	....	....	62 00
August...........	155 00	3 00	1 50	....	35 22	194 72	14 00	5 00	....	36 00	55 00
September......	155 00	11 50	1 00	....	20 18	187 68	35 00	15 00	....	33 00	83 00
Totals..........	$1,808 84	$80 57	$43 52	$15 60	$437 42	$2,415 95	$201 00	$70 00	$10 50	$216 50	$198 00

TABLE THIRD.

MONTHS.	RESIDENT PHYSICIAN.				ASSISTANT PHYSICIAN.		
	Pay Roll	Steward's Account	Fuel	Total	Steward's Account	Fuel	Total
1863.							
October	$29 04	$34 38	$11 40	$74 82	$17 60	$7 13	$24 73
November	75 00	133 04	19 95	227 99	61 18	11 40	72 58
December	72 98	153 10	28 50	254 58	102 12	17 10	119 22
1864.							
January	66 52	75 79	25 65	167 96	84 38	19 95	104 33
February	70 00	114 96	18 53	203 49	73 36	17 10	90 46
March	57 50	87 82	8 55	153 87	69 92	7 12	77 04
April	75 00	123 26	6 12	204 38	89 34	5 70	95 04
May	75 00	125 98	8 55	209 53	92 59	5 70	98 29
June	75 00	103 01	9 98	187 99	102 09	7 13	109 22
July	75 00	124 93	8 55	208 48	84 94	7 13	92 07
August	75 00	102 52	5 45	182 97	67 70	5 45	73 15
September	75 00	121 66	6 53	203 19	78 42	5 45	83 87
Totals	$821 04	$1,299 45	$157 76	$2,279 25	$923 64	$116 36	$1,040 00

TABLE FOURTH

MONTHS.	IMPROVEMENTS.				REPAIRS.				Extraordinary Expenses	GRAND TOTALS
	Pay Roll	Lumber	Painting	Miscellaneous	Total	Pay Roll	Lumber	Miscellaneous	Total		
1863.											
October	$35 05	$116 01	$23 75	$1,589 48	$1,764 29	$13 31	$69 63	$26 00	$108 94	$91 50	$1,964 73
November	101 24	1,092 17	130 00	1,464 41	2,787 82	23 76	65 50	37 75	127 01	570 56	3,485 39
December	95 57	676 69	178 39	3,088 11	4,038 76	29 43		4 00	33 43	932 87	5,005 06
1864.											
January	101 00	236 92	94 17	2,120 52	2,552 61	24 00		16 75	40 75	1,045 89	3,639 25
February						75 00		69 63	144 63	688 89	833 52
March						75 00	14 68	128 92	218 60	308 28	526 88
April						75 00	17 39	88 33	180 72	494 91	675 63
May						75 00		73 22	148 22	100 28	248 50
June						75 00	35 40	159 13	269 53	76 21	345 74
July						75 00	15 99	484 83	575 82	707 75	1,283 57
August						75 00	3 60	149 17	227 77	931 35	1,159 12
September	75 00							55 20	130 20	121 49	251 69
Totals	$332 86	$2,121 79	$426 31	$8,262 52	$11,143 48	$690 50	$222 19	$1,292 93	$2,205 62	$6,069 98	$19,419 08

TABLE FIFTH,
General Summary.

MONTHS.	Asylum.	Office.	Passages paid discharged Patients.	Resident Physician.	Assistant Physician.	Improvements.	Repairs.	Extraordinary Expenses.	TOTALS.
1863.									
October	$3,713 57	$91 19	$27 50	$74 82	$24 73	$1,764 29	$103 94	$91 50	$5,896 54
November	7,977 70	272 48	51 50	227 99	72 58	2,787 82	127 01	570 56	12,087 64
December	11,762 81	258 53	26 00	254 58	119 22	4,036 76	33 43	932 87	17,426 20
1864.									
January	8,278 54	224 36	60 00	167 96	104 33	2,552 61	40 75	1,015 89	12,474 44
February	6,693 24	237 54	24 00	203 49	90 46		144 63	688 89	8,082 25
March	6,463 08	209 07	39 50	153 87	77 04		218 60	308 28	7,469 41
April	6,744 93	192 10	21 50	204 38	95 04		180 72	494 91	7,933 58
May	6,841 55	179 80	29 00	209 53	98 29		148 22	100 28	7,609 67
June	6,623 38	175 75	19 00	187 99	109 22		269 53	76 21	7,461 08
July	7,188 02	192 73	62 00	208 48	92 07		575 82	707 75	9,026 87
August	6,918 46	194 72	55 00	182 97	73 15		227 77	931 35	8,583 42
September	6,308 53	187 68	83 00	203 19	83 87		130 20	121 49	7,617 96
Totals	$86,016 81	$2,415 95	$498 00	$2,279 25	$1,010 00	$11,143 48	$2,205 62	$6,069 98	$111,669 09

TABLE SIXTH.

Produce of the Farm, Garden, and Dairy.

MONTHS.	Expenses	Number of days labor by Patients	Number pounds of Cabbage	Number pounds of Tomatoes	Number pounds Beets and Turnips	Number pounds of Squashes	Number pounds Beans and Peas	Number pounds other Vegetables	Number dozens of other Vegetables	Number bunches other Vegetables
1863.										
October	$275 98	108	736	2,385	336	......	200	171	458	21
November	638 47	357	2,173	2,821	932	9,010	450	351	......	187
December	513 49	504	3,768	277	3,686	......	......	466	......	441
1864.										
January	762 71	684	8,480	......	24,964	......	......	914	......	787
February	893 09	590	4,309	170	604	......	......	......	......	182
March	537 48	580	2,421	......	......	......	......	1,200	......	133
April	533 47	514	1,949	......	1,066	......	......	17	......	1,555
May	638 18	557	1,638	......	2,427	1,052	5,811	621	......	2,725
June	708 55	609	3,275	1,899	2,409	998	1,253	1,409	68	2,882
July	643 55	551	3,253	7,324	3,625	1,023	2,535	5,117	148	57
August	600 06	559	1,018	9,180	71,880	1,290	1,179	1,478	73	59
September	684 57	547	3,679	......	......	......	970	......	......	56
Totals	$7,369 60	6,160	37,029	24,056	111,929	13,373	12,509	11,744	747	9,085

TABLE SIXTH—Continued.

Produce of the Farm, Garden, and Dairy.

MONTHS.	Number of Melons	Number pounds of Peaches	Number pounds of other Fruits	Number gallons Milk from Dairy	Pounds Meat and Lard from Dairy	Number dozens of Eggs	Number of Chickens	Number pounds of Corn Fodder	Number Gallons of Pickles	Value of Products
1863.										
October	21			180	965					$209 47
November				486	851	4	17		60	570 96
December				370		11				515 95
1864.										
January				411		15	12			850 91
February				689	2,462	19	18			669 12
March				1,017	1,563	11	5			659 07
April				984	418	18	8			645 10
May				949		17				1,006 55
June		657	78	1,013		9	6			1,003 14
July		11,197	197	1,075	511	6	3			1,473 95
August	3,029	3,759	2,819	1,023		10	19	18,000		1,418 13
September	1,506	133	818	916		9	2			1,757 74
Total	4,615	15,716	3,912	9,122	6,770	129	90	18,000	60	$10,780 69

TABLE SEVENTH.

Averages.

MONTHS.	Number of Patients on hand daily	Daily expenses	Cost per capita per day	Cost per capita per month	Cost per Patient per month for Boots and Shoes	Cost per Patient per month for Clothing
1863.						
October	583	$290 77	$ 50	$15 46	$ 43	$1 27
November	587	309 99	53	15 84	22	2 72
December	579	431 85	75	23 12	40	5 19
1864.						
January	570	320 06	56	17 41	10	57
February	560	278 70	50	14 43	18	27
March	562	240 95	43	13 29	16	56
April	565	264 45	47	14 04	25	55
May	567	245 47	43	13 42	14	28
June	570	248 70	44	13 09	25	24
July	576	291 19	51	15 67	15	45
August	575	276 88	48	14 93	18	34
September	584	253 93	43	13 04	18	27
Averages	573	$287 75	$ 50¼	$15 31	$ 22	$1 06

OF THE

OFFICERS AND TRUSTEES

OF THE

CALIFORNIA PRISON COMMISSION.

PETITION

OF THE

OFFICERS AND TRUSTEES

OF THE

CALIFORNIA PRISON COMMISSION.

D. W. GELWICKS.........STATE PRINTER.

PETITION.

To the Honorable Senate and Assembly of the State of California:

The undersigned, officers and Trustees of the California Prison Commission, would respectfully represent:

The Association named has been in existence for a little more than two years, having for its object, according to Article second of the Constitution, "The amelioration of the condition of prisoners, whether detained for trial or as witnesses, or finally convicted; the improvement of prisons and prison discipline; the government of prisons, whether for cities, or counties or the State; the aid and encouragement of discharged prisoners, whenever such aid and encouragement seems hopeful and wise." Our aims are identical with the general interests of the State. We seek to meet the discharged prisoner at the threshold of his prison house, just as he is entering the world again to begin life over, and by words of kindness and of counsel, and the use of such other means as lie at our command, endeavor to guide the current of that life into the channels of respectability and happiness. We strive to induce and to help him to become a useful citizen, instead of a public burden and expense. The result of our labors for two years in this direction is such as to give us abundant encouragement to persevere in our efforts. Our last annual report, a copy of which was placed in the hands of each member of your joint body, we think, gives ample evidence of this.

Our Association is also a bureau for the collection of information on prison matters in general. We are in correspondence with Associations of the same character with our own in the East, and with persons who make the subject of penalogy a special study. From these we receive whatever books or reports that are written upon the subject; and by observation concerning our own prison system, as shown in the different penal institutions of the State, we design to obtain, and from time to time to present, such facts and suggestions as will aid in the formation of correct ideas with regard to it. We propose, if authorized by the Legislature so to do, and if the means to defray the expense can be obtained, to make a thorough examination of our prison system by personal visitation and inspection of the jails and prisons of the State, and to make a full report of the result to the Legislature at its next session. But we can do nothing without money, and a sufficiency of this we find it difficult to procure. It has been only by the practice of the most rigid economy that we have been able to maintain our organization and work till the present time, and now we find ourselves in debt to the amount of a thousand dollars, with the indebtedness constantly increasing. As the money which we expend is really for the benefit, financially as well as morally, of the entire State, we are constrained to ask you to aid us by an appropriation from the public treasury. The amount which we ask of you at this time is five thousand dollars, which, in consideration of the importance of our work and the urgency of the case, we cannot think you will refuse, and for which if received we shall feel truly and profoundly grateful.

    Respectfully,

           ALPHEUS BULL,
               Vice President.

           JAS. WOODWORTH,
               Secretary.

           NATHANIEL GRAY,
           W. T. ANDREWS,
           M. J. O'CONNOR,
           ROBT. B. SWAIN,
           GEO. W. DAM,
           THOS. H. CAMPBELL,
           JAMES LINFORTH,
           L. B. BENCHLEY,
           ANNIS MERRILL,
           D. N. HAWLEY,
           WILLIAM ALVORD,

San Francisco, February 18th, 1868.

REPORT AND PETITION

OF THE

MANAGERS OF THE MAGDALEN ASYLUM

OF

SAN FRANCISCO,

From January, 1864, to February 1st, 1868.

SACRAMENTO:
D. W. GELWICKS, STATE PRINTER,
1868.

REPORT AND PETITION

OF THE

MANAGERS OF THE MAGDALEN ASYLUM

OF

SAN FRANCISCO,

From January, 1864, to February 1st, 1868.

D. W. GELWICKS.........STATE PRINTER.

REPORT AND PETITION.

To the Honorable the Senate and Assembly of the State of California:

The undersigned, managers of the Magdalen Asylum of San Francisco, beg leave to present the following report and petition:

Following the report of January, eighteen hundred and sixty-four, the number of inmates increased so rapidly that the building in Hayes' Valley then occupied was very soon found inadequate for their accommodation, so that, early in eighteen hundred and sixty-five, it became necessary to provide more commodious apartments. To this end, an eligible site was purchased in a better locality near the city, and a substantial brick building erected thereon, the grounds fenced, and other necessary improvements made, costing in the aggregate a large sum of money—about twenty thousand dollars of which was contributed by persons whose appreciation of this great work of mercy is commensurate with their generous liberality.

The increased number of inmates and consequent growing necessities of the establishment, added to the large balance due for the land and improvements above mentioned, leaves the institution heavily involved, and renders aid from your honorable body imperatively necessary if this beneficent work of charity and reformation is to be continued.

The field of usefulness is daily being enlarged, and the management can plainly see the necessity very soon of adding to the capacity of the present buildings, thereby incurring additional outlay of money.

At the last session of the Legislature the usual appropriation was withheld, and the institution, being without endowment or revenue from any source, is left to depend solely upon the means derived from the sale of needle-work executed by the inmates and the contributions of the charitable, which form but a slender basis for the maintenance of such an establishment.

The following tabular statement exhibits summarily the number of persons admitted to the institution, the date of admission, age, place of nativity, and the disposition of each:

TABULAR STATEMENT.

No.	Date of admission.	Age.	Place of nativity.	Remarks.
	1859.			
1	August 29	46	Louisiana	Became insane and transferred to Lunatic Asylum, July 9, 1864.
	1860.			
2	January 23	19	New York	Remaining in Asylum.
3	January 26	18	Virginia	Taken home by her aunt, January 28, 1864.
4	November 8	19	Germany	Died March 18, 1865.
	1861.			
5	September 29	14	New York	Remaining in Asylum.
6	September 30	27	Ireland	Remaining in Asylum.
7	October 2	18	Pennsylvania	Provided with situation, October, 1863, since well married.
8	October 30	18	Australia	Dismissed as incorrigible, March 14, 1864.
	1862.			
9	February 18	19	Mexico	Sent to St. Mary's Hospital, October 11, 186?.
10	March 19	38	Ireland	Provided with situation, April 26, 1863.
11	April 4	16	Massachusetts	Taken home by her parents, January 19, 1864.
12	June 2	14	New York	Remaining in Asylum.
13	August 5	16	New York	Remaining in Asylum.
14	August 6	11	New York	Provided with situation, November 18, 1863.
15	September 12	44	Ireland	Provided with situation, November 21, 1863.
16	September 12	10	California	Transferred to school by her father, Jan. 3, 1864.
17	September 13	24	Ireland	Left the Asylum, March 10, 1863.
18	October 2	19	Louisiana	Left the Asylum, November 21, 1863.
19	October 25	11	California	
20	October 31	40	Ireland	Provided with situation.
21	October 31	20	California	Remaining in Asylum.
22	November 7	38	Ireland	Died July 28, 1863, in St. Mary's Hospital.
23	November 19	10	California	Remaining in Asylum.
24	November 22	14	New York	Removed by her father, June 19, 1863.
	1863.			
25	January 3	22	Ireland	Left Asylum, July 26, 1863.
26	January 9	32	Ireland	Left Asylum, August 6, 1863.
27	February 14	38	Ireland	
28	February 14	10	California	Given to a good family, October 19, 1864.
29	February 27	24	Maine	Left Asylum, August 29, 1863.
30	March 14	32	Ireland	Left Asylum, July 9, 1863.
31	April 14	14	Kentucky	Remaining in Asylum.
32	April 25	18	Pennsylvania	Sent to the Eastern States by her family.
33	May 9	32	Ireland	} Left Asylum, July 8, 1862—mother and child.
34	May 9	12	California	
35	May 11	9	Pennsylvania	Remaining in Asylum.
36	May 14	18	Pennsylvania	Brought to Asylum by officer, afterward ran away.
37	July 4	14	Massachusetts	Remaining in Asylum.
38	July 4	8	California	Transferred from Protestant Orphan Asylum; given to a family, August 6, 1867.
39	July 6	26	Ireland	Left Asylum, July 28, 1864.
40	July 29	30	England	Left Asylum, September 11, 1863.
41	August 2	10	California	Remaining in Asylum.
42	August 3	15	New York	Left Asylum, August 27, 1863.
43	September 6	19	Illinois	Left Asylum, September 21, 1863.
44	September 19	14	California	Remaining in Asylum.
45	September 21	14	Maine	Left Asylum, June 20, 1864.
46	September 29	36	Ireland	Left Asylum, February 7, 1864.
47	September 30	24	New York	Left Asylum, January 18, 1864.
48	October 29	17	Australia	Left Asylum, January 23, 1865.
49	November 15	24	Ireland	Left Asylum, January 31, 1864.
50	November 15	6½	California	Adopted by a good family, March 21, 1865.
51	November 26	22	Ireland	Left Asylum, February 22, 1864.
52	November 26	15	California	Left Asylum, December 4, 1864.
53	November 28	18	Maine	Second time in Asylum; escaped Jan. 24, 1864.

No.	Date of admission.	Age.	Place of nativity.	Remarks.
	1863.			
54	December 16....	13	Missouri............	Brought to Asylum by Sup't of the Industrial School, Marysville; taken home by stepmother, March 10, 1864; died.
55	December 26....	11	California..........	Removed by her mother, January 10, 1865.
	1864.			
56	May 9	14	California..........	Remaining in Asylum.
57	May 27	30	Ireland	Left Asylum, August 4, 1864.
58	February 1......	15	Illinois.............	Left Asylum, November 14, 1864.
59	February 10.....	15	New York..........	Removed by her father, March 26, 1865.
60	February 17.....	26	Ireland	Left Asylum, March 19, 1864.
61	March 5..........	12	California..........	Left Asylum, June 5, 1864.
62	March 22.........	23	Ireland	Left Asylum, September 19, 1864.
63	March 23.........	13	New York..........	Provided with a situation, May 31, 1865.
64	April 19..........	12	California..........	Provided with a situation, January, 1866.
65	May 9	14	New Jersey........	Remaining in Asylum.
66	May 10...........	40	Ireland.............	Left Asylum, July 10, 1864.
67	May 13...........	30	England	Left Asylum, May 25, 1864.
68	July 16...........	41	Ireland	Left Asylum, September 20, 1864.
69	July 19...........	21	Virginia............	Remaining in Asylum.
70	July 20...........	16	New York..........	Removed by her sister, July 1, 1866.
71	August 4.........	20	California..........	Sent to C. O. Asylum by order of Archbishop.
72	August 5.........	42	Ireland	Remaining in Asylum.
73	August 5.........	40	Ireland	Ran away, September 25, 1864; afterward sent to Lunatic Asylum.
74	August 27........	22	Louisiana..........	Ran away, October 13, 1864.
75	September 3.....	12	Massachusetts.....	Removed by her father, December 22, 1866.
76	September 22...	13	New York..........	Removed by her father.
77	September 23...	35	Ireland	Returned home, December 10, 1864.
78	September 25....	37	Ireland	Remaining in Asylum.
79	October 4.........	17	United States......	Went to San José, June 9, 1866.
80	October 18.......	36	Ireland	Left Asylum, December 24, 1864.
81	October 22......	23	Pennsylvania.....	Left Asylum, June 24, 1864.
82	November 3.....	17	Illinois.............	Remaining in Asylum.
83	November 22 ...	17	England	Taken from the Asylum by an adopted sister.
	1865.			
84	January 1........	16	Missouri	Taken home, January 23, 1866.
85	January 3	37	Ireland	Left Asylum, July 19, 1865.
86	January 5	28	Ireland	Left Asylum, October 3, 1865.
87	January 5........	16	New York	Left Asylum, March 26, 1865.
88	January 16......	16	Pennsylvania.....	Remaining in Asylum.
89	April 20..........	16	New York..........	Remaining in Asylum.
90	April 30..........	24	Ireland	Sent to New York to her brothers, Oct. 13, 1865.
91	March 10.........	50	Ireland	Left Asylum, December 28, 1864. } Mother
92	March 10.........	22	Australia...........	Left Asylum, January 4, 1865. } and child.
93	May 12	16	New York..........	Sent from Industrial School.
94	May 19	15	Louisiana..........	Sent from Industrial School; removed by her brother-in-law.
95	May 29	25	Ireland	Remaining in Asylum.
96	June 12	13	New York	Provided with a situation, October 1, 1866.
97	June 22	25	Canada	Dismissed.
98	July 2	45	England	Dismissed, October 2, 1865.
99	July 2	50	Ireland	Left Asylum, March 18, 1866.
100	July 3	28	Ireland	Went to New York, October 13, 1866.
101	July 5	23	Australia...........	Scaled the wall.
102	July 19	27	Liverpool..........	Summoned to her father's trial, Dec. 6, 1866.
103	July 27...........	15	Maine...............	Remaining in Asylum.
104	July 28...........	16	England	Taken from the Sacramento Jail at instance of Judge Holl: left October 21, 1866.
105	July 29...........	14	Massachusetts.....	Left Asylum, January 3, 1867.
106	August 7	13	California.........	Remaining in Asylum.
107	August 7........	20	Maine...............	Left Asylum, October 27, 1865.
108	August 25.......	16	New York.........	Left Asylum, November 28, 2865.
109	August 25.......	40	Ireland.............	Remaining in Asylum.
110	September 8.....	30	Ireland.............	Provided with a situation, September 25, 1866.
111	September 14...	35	Ireland.............	Removed by her husband, October 19, 1865.

No.	Date of admission.	Age.	Place of nativity.	Remarks.
	1865.			
112	October 12.......	14	Massachusetts.....	Left Asylum, April 25, 1866.
113	October 16	13	California..........	Provided with a situation, May, 1867.
114	October 16	21	Ireland	Remaining in Asylum.
115	October 17.......	11	California..........	Left Asylum, October 23, 1866.
116	October 17.......	11	California..........	Removed by her mother, November 3, 1867.
117	October 19.......	55	Ireland	Left Asylum, January 10, 1866.
118	October 24.......	9	California..........	Remaining in Asylum.
119	October 25.......	30	Ireland	Left Asylum, November 26, 1865.
120	December 30....	24	Ireland	Remaining in Asylum.
	1866.			
121	January 2........	13	California..........	Remaining in Asylum.
122	January 2........	8	California..........	Remaining in Asylum.
123	January 12......	40	Ireland	Left Asylum, June 29, 1866.
124	January 27......	7	California..........	Remaining in Asylum.
125	February 1......	20	Ireland	Left Asylum, March 24, 1866.
126	March 27........	35	Ireland	Left Asylum, April 10, 1866.
127	March 13........	17	Connecticut........	Left Asylum, August 18, 1867.
128	March 20........	19	Illinois.............	Went to friends in Oregon.
129	April 2...........	27	Liverpool..........	Taken from station-house and sent to Lunatic Asylum.
130	April 2...........	30	Ireland	Provided with a situation, October 1, 1867.
131	April 5...........	16	United States......	Left Asylum, May 20, 1866; married soon after.
132	April 6...........	42	Ireland	Sent to County Hospital, October 20, 1866.
133	April 6...........	12	California..........	Provided with a situation, July 1, 1867.
134	April 6...........	4	California..........	Sent to Boys' Orphan Asylum, July 1, 1866.
135	April 6...........	2	California..........	Adopted, August 28, 1866. (These three, children of No. 132.)
136	April 10.........	35	Ireland	Left Asylum, October 3, 1866.
137	April 10.........	38	Ireland	Died, February 20, 1867.
138	April 11.........	12	Massachusetts.....	Sent to brother, (Boston,) October 30, 1866.
139	April 24.........	17	New York	Removed by aunt, August 30, 1866.
140	April 25.........	15	New York	Remaining in Asylum.
141	May 8	14	Massachusetts.....	Removed by mother, November 23, 1866.
142	May 8	16	California..........	Left Asylum, October 29, 1866.
143	May 8	25	Ireland	Left Asylum, September 10, 1866.
144	May 15...........	30	Ireland.............	Escaped, June 29, 1866.
145	May 24...........	15	Massachusetts.....	Remaining in Asylum.
146	May 20...........	32	England	Died, June 29, 1866.
147	June 2............	30	Australia...........	Left Asylum, October 29, 1866.
148	June 2............	5	California..........	Left Asylum, October 29, 1866. } Children of No. 147.
149	June 2............	3	California..........	Left Asylum, October 29, 1866. }
150	June 4............	17	Dist. of Columbia.	Remaining in Asylum.
151	June 6............	37	Ireland..	Left Asylum, January 2, 1867.
152	June 12...........		New York	Left Asylum, June 29, 1866.
153	July 10...........		California..........	Removed by mother, January 6, 1867.
154	July 13...........	23	Ireland.............	Removed by husband, August 30, 1866.
155	July 13...........	14	California..........	Left Asylum, August 30, 1866.
156	July 13...........	33	Ireland.............	Left Asylum, October 29, 1866.
157	July 20...........	22	New York	Remaining in Asylum.
158	July 27...........	33	Ireland.............	Left Asylum, October 13, 1866.
159	July 30...........	13	California..........	Remaining in Asylum.
160	September 5.....	34	Ireland.............	Left Asylum, December 10, 1866.
161	September 24...	16	Germany...........	Remaining in Asylum.
162	September 28...	40	Ireland.............	Provided with situation, July, 1867.
163	October 2........	3	California..........	Remaining in Asylum.
164	October 5........	30	New York..	Left Asylum, April 3, 1867.
165	October 20......	14	Buenos Ayres.....	Remaining in Asylum.
166	October 21	25	Louisiana..........	Broke her leg, August 20, and sent to St. Mary's Hospital.
167	November 6.....	18	Massachusetts.....	Remaining in Asylum.
168	November 16 ...	33	Ireland.............	Remaining in Asylum.
169	December 17....	4	California..........	Remaining in Asylum.
170	December 29....		California..........	Remaining in Asylum.
171	December 31....	17	Australia...........	Remaining in Asylum.

No.	Date of admission.	Age.	Place of nativity.	Remarks.
	1867			
172	January 8	2	California	Left Asylum, October 22, 1867.
173	January 18	32	England	Left Asylum, May 21, 1867.
174	January 19	11	California	Remaining in Asylum.
175	January 20		California	Remaining in Asylum.
176	January 23	21	Ireland	Sent to County Hospital, July 13, 1867.
177	January 27	15	California	Remaining in Asylum.
178	February 3	35	Ireland	Returned home, June 1, 1867.
179	February 12	12	California	Sent from R. C. O. Asylum. Remaining in Asylum
180	February 12	11	California	Sent from R. C. O. Asylum. Remaining in Asylum
181	March 16	13	Sandwich Islands.	Left Asylum, August 18, 1867.
182	March 27	32	Ireland	Left Asylum, May 30, 1867.
183	March 30	17	Maryland	Sent from Industrial School, San Francisco. Remaining in Asylum.
184	March 30	18	Louisiana	Sent from Industrial School, San Francisco. Remaining in Asylum.
185	March 30	14		Remaining in Asylum.
186	April 13	30	Ireland	Left Asylum, July 1, 1867.
187	April 27	25	Ireland	Left Asylum, May 27, 1867.
188	April 22	4	California	Left Asylum, July 2, 1867.
189	April 30	17	England	From Industrial School, San Francisco. Remaining in Asylum.
190	May 20	14	Massachusetts	Remaining in Asylum.
191	May 25	14	New York	Remaining in Asylum.
192	May 26	40	Ireland	Remaining in Asylum.
193	May 28	15	Massachusetts	Remaining in Asylum.
194	May 31	45	Missouri	Remaining in Asylum.
195	June 12	17	California	Remaining in Asylum.
196	June 26	11	China	Sent by Chief of Police, and removed by his orders, July 23, 1867.
197	June 28		California	Left Asylum, July 8, 1867.
198	July 12	25	Ireland	Left Asylum, September 29, 1867.
199	July 16	14	California	Removed by her parents, November 30, 1867.
200	July 24	23	Ireland	Left Asylum, July 28, 1867.
201	August 4	13	California	Remaining in Asylum.
202	August 6	14	Massachusetts	Left Asylum, October 1, 1867.
203	August 7	27	Ireland	Left Asylum, September 1, 1867.
204	August 15	17	Ireland	Remaining in Asylum.
205	August 20	11	California	Remaining in Asylum.
206	August 27	40	New York	Left Asylum, December 20, 1867.
207	August 28	16	New York	Remaining in Asylum.
208	September 4	15	California	Remaining in Asylum.
209	September 18	32	Ireland	Remaining in Asylum.
210	September 20	14	California	Remaining in Asylum.
211	September 29		California	Left Asylum, October 31, 1867.
212	October 17	36	Ireland	Removed by husband, November 30, 1867.
213	October 28	17	New York	Remaining in Asylum.
214	November 9	14	Michigan	Remaining in Asylum.
215	November 9	25	Louisiana	Removed by sister, December 1, 1867.
216	December 14	50	Illinois	Remaining in Asylum.
217	December 30	17	California	Remaining in Asylum.

SUMMARY.

In Asylum at date of last report	30	
Admitted since	187	
Total		217
Sent to Lunatic Asylum	2	
Variously provided for	92	
Died	5	
Returned to friends	33	
Sent away, or left incorrigible	9	
Still remaining in the Asylum	76	
Total		217
Discharged prior to last report		77
Total number admitted since the opening of the Asylum		294

The undersigned confidently hope that in view of the reformation already accomplished, and the great benefits that are to flow from the labors of this institution, that the Legislature, in its generous wisdom, will make such an appropriation at the present session as will relieve the establishment from its embarrassment and enable the management to continue and enlarge their mission of charity, mercy, and usefulness.

Respectfully submitted.

Sister MARY G. BROWN,
Superioress of Sisters of Mercy.
Sister MARY B. RUSSELL.
Sister MARY DE CHANTAL FLEMING.

REPORT

OF THE

Directors of the California State Prison.

DECEMBER 1, 1867.

SACRAMENTO:
D. W. GELWICKS, STATE PRINTER.
1867.

REPORT

OF THE

Directors of the California State Prison.

DECEMBER 1, 1867.

D. W. GELWICKS..........STATE PRINTER.

OFFICE OF THE BOARD OF STATE PRISON DIRECTORS,
December 2d, 1867.

To His Excellency,
    FREDERICK F. LOW,
        Governor of California:

In compliance with the requirements of the statute, we beg leave to submit the following report of the transactions of the Board of Directors of the California State Prison, and statistics relating to the inmates of the prison, from November first, eighteen hundred and sixty-five, to December first, eighteen hundred and sixty-seven.

        Respectfully,

                T. N. MACHIN,
                B. B. REDDING,
                      State Prison Directors.

REPORT.

To His Excellency,
    FREDERICK F. LOW,
        Governor:

SIR:—Accompanying this will be found tables showing the financial condition of the California State Prison, monthly, since our last report, and up to December first, eighteen hundred and sixty-seven. The Turnkey's report, exhibiting the number of prisoners, the crimes for which they were sentenced, places of nativity, educational acquirements, pardons, escapes, etc., is complete to November first, eighteen hundred and sixty-seven. The report of the Physician is to December first, eighteen hundred and sixty-seven.

The financial tables show the net indebtedness of the prison, December first, eighteen hundred and sixty-seven, to be three thousand eight hundred and ninety-three dollars and fifty cents, ($3,893 50.) While this is correct, it is but proper to state that, to produce this result and to avoid making purchases of supplies on credit, we have been compelled to anticipate the appropriation made by the State, so that unless a special appropriation be made by the Legislature, the prison will be largely in debt by July first, eighteen hundred and sixty-eight.

The ordinary annual appropriation made by the State when the average number of prisoners was four hundred, was fifty thousand dollars. During the past three years the average number of prisoners has been nearly seven hundred, while the annual appropriation has not been increased. Argument is not necessary to prove that the feeding, clothing, and guarding of seven hundred prisoners costs nearly double what it would to feed, clothe, and guard three hundred and fifty. The labor of the prisoners for the past two years has brought an income to the prison of seventy-eight thousand seven hundred and twenty-three dollars and thirty-two cents ($78,723 32,) an increase of twenty-five thousand six hundred and forty-five dollars and twenty-two cents ($25,645 22) over the previous two years. This satisfactory increase only lessens the total expenses—it does not avoid the necessity for increased appropriations. We would recommend an appropriation of forty thousand dollars ($40,000) to meet the liabilities that will accrue from December first, eighteen hundred and sixty-seven, to July first, eighteen hundred and sixty-eight, the close of the present fiscal year, and an annual appropriation of seventy-five thousand dollars, which should continue so long as the prison contains seven hundred prisoners, or until the State becomes so largely interested in manufactures that convict labor will be worth one dollar per day.

The construction of the two prison buildings, containing three hundred and ninety-two cells, would have been of some benefit in facilitating the classifying of prisoners, had not the increase of prisoners kept pace with the increase of cells. Some plan should be devised for the separation of the young convicts from those hardened in crime. It does not seem possible that this can be done within the walls of the present prison. If the only object of a State Prison is to confine and punish men who have committed crime, then men can be safely kept and made to work within the walls of the present prison; but if in addition to this it is expected that a prison shall, in some measure, be a reformatory institution, or at least that men shall leave it no worse in knowledge of crime than when they entered it, then it is necessary to classify the prisoners, and remove those who, through intoxication or other cause, have been induced to commit a first offence from contact and communication with old offenders and hardened thieves, highwaymen and burglars, whose constant boast is of the crimes they have committed. The prison has been kept a model of cleanliness; the prisoners are well clothed, and are supplied with abundant and good food; the officers have been humane; there has been no unnecessary punishment; and all this may continue, and yet the prison will fail to earn the commendations or meet the anticipations of thoughtful men, unless when its inmates are discharged they are better men than when they entered its gates. We earnestly request you to present the subject to the Legislature, that in its wisdom it may devise some means whereby the prison can be made a reformatory as well as a penal institution.

The shop room of the prison is inadequate. the buildings containing many of the shops are old, badly constructed, and poorly lighted. If the demand for prison labor shall hereafter increase in the ratio it has increased during the past two years, it will soon be necessary that some of the buildings now used for shops be torn down, and others upon a better plan be constructed. The increase of prisoners and constant enlargement of manufacturing pursuits within the prison, necessitates the use of a larger supply of water than the present water works can furnish. That an increased revenue may be derived from prison labor, and that a greater number of prisoners may be employed by contractors at higher rates, it will be necessary to construct new buildings for shop room, and increase the supply of water. To accomplish this the Legislature should levy a tax of five per cent. on each one hundred dollars of taxable property in the State, to create a fund from which these improvements can be made.

The report of Dr. Charles Burrell, the Physician of the prison, will be read with interest. A comparison as to the average sickness in the California State Prison and the prisons of the Atlantic States and Europe, will show no other prison where the average sickness is so small. The percentage of deaths is less than in any other prison the published reports of which have reached us.

We desire to express our thanks to the officers and guards who have assisted us in the care of the prison during the past four years. With one exception the officers have been honest, and faithfully and economically administered the trust confided to them. The prisoners have been treated humanely, and have been faithfully guarded. During the past four years but five prisoners have escaped, and of these three were recaptured.

We desire to repeat the statement made in our last report, and confirmed by continued observation and investigation: There are many men in the prison who have been sentenced for longer terms than the crime committed seems to warrant. The disparity in sentences for the same crime, by different Courts, is an evil for which there seems no remedy. Many of these cases deserve investigation. There is not time for the Executive to make this investigation, and sort out from the seven hundred prisoners all whose crimes have been adequately punished, or whose faithful labor and uniform good conduct give assurance of the sincerity of repentance. Yet that this should be faithfully done, under authority of law, by some commission appointed for the purpose, and whose recommendation to the Executive would be his warrant upon which to grant pardons, is the concurrent observation and testimony of all who have the immediate control of the prisoners.

Respectfully submitted.

T. N. MACHIN,
B. B. REDDING,
    State Prison Directors.

EXHIBITS.

LIST OF EXHIBITS CONTAINED IN THE REPORT OF THE CALIFORNIA STATE PRISON.

[A]

Shows the "Monthly Cost" of maintaining prison, including improvements, from November first, eighteen hundred and sixty-five, to December first, eighteen hundred and sixty-seven.

[B]

Shows the "Earnings" of the prison each month, from November first, eighteen hundred and sixty-five, to December first, eighteen hundred and sixty-seven.

[C]

Shows the "Cash Receipts" of the prison each month, from November first, eighteen hundred and sixty-five, to December first, eighteen hundred and sixty-seven.

[D]

Shows the "Cash Disbursements" of the prison per month, from November first, eighteen hundred and sixty-five, to December first, eighteen hundred and sixty-seven.

[E]

Is a "General Summary" of expenditures and receipts.

[F]

Shows the "Financial Condition" of the prison on the first day of December, eighteen hundred and sixty-seven.

[A]

Showing the Cost of Maintaining the California State Prison from November 1st, 1865, to December 1st, 1867.

Month.	Nature of Expenditure.		Amount.
Nov., 1865	Subsistence	$2,996 39	
	State Prison improvements	478 13	
	Clothing, bedding, and shoes	1,308 58	
	General use	285 42	
	Water	100 00	
	Freight	17 40	
	Forage	69 55	
	Paint, tin and blacksmith shops	43 37	
	Medicines	71 38	
	Stationery	29 75	
	Fuel	296 37	
	Ordnance	8 25	
	Wash house	40 14	
	Discharged prisoners	41 00	
	Incidental expenses	50 00	
	Salaries	2,666 64	
	Discount	44 30	
			$8,546 67
December	Subsistence	$2,865 26	
	State Prison improvements	290 92	
	Clothing, bedding, and shoes	1,488 30	
	General use	307 56	
	Water	100 00	
	Freight	562 40	
	Forage	87 74	
	Paint, tin and blacksmith shops	88 50	
	Medicines	79 50	
	Stationery	13 25	
	Wash-house	25 00	
	Discharged prisoners	45 00	
	Incidental expenses	75 00	
	Salaries	2,734 15	
			8,262 58
Jan., 1866	Subsistence	2,366 59	
	State Prison improvements	298 70	
	Clothing, bedding, and shoes	1,034 22	
	General use	243 15	
	Water	100 00	
	Freight	49 02	
			4,091 68
	Carried forward		$20,900 93

EXHIBIT A—Continued.

Month.	Nature of Expenditure.		Amount.
	Brought forward................		$20,900 93
Jan., 1866..	Forage...............................	89 87	
	Paint and tin shops................	43 50	
	Medicines............................	218 50	
	Stationery...........................	23 75	
	Fuel..................................	569 50	
	Ordnance.............................	16 50	
	Wash-house..........................	36 57	
	Discharged prisoners................	54 00	
	Incidental expenses.................	130 50	
	Salaries..............................	2,898 32	
			4,081 01
February...	Subsistence..........................	$2,193 21	
	State Prison improvements...........	587 73	
	Clothing, bedding, and shoes........	557 55	
	General use..........................	285 31	
	Water.................................	100 00	
	Freight...............................	5 20	
	Forage................................	106 89	
	Paint and tin shops.................	136 31	
	Medicines............................	72 00	
	Stationery...........................	29 50	
	Fuel..................................	466 07	
	Ordnance.............................	21 00	
	Wash-house..........................	23 28	
	Discharged prisoners................	72 00	
	Incidental expenses.................	45 00	
	Salaries..............................	2,975 00	
			7,676 05
March......	Subsistence..........................	$5,231 49	
	State Prison improvements...........	867 70	
	Clothing, bedding, and shoes........	1,169 07	
	General use..........................	409 42	
	Water.................................	100 00	
	Freight...............................	287 89	
	Forage................................	57 87	
	Paint and tin shops.................	53 13	
	Medicines............................	51 88	
	Stationery...........................	22 00	
	Fuel..................................	382 50	
	Wash-house..........................	27 65	
	Discharged prisoners................	21 00	
	Incidental expenses.................	47 50	
	Salaries..............................	3,038 31	
			$9,007 41
	Carried forward................		$41,665 40

Exhibit A—Continued.

Month.	Nature of Expenditure.		Amount.
	Brought forward....................		$41,665 40
April, 1866	Subsistence...........................	$2,820 90	
	State Prison improvements.........	303 21	
	Clothing, bedding, and shoes......	1,454 20	
	General use...........................	391 33	
	Water, (contract purchased).......	1,500 00	
	Freight................................	213 62	
	Forage................................	211 87	
	Paint and tin shops..................	148 95	
	Medicines.............................	117 63	
	Stationery............................	51 00	
	Wash-house..........................	44 37	
	Discharged prisoners................	30 00	
	Incidental expenses..................	66 50	
	Salaries...............................	3,037 46	
	Profit and loss.......................	2,532 35	
			12,923 39
May........	Subsistence...........................	$2,759 42	
	State Prison improvements.........	1,300 81	
	Clothing, bedding, and shoes......	444 73	
	General use..........................	312 07	
	Freight................................	153 75	
	Forage................................	153 21	
	Paint and tin shops..................	15 75	
	Medicines.............................	122 25	
	Stationery............................	28 13	
	Fuel...................................	774 50	
	Ordnance.............................	91 00	
	Wash-house..........................	31 50	
	Discharged prisoners................	54 00	
	Incidental expenses..................	80 00	
	Salaries...............................	3,191 66	
	Profit and loss.......................	65 06	
			9,577 84
June.......	Subsistence...........................	$2,627 95	
	State Prison improvements.........	84 97	
	Clothing, bedding, and shoes......	448 44	
	General use..........................	196 30	
	Freight................................	90 50	
	Forage................................	55 62	
	Paint and tin shops..................	170 20	
	Medicines.............................	136 51	
	Stationery............................	21 50	
	Wash-house..........................	33 30	
	Discharged prisoners................	45 00	
	Incidental expenses..................	84 50	
	Salaries...............................	3,221 65	
			7,216 44
	Carried forward.....................		$71,383 07

Exhibit. A—Continued.

Month.	Nature of Expenditure.		Amount.
	Brought forward....................................		$71,888 07
July, 1866..	Subsistence................................	$2,873 56	
	State Prison improvements...............	71 13	
	Clothing, bedding, and shoes............	615 24	
	General use....................................	157 60	
	Freight..	97 25	
	Forage...	60 34	
	Paint and tin shops.........................	140 90	
	Medicines......................................	27 00	
	Fuel...	666 41	
	Ordnance..	21 28	
	Wash-house....................................	77 85	
	Discharged prisoners......................	46 00	
	Incidental expenses........................	62 16	
	Salaries...	3,223 33	
			8,140 14
August......	Subsistence...................................	$2,829 18	
	State Prison improvements...............	87 25	
	Clothing, bedding, and shoes............	790 46	
	General use....................................	169 26	
	Freight...	112 01	
	Forage..	42 53	
	Paint and tin shops.........................	39 83	
	Medicines......................................	76 45	
	Stationery......................................	15 25	
	Fuel...	39 19	
	Ordnance..	3 25	
	Wash-house....................................	25 69	
	Discharged prisoners......................	80 00	
	Incidental expenses........................	75 50	
	Salaries...	3,233 83	
	Discount (on currency)..................	829 42	
			8,448 60
September.	Subsistence...................................	$2,759 78	
	State Prison improvements...............	125 23	
	Clothing, bedding, and shoes............	721 98	
	General use....................................	183 92	
	Freight...	110 30	
	Forage..	65 99	
	Paint and tin shops.........................	30 65	
	Medicines......................................	21 25	
	Stationery......................................	16 00	
	Ordnance..	2 50	
	Wash-house....................................	42 71	
	Discharged prisoners......................	45 00	
	Incidental expenses........................	101 75	
			4,227 06
	Carried forward...........................		$92,198 87

Exhibit A—Continued.

Month.	Nature of Expenditure.		Amount.
	Brought forward............		$92,198 87
Sep., 1866..	Salaries	3,201 65	
	Discount (on currency)........	202 07	
			3,403 72
October.....	Subsistence.............	$3,367 98	
	State Prison improvements	157 33	
	Clothing, bedding, and shoes..........	733 40	
	General use	168 29	
	Freight........	114 50	
	Forage...........	364 90	
	Paint and tin shops........	66 78	
	Medicines........	61 63	
	Ordnance........	7 50	
	Wash-house	29 31	
	Discharged prisoners	49 00	
	Incidental expenses........	118 60	
	Salaries	3,235 00	
			8,474 22
November.	Subsistence...........	$3,634 03	
	State Prison improvements	109 13	
	Clothing, bedding, and shoes	851 25	
	General use........	208 46	
	Freight........	136 75	
	Forage.........	119 83	
	Paint and tin shops........	13 63	
	Medicines........	24 26	
	Stationery.........	75 50	
	Fuel........	1,332 47	
	Wash-house.........	45 36	
	Discharged prisoners........	33 00	
	Incidental expenses	68 72	
	Salaries.........	3,226 66	
	Profit and loss..........	106 50	
			9,990 55
December..	Subsistence.	$3,065 85	
	State Prison improvements........	732 85	
	Clothing, bedding, and shoes........	667 73	
	General use	258 99	
	Freight........	169 20	
	Forage	31 10	
	Paint and tin shops........	88 65	
	Medicines........	73 85	
	Stationery........	9 00	
	Fuel	18 84	
	Wash-house........	38 75	
	Discharged prisoners........	57 00	
			5,211 81
	Carried forward........		$119,279 17

EXHIBIT A—Continued.

Month.	Nature of Expenditure.		Amount.	
	Brought forward...................		$119,279	17
Dec., 1866..	Incidental expenses..................	65 00		
	Salaries..............................	3,236 66		
	Discount (on currency)...............	276 36		
			3,578	02
Jan., 1867..	Subsistence...........................	3,538 30		
	State Prison improvements............	55 55		
	Clothing, bedding, and shoes.........	746 88		
	General use.........................	337 07		
	Freight..............................	161 00		
	Forage..............................	118 90		
	Paint and tin shops..................	36 89		
	Medicines...........................	48 53		
	Fuel................................	32 02		
	Wash-house.........................	29 25		
	Discharged prisoners................	78 00		
	Incidental expenses.................	154 00		
	Salaries.............................	3,235 00		
	Discount (on currency)..............	738 19		
			9,309	58
February..	Subsistence..........................	$3,143 27		
	State Prison improvements...........	137 06		
	Clothing, bedding, and shoes.........	1,150 69		
	General use.........................	296 97		
	Freight..............................	112 25		
	Forage..............................	91 72		
	Paint and tin shops..................	77 83		
	Medicines...........................	38 43		
	Stationery..........................	31 00		
	Fuel................................	18 72		
	Ordnance...........................	17 25		
	Wash-house.........................	28 14		
	Discharged prisoners................	60 00		
	Incidental expenses.................	55 15		
	Salaries.............................	3,205 00		
			8,463	48
March	Subsistence..........................	$3,282 02		
	State Prison improvements...........	103 67		
	Clothing, bedding, and shoes.........	885 23		
	General use.........................	192 83		
	Freight..............................	138 50		
	Forage..............................	118 44		
	Paint and tin shops..................	63 85		
	Medicines...........................	50 68		
	Fuel................................	1,292 30		
	Wash-house.........................	62 15		
			6,189	12
	Carried forward...................		$146,819	37

EXHIBIT A—Continued.

Month.	Nature of Expenditure.		Amount.
	Brought forward....................................		$146,819 37
	Discharged prisoners......................	106 00	
	Incidental expenses......................	94 60	
	Salaries	3,235 00	
			3,435 60
April, 1867	Subsistence...................	$3,693 24	
	State Prison improvements...............	185 10	
	Clothing, bedding, and shoes............	1,129 85	
	General use.....................................	235 85	
	Freight...	132 10	
	Forage.............................	18 46	
	Paint and tin shops.......................	74 87	
	Medicines.........	38 99	
	Stationery	56 65	
	Fuel.........	210 05	
	Wash-house.....................................	32 00	
	Discharged prisoners......................	55 00	
	Incidental expenses............	61 00	
	Salaries	3,225 00	
			9,148 16
May...........	Subsistence..	$3,900 00	
	State Prison improvements............ ...	171 12	
	Clothing, bedding, and shoes............	275 78	
	General use.....................................	132 22	
	Freight..........	118 60	
	Forage...	79 85	
	Paint and tin shops.......................	177 57	
	Medicines...	73 57	
	Stationery	9 00	
	Fuel..........	655 40	
	Wash-house.....................................	50 69	
	Discharged prisoners.........	60 00	
	Incidental expenses.......................	50 00	
	Salaries..	3,235 00	
			8,988 30
June........	Subsistence........................	$3,873 26	
	State Prison improvements.........	119 77	
	Clothing, bedding, and shoes............	788 76	
	General use.....................................	162 42	
	Freight...	122 10	
	Forage	90 63	
	Medicines...	37 00	
	Ordnance...	19 50	
	Wash-house.....................................	23 71	
	Discharged prisoners......................	62 00	
	Incidental expenses...................	50 00	
			5,349 15
	Carried forward....................................		$173,735 58

Exhibit A—Continued.

Month.	Nature of Expenditure.		Amount.	
	Brought forward......		$173,735	58
June, 1867.	Salaries............	3,225 00		
	Profit and loss............	15 00		
			3,240	00
July	Subsistence............	$3,827 10		
	State Prison improvements............	1,021 54		
	Clothing, bedding, and shoes............	933 93		
	General use............	167 03		
	Freight............	142 80		
	Forage............	389 67		
	Paint and tin shops............	65 48		
	Medicines............	108 25		
	Stationery............	33 50		
	Fuel............	21 28		
	Wash-house............	73 30		
	Incidental expenses............	181 00		
	Discharged prisoners............	72 00		
	Salaries............	3,235 00		
	Discount (on silver)............	10 00		
			10,281	88
August	Subsistence............	$4,058 65		
	State Prison improvements............	225 11		
	Clothing, bedding, and shoes............	625 86		
	General use............	126 00		
	Freight............	143 60		
	Forage............	80 29		
	Paint, tin and blacksmith shops............	134 63		
	Medicines............	38 13		
	Stationery............	5 75		
	Wash-house............	37 50		
	Discharged prisoners............	59 00		
	Incidental expenses............	50 50		
	Salaries............	3,235 00		
	Profit and loss (damaged beef)............	1,267 50		
	Discount (on silver)............	5 00		
			10,092	52
September.	Subsistence............	$4,031 64		
	State Prison improvements............	316 31		
	Clothing, bedding, and shoes............	872 74		
	General use............	199 64		
	Freight............	142 50		
	Forage............	333 63		
	Paint, tin and blacksmith shops............	82 48		
	Medicines............	39 80		
	Stationery............	22 50		
	Wash-house............	44 05		
			$ 6,085	29
	Carried forward......		$203,435	27

EXHIBIT A—Continued.

Month.	Nature of Expenditure.			Amount.	
	Brought forward............			$203,435	27
Sep., 1867..	Discharged prisoners............	60	00		
	Incidental expenses............	50	00		
	Salaries............	2,831	65		
	Profit and loss (damaged beef)........	634	18		
	Discount (on currency)............	148	40		
				3,724	23
October ...	Subsistence............	$4,875	63		
	State Prison improvements............	145	31		
	Clothing, bedding, and shoes............	601	22		
	General use............	181	51		
	Freight............	153	75		
	Forage............	297	12		
	Paint, tin and blacksmith shops.......	8	38		
	Medicines............	69	85		
	Stationery............	17	00		
	Wash-house............	21	55		
	Discharged prisoners............	87	00		
	Incidental expenses............	216	00		
	Salaries............	3,461	54		
	Profit and loss............		70		
	Discount (on silver)............	10	00		
				9,646	56
November.	Subsistence	$4,157	21		
	Forage............	170	20		
	Clothing, bedding, and shoes............	554	80		
	General use............	155	75		
	Medicines............	33	00		
	Fuel............	1,756	75		
	State Prison improvements	181	79		
	Ordnance............	5	25		
	Wash-house............	36	36		
	Paint, tin and blacksmiths shops.......	100	92		
	Discharged prisoners............	99	00		
	Incidental expenses............	99	10		
	Discount (on currency and silver).....	246	58		
	Profit and loss (on account of T. H. Loehr)	55	00		
	Freight............	153	10		
	Salary............	3,075	25		
				10,880	06
	Total............			$227,686	12

RECAPITULATION.

Subsistence	$81,071 91
State Prison improvements	8,157 42
Clothing, bedding, and shoes	20,790 89
General use	5,764 46
Water	2,000 00
Freight	3,635 09
Forage	3,305 72
Paint, tin and blacksmith shops	1,902 55
Medicines	1,780 27
Stationery	510 03
Fuel	8,532 37
Ordnance	213 28
Wash-house	960 18
Discharged prisoners	1,475 00
Incidental expenses	2,132 08
Salaries	78,318 26
Profit and loss	4,676 29
Discount	2,510 32
Total	$227,686 12

[B]

Showing the earnings of the California State Prison, from November 1st, 1865, to November 1st, 1867.

Date.	From what source.		Amount.
Nov., 1865.	Labor	$2,173 85	
	Contributions at gate	3 50	
			$2,177 35
December..	Labor	$1,968 05	
	Subsistence U. S. prisoners	1,035 00	
			3,003 05
Jan., 1866..	Labor	$1,926 08	
	Subsistence U. S. prisoners	496 00	
			2,422 08
February ..	Labor	$1,708 27	
	Drayage	129 00	
	Subsistence U. S. prisoners	153 00	
			1,990 27
March	Labor	$2,405 35	
	Drayage	65 00	
	Subsistence U. S. prisoners	524 00	
	Profit and loss	03	
			2,994 38
April	Labor	$2,344 60	
	Drayage	64 00	
	Subsistence U. S. prisoners	480 00	
	Profit and loss	61 50	
			2,950 10
May	Labor	$2,552 75	
	Drayage	88 50	
	Contributions at gate	103 75	
	Subsistence U. S. prisoners	345 00	
			3,090 00
June	Labor	$3,053 80	
	Drayage	86 50	
	Contributions at gate	94 75	
	Sale of hogs	597 31	
	Subsistence U. S. prisoners	309 00	
	Profit and loss	30	
	Sale of stores	32 50	
			4,174 16
July	Labor	$2,989 30	
	Drayage	89 00	
	Contributions at gate	48 00	
			3,126 30
	Carried forward		$25,927 69

Exhibit B—Continued.

Date.	From what source.		Amount.
	Brought forward		$25,927 69
July, 1866..	Sale of hogs	5 00	
	Subsistence U. S. prisoners	310 00	
	Sale of stores	24 85	
			339 85
August	Labor	$3,843 82	
	Drayage	89 50	
	Contributions at gate	12 50	
	Subsistence U. S. prisoners	267 00	
	Sale of stores	11 25	
			4,224 07
September.	Labor	$3,082 91	
	Drayage	103 00	
	Contributions at gate	7 00	
	Sale of hogs	437 15	
	Subsistence U. S. prisoners	102 00	
	Sale of stores	166 79	
			3,898 85
October	Labor	$3,400 07	
	Drayage	94 00	
	Contributions at gate	13 50	
	Subsistence U. S. prisoners	93 00	
	Sale of stores	35 19	
			3,635 76
November.	Labor	$2,775 15	
	Drayage	91 00	
	Contributions at gate	7 50	
	Sale of hogs	14 25	
	Subsistence U. S. prisoners	90 00	
	Sale of stores	4 25	
			2,982 15
December..	Labor	$2,501 71	
	Drayage	90 50	
	Sale of hogs	54 91	
	Subsistence U. S. prisoners	79 00	
	Sale of stores	6 40	
			2,732 52
Jan., 1867..	Labor	$2,682 05	
	Drayage	91 50	
	Subsistence U. S. prisoners	62 00	
	Sale of stores	7 25	
			2,842 80
February ..	Labor	$2,310 96	
	Drayage	90 00	
	Contributions at gate	1 00	
			2,401 96
	Carried forward		$48,985 65

EXHIBIT B—Continued.

Date.	From what source.		Amount.
	Brought forward..................		$48,985 65
Feb., 1867..	Subsistence U. S. prisoners..............	108 00	
	Sale of stores.................................	37 41	
			145 41
March......	Labor..	$2,534 38	
	Drayage..	93 00	
	Subsistence U. S. prisoners..............	268 00	
	Sale of stores....................................	37 39	
			2,932 77
April........	Labor..	$2,942 20	
	Drayage..	95 00	
	Contributions at gate.......................	9 50	
	Subsistence U. S. prisoners..............	270 00	
	Sale of stores...................................	14 00	
			3,330 70
May.........	Labor..	$3,482 85	
	Drayage..	110 00	
	Contributions at gate.......................	54 00	
	Subsistence U. S. prisoners..............	200 00	
	Sale of stores...................................	47 75	
			3,894 60
June........	Labor..	$3,197 30	
	Drayage..	100 00	
	Contributions at gate.......................	106 50	
	Subsistence U. S. prisoners..............	103 00	
	Sale of stores...................................	20 90	
			3,527 70
July.........	Labor..	$3,238 05	
	Drayage..	98 50	
	Contributions at gate.......................	70 50	
	Subsistence U. S. prisoners..............	93 00	
	Sale of stores...................................	30 00	
			3,530 05
August......	Labor..	3,422 05	
	Drayage..	100 00	
	Contributions at gate.......................	26 00	
	Subsistence U. S. prisoners..............	93 00	
	Profit and loss..................................	1 00	
	Sale of stores...................................	6 75	
			3,648 80
September	Labor..	$2,679 25	
	Drayage..	86 50	
	Contributions at gate.......................	6 50	
	Sale of hogs.....................................	34 00	
	Subsistence U. S. prisoners..............	90 00	
	Sale of stores...................................	35 05	
			2,931 30
	Carried forward................................		$72,926 98

EXHIBIT B—Continued.

Date.	From what source.		Amount.	
	Brought forward		$72,926	98
Oct., 1867..	Labor	$2,980 33		
	Drayage	86 50		
	Contributions at gate	15 00		
	Subsistence U. S. prisoners	93 00		
	Sale of stores	29 05		
			3,203	88
November.	Labor	$2,659 05		
	Drayage	74 50		
	Subsistence U. S. prisoners	133 00		
	Sale of hogs	593 50		
	Contributions at gate	11 50		
	Sale of stores	26 38		
			3,497	93
	Total		$79,628	79

RECAPITULATION.

Labor	$68,854	18
Drayage	2,015	50
Contributions at gate	591	00
Sale of hogs	1,736	12
Subsistence U. S. prisoners	5,769	00
Profit and loss	62	83
Sale of stores	573	16
Total	$79,628	79

[C]

Showing the Cash Receipts of the California State Prison, from November 1st, 1865, to November 1st, 1867.

Date.	From what source.		Amount.
Nov., 1865.	Labor	$3,590 30	
	State Treasurer	1,500 00	
	Contributions at gate	3 50	
	Sale of stores	23 65	
			$5,117 45
December..	Labor	$875 05	
	State Treasurer	5,000 00	
	Sale of stores	19 50	
			5,894 55
Jan., 1866..	Labor	$2,102 57	
	State Treasurer	3,500 00	
	Sale of stores	33 25	
			5,635 82
February ..	Labor	$1,621 10	
	State Treasurer	3,425 00	
			5,046 10
March......	Labor	$2,450 64	
	State Treasurer	10,000 00	
	Sale of stores	68 15	
			12,518 79
April.......	Labor	$3,795 45	
	State Treasurer	15,000 00	
	Sale of stores	15 55	
			18,811 00
May........	Labor	$4,782 27	
	State Treasurer	4,000 00	
	Contributions at gate	103 75	
	Sale of stores	23 15	
			8,909 17
June	Labor	$4,265 18	
	State Treasurer	4,000 00	
	Sale of stores	45 20	
	Contributions at gate	94 75	
	Sale of hogs	597 31	
			9,002 44
July........	Labor	$2,537 75	
	State Treasurer	3,875 00	
	Contributions at gate	48 00	
	Sale of stores	31 40	
			6,492 15
	Carried forward		$77,427 47

EXHIBIT C—Continued.

Date.	From what source.		Amount.
	Brought forward.................................		$77,427 47
Aug., 1866.	Labor.................................	$3,369 90	
	State Treasurer.................................	4,000 00	
	Contributions at gate.....................	12 50	
	Sale of stores.................................	21 50	
	United States (in currency)............	2,936 00	
			10,339 90
September	Labor.................................	$2,855 00	
	Contributions at gate.....................	7 00	
	Sale of stores.................................	15 50	
	Sale of hogs.................................	577 15	
			3,454 65
October.....	Labor.................................	$3,401 59	
	State Treasurer.................................	11,000 00	
	Contributions at gate.....................	13 50	
	Sale of stores.................................	12 30	
			14,427 39
November.	Labor.................................	$2,538 32	
	State Treasurer.................................	4,000 00	
	Contributions at gate.....................	7 50	
	Sale of stores.................................	17 50	
			6,563 32
December..	Labor.................................	$2,402 85	
	State Treasurer.................................	5,000 00	
	Sale of stores.................................	63 56	
	United States (in currency)............	987 00	
			8,453 41
Jan., 1867..	Labor.................................	$2,814 37	
	State Treasurer.................................	5,000 00	
	Sale of stores.................................	12 75	
	United States (in currency)............	2,774 00	
			10,101 12
February...	Labor.................................	$3,185 36	
	Sale of stores.................................	43 70	
			3,229 06
March......	Labor.................................	$1,786 15	
	State Treasurer.................................	3,000 00	
	Sale of stores.................................	20 40	
			4,806 55
April........	Labor.................................	$3,363 70	
	State Treasurer.................................	4,000 00	
	Contributions at gate.....................	9 50	
	Sale of stores.................................	15 25	
			7,388 45
May........	Labor and drayage.....................	$2,852 10	
	State Treasurer.................................	4,000 00	
			6,852 10
	Carried forward.................................		$153,043 42

EXHIBIT C—Continued.

Date.	From what source.			Amount.	
	Brought forward.			$153,043	42
May, 1867.	Contributions at gate	54	00		
	Sale of stores	38	75		
				92	75
June	Labor and drayage	$2,715	79		
	State Treasurer	4,290	00		
	Contributions at gate	106	50		
	Sale of stores	30	00		
				7,142	29
July	Labor and drayage	$5,412	95		
	State Treasurer	10,000	00		
	Contributions at gate	70	50		
	Sale of stores	43	00		
				15,526	45
August	Labor and drayage	$2,695	15		
	Contributions at gate	26	00		
	State Treasurer	5,000	00		
				7,721	15
September.	Labor and drayage	$2,625	40		
	State Treasurer	5,000	00		
	Contributions at gate	6	50		
	Sale of hogs	34	00		
	Sale of stores	35	05		
	United States (in currency)	478	00		
				8,178	95
October	Labor and drayage	$3,660	35		
	State Treasurer	10,000	00		
	Contributions at gate	15	00		
	Sale of stores	24	85		
				13,700	20
November.	State Treasurer	15,000	00		
	Labor and drayage	7,524	03		
	Contributions at gate	11	50		
	Sale of hogs	593	50		
	Sale of stores	24	50		
				23,153	53
	Total			$228,558	74

RECAPITULATION.

Labor and drayage...	$78,723 82
State Treasurer..	139,590 00
Contributions at gate	590 00
Sale of hogs...	1,801 96
Sale of stores...	678 46
Subsistence U. S. prisoners.....................................	7,175 00
Total	$228,558 74

[D]

Showing the Cash Disbursements of the California State Prison, from November 1st, 1865, to December 1st, 1867.

Date.	Nature of Disbursement.		Amount.	
Nov., 1865.	Commissary supplies	$4,658 16		
	Salaries	156 00		
	Water	600 00		
	Freight	17 40		
	Redemption of scrip	50 00		
	Incidental expenses	50 00		
	Discharged prisoners	41 00		
			$5,572 56	
December.	Commissary supplies	$5,328 71		
	Redemption of scrip	479 20		
	Discharged prisoners	45 00		
	Incidental expenses	75 00		
	Salaries	25 00		
	Freight	20 00		
			5,972 91	
Jan., 1866.	Commissary supplies	$5,303 76		
	Discharged prisoners	54 00		
	Incidental expenses	130 50		
	Freight	49 02		
			5,537 28	
February.	Commissary supplies	$5,326 27		
	Discharged prisoners	72 00		
	Incidental expenses	45 00		
	Freight	547 60		
	Robert Dixon	19 50		
			6,010 37	
March	Commissary supplies	$5,012 32		
	Salaries	2,000 00		
	Freight	603 37		
	Incidental expenses	47 50		
	Discharged prisoners	21 00		
	J. F. Chellis	3,024 56		
			10,708 75	
April	Commissary supplies	$4,783 49		
	Redemption of scrip	12,138 15		
	Salaries	2,667 36		
	J. F. Chellis	15 87		
	Discharged prisoners	30 00		
	Incidental expenses	66 50		
			19,701 37	
	Carried forward		$53,503 24	

Exhibit D—Continued.

Date.	From what source.		Amount.
	Brought forward..............................		$53,503 24
May, 1866..	Commissary supplies........................	$5,364 35	
	Redemption of scrip	1,322 66	
	Freight..	64 62	
	Discharged prisoners......................	54 00	
	Incidental expenses........................	73 50	
	S. D. Thompson.............................	65 00	
			6,914 13
June.........	Commissary supplies........................	$5,208 51	
	Redemption of scrip........................	2,479 23	
	Discharged prisoners......................	45 00	
	Incidental expenses........................	84 50	
			7,817 24
July	Commissary supplies........................	$3,922 64	
	Redemption of scrip........................	3,132 90	
	Discharged prisoners......................	46 00	
	Freight..	1 50	
	Incidental expenses........................	62 16	
			7,165 20
August	Commissary supplies........................	$4,235 01	
	Redemption of scrip........................	3,901 45	
	Salaries..	100 00	
	Discharged prisoners......................	80 00	
	Incidental expenses........................	50 00	
	Discount (on currency)...................	829 42	
			9,195 88
September.	Commissary supplies........................	$4,528 45	
	Redemption of scrip........................	1,743 49	
	W. S. Pierce (estate of)..................	612 14	
	Salaries..	58 33	
	Discount (on currency)...................	202 07	
	Discharged prisoners......................	45 00	
	Incidental expenses........................	101 75	
			7,291 23
October	Commissary supplies........................	$3,711 66	
	Redemption of scrip	9,764 07	
	Salaries..	50 00	
	Discharged prisoners......................	49 00	
	Freight..	50	
	Incidental expenses........................	118 60	
			13,693 88
November.	Commissary supplies........................	$4,412 89	
	Redemption of scrip........................	2,758 85	
	Discharged prisoners......................	38 00	
	H. T. Libkisher.............................	106 50	
	Incidental expenses........................	68 72	
			7,384 96
	Carried forward..............................		$112,995 71

Exhibit D—Continued.

Date.	From what source.		Amount.	
	Brought forward..................................		$112,995	71
Dec., 1866..	Commissary supplies.....................	$5,892 49		
	Redemption of scrip.....................	847 87		
	Discount (on currency)..................	276 36		
	Incidental expenses.......................	65 00		
	Discharged prisoners.....................	57 00		
	Freight....................................	1 50		
	Salaries...................................	1 66		
			7,141	88
Jan., 1867..	Commissary supplies.....................	$7,960 60		
	Redemption of scrip.....................	560 16		
	Discount (on currency)..................	738 19		
	Salaries...................................	100 00		
	Discharged prisoners.....................	78 00		
	Incidental expenses......................	50 00		
			9,486	95
February..	Commissary supplies.....................	$4,720 88		
	Salaries...................................	50 00		
	Freight....................................	27 00		
	Incidental expenses......................	50 00		
	Discharged prisoners.....................	60 00		
			4,907	88
March......	Commissary supplies.....................	$5,082 40		
	Salaries...................................	108 00		
	Incidental expenses......................	94 60		
	Discharged prisoners.....................	106 00		
			5,391	00
April.......	Commissary supplies.....................	$6,479 07		
	Salaries...................................	50 00		
	Incidental expenses......................	51 00		
	Discharged prisoners.....................	55 00		
	Freight....................................	9 50		
			6,644	57
May........	Commissary supplies.....................	$5,368 61		
	Discharged prisoners.....................	60 00		
	Salaries...................................	50 00		
	Incidental expenses......................	50 00		
			5,528	61
June	Commissary supplies.....................	$4,866 33		
	Salaries...................................	50 00		
	Discharged prisoners.....................	62 00		
	J. Long...................................	15 00		
	Incidental expenses......................	50 00		
			5,043	33
July........	Commissary supplies.....................	$5,808 95		
	Salaries...................................	50 00		
			5,858	95
	Carried forward...................................		$162,998	88

EXHIBIT D—Continued.

Date.	From what source.			Amount.	
	Brought forward....			$162,998	88
July, 1867..	Incidental expenses..................	181	00		
	Discount (on silver)...................	10	00		
	Redemption of scrip...................	12,203	05		
	Discharged prisoners	72	00		
				12,466	05
August......	Commissary supplies	$6,010	96		
	Incidental expenses...................	50	50		
	Discount (on silver)...................	5	00		
	Redemption of scrip...................	948	32		
	Salaries	50	00		
	Discharged prisoners.................	59	00		
				7,123	78
September	Commissary supplies.................	$4,900	68		
	Salaries	6	65		
	Incidental expenses...................	50	00		
	Discount (on currency and silver).....	148	40		
	Redemption of scrip...................	50	00		
	Freight	26	00		
	Discharged prisoners.................	60	00		
				5,241	73
October	Commissary supplies.................	$5,033	44		
	Redemption of scrip...................	10,194	66		
	Salaries	100	00		
	Discharged prisoners.................	87	00		
	Incidental expenses...................	106	00		
	Discount (on silver)...................	10	00		
				15,531	10
November.	Commissary supplies.................	$203	87		
	Redemption of scrip...................	22,064	58		
	Profit and loss, (acc't of T. H. Loehr)..	55	00		
	Incidental expenses...................	99	10		
	Discount (on currency and silver).....	246	58		
	Discharged prisoners.................	99	00		
				22,768	13
	Total.....................................			$226,129	67

RECAPITULATION.

Commissary supplies	$124,124	50
Salaries	5,673	00
Water	600	00
Freight	1,868	01
Redemption of scrip	84,638	64
Incidental expenses	1,870	93
Discharged prisoners	1,475	00
Discount	2,466	02
J. F. Chellis	3,040	43
W. S. Pierce (estate of)	612	14
Robert Dixon	19	50
S. D. Thompson	65	00
H. T. Libkisher	106	50
J. Long	15	00
A. A. Cummings (profit and loss)	40	00
Peter Metz (profit and loss)	15	00
Total	$226,129	67

Balance cash, November 1, 1865	$1,922 35		
Total receipts to November 30, 1867	$228,558 74		
		$230,481	09
Total disbursements to November 30, 1867	$226,129 67		
Balance cash, November 30, 1867	4,351 42		
		230,481	09

[E]

GENERAL SUMMARY

Of Expenditures and Receipts of the California State Prison from November 1st, 1865, to December 1st, 1867, and the average amount of same per month.

Total expenditures, as per Exhibit A............................		$227,686 12
Total earnings, as per Exhibit B.....................	$79,628 79	
Deficiency of support by prison earnings..........	148,057 33	
		227,686 12
Balance deficiency, brought down..	$148,057 33	
Liabilities of prison, November 1, 1865.............	19,720 55	
		$167,777 88
Appropriations by State, per Exhibit C............	$139,590 00	
Commissary stores, per inventory	1,208 88	
Assets of prison, per inventory.......................	23,085 50	
Net indebtedness, December 1, 1867..	3,893 50	
		167,777 88
Average expenditure per month.......................................		$9,107 44.48
Average earnings per month..		3,185 15.16
Average deficiency per month		5,922 29.32

The item, $28 23, which is charged as a balance due on old debt, in the report of November 1st, 1865, was closed to profit and loss, and does not appear on the books of the present administration.

[F]

STATEMENT

Showing the Liabilities and Available Assets of the California State Prison, December 1st, 1867.

LIABILITIES.	
For bills payable (outstanding scrip)	$18,887 55
For commissary supplies	14,761 70
For medical services (A. W. Taliaferro)	110 00
For salary (T. N. Machin)	910 00
For balance due Ireland & Huntoon	58 70
	$34,727 95
ASSETS.	
Cash on hand	$4,351 42
United States, for subsistence of prisoners	502 00
Commissary stores on hand	2,895 53
Valuation of property of prison, per inventory	23,085 50
Net indebtedness, December 1, 1867	3,893 50
	$34,727 95

TURNKEY'S REPORT.

CON. MURPHY, Turnkey.

TABLE FIRST.
Prison Account from 1851, to November 1st, 1867.

YEARS.	Total receipts	Total discharges	New trial and habeas corpus	Sent to Insane Asylum	Returned from Insane Asylum	Died and killed	Restored to citizenship by the Governor	Pardoned by the Governor	Pardoned by the President	Sentence remitted by the Secretary of War	Sentence remitted by the Secretary of the Navy	Escaped	Discharged by expiration of sentence	Discharged under the Act	Escapes recaptured	Pardons revoked	Prisoners received
1851	35	1	..	..	..	1	..	2	..	..	..	1	..	..	3	..	35
1852	108	21	..	..	..	3	..	9	..	..	..	6	12	..	2	..	105
1853	165	58	..	..	..	6	..	14	..	..	..	8	38	..	16	..	163
1854	227	209	..	..	..	..	..	29	..	..	..	87	102	..	25	..	211
1855	201	157	..	..	..	5	..	18	..	..	..	28	94	..	29	..	266
1856	287	196	4	2	..	14	1	28	..	..	..	65	103	..	32	..	258
1857	277	234	1	3	..	5	4	27	..	..	..	72	114	..	33	..	245
1858	259	191	4	1	..	17	..	38	..	..	..	23	94	..	50	..	226
1859	270	299	7	2	..	7	32	25	..	..	..	95	119	..	20	..	220
1860	315	314	13	1	..	8	16	34	..	..	..	127	145	..	9	..	295
1861	247	212	7	8	..	15	1	11	..	..	..	35	130	..	71	..	238
1862	264	282	4	..	..	4	4	24	..	..	..	90	153	..	4	..	190
1863	167	193	5	..	..	17	..	11	..	..	..	24	134	..	2	..	163
1864	234	196	3	..	..	8	..	11	..	..	..	..	66	98	1	..	232
1865	236	176	10	3	1	17	43	23	8	3	3	1	3	134	2	1	225
1866	258	212	8	1	..	8	7	11	..	..	6	4	3	126	..	..	251
1867	287	289	11	3	..	16	25	23	..	..	..	..	4	171	..	..	257

TABLE SECOND.

Classification of Crimes.

Character.	No.	Character.	No.
Murder	12	Perjury	3
Murder, second degree	77	Embezzlement	2
Manslaughter	50	Counterfeiting	1
Assault to murder	16	Having tools in possession for counterfeiting	1
Assault with deadly weapon	13	Breaking jail	3
Mayhem	2	Felony	14
Rape	9	Grand larceny	252
Assault to rape	12	Attempt to commit grand larceny	1
Robbery	65	House breaking	13
Assault to rob	7	Incest	3
Burglary	114	Attempt to poison	1
Arson	5	Resisting a United States officer	1
Arson, second degree	5		
Attempt to commit arson	1		
Forgery	9	Total	692

TABLE THIRD.

Number of Prisoners from each County.

County.	No.	County.	No.
Alameda	23	San Bernardino	14
Alpine	1	San Diego	2
Amador	18	San Francisco	193
Butte	14	San Joaquin	10
Calaveras	26	San Luis Obispo	4
Colusa	6	San Mateo	13
Contra Costa	11	Santa Barbara	5
El Dorado	25	Santa Clara	22
Fresno	2	Santa Cruz	7
Humboldt	1	Sierra	10
Inyo	2	Siskiyou	13
Lake	1	Solano	6
Los Angeles	46	Sonoma	16
Marin	8	Stanislaus	2
Mariposa	15	Sutter	2
Mendocino	6	Tehama	5
Merced	4	Trinity	1
Monterey	6	Tulare	4
Napa	9	Tuolumne	11
Nevada	25	Yolo	4
Placer	30	Yuba	5
Plumas	1	Mare Island	1
Shasta	6		
Sacramento	56	Total	692

TABLE FOURTH.

Term of Imprisonment.

Duration of Sentence.	No.	Duration of Sentence.	No.
Life...	22	Four years	56
Twenty years and upwards................	18	Three years...............................	132
Fifteen to twenty years.....................	2	Two years.................................	100
Ten to fifteen years.........................	54	One year...................................	51
Seven to ten years..........................	109		
Five to seven years.........................	55	Total..................................	692
Five years....................................	93		

TABLE FIFTH.

Ages of Prisoners.

Age.	No.	Age.	No.
Twenty years and less.....................	66	Forty to fifty years.......................	71
Twenty to twenty-five years..............	155	Fifty years and upwards.................	19
Twenty-five to thirty years................	156		
Thirty to thirty-five years.................	149	Total..................................	692
Thirty-five to forty years..................	76		

TABLE SIXTH—*Nativity of Prisoners.*

UNITED STATES.

State.	No.	State.	No.
Alabama	3	Mississippi	1
Arkansas	8	New Hampshire	4
Connecticut	5	New York	39
District of Columbia	1	New Jersey	2
Florida	1	North Carolina	4
Georgia	3	Ohio	18
Illinois	12	Pennsylvania	22
Indiana	6	Rhode Island	3
Iowa	1	South Carolina	1
Kansas	1	Tennessee	11
Kentucky	23	Texas	2
Louisiana	7	Vermont	3
Maine	10	Virginia	3
Massachusetts	14	Utah	1
Maryland	12		
Michigan	2	Total	243
Missouri	20		

FOREIGN.

Country.	No.	Country.	No.
England	46	Manila	3
Ireland	85	China	78
Scotland	4	Australia	4
Wales	3	Austria	1
France	9	Russia	1
Sweden	1	Isle of Man	1
Germany	33	Denmark	2
Italy	10	Greece	2
Portugal	3	Canada	5
Mexico	53	Switzerland	4
California	74	Argentine Republic	1
Chile	13	Belgium	1
Brazil	1	Spain	1
West Indies	3		
British America	2	Total	449
Poland	2	United States, brought forward	243
Prussia	2		
Peru	1	Total	692

TABLE SEVENTH.

Occupation when Sentenced.

Occupation.	No.	Occupation.	No.
Blacksmiths	10	Silversmiths	4
Bakers	4	Saddlers	5
Butchers	9	Tailors	12
Brickmasons	2	Upholsterers	2
Barkeepers	3	Vaqueros	10
Cooks	28	Waiters	6
Cabinetmakers	4	Wheelwrights	3
Cigarmakers	2	Washmen	15
Carpenters	20	Fishermen	3
Coopers	2	Shoemakers	9
Clerks	14	Goldbeater	1
Farmers	35	Gunsmiths	2
Laborers	360	Seamstresses	4
Moulders	4	Weavers	3
Miners	42	Sailmakers	2
Machinists	3	Dyer	1
Merchants	4	Stonecutter	1
Barbers	5	Teamsters	3
Hatters	2	Gilder	1
Printer	1	Engineers	2
Seamen	39	Millwright	1
Boilermakers	2		
Physician	1	Total	692
Painters	6		

TABLE EIGHTH.

Number of Prisoners at various periods during the years 1865, 1866, 1867.

Time.	No.	Time.	No.
October 31, 1865	648	November 30, 1866	725
November 30, 1865	661	December 31, 1866	710
December 31, 1865	671	January 31, 1867	703
January 31, 1866	669	February 28, 1867	706
February 28, 1866	659	March 31, 1867	709
March 31, 1866	675	April 30, 1867	707
April 30, 1866	699	May 31, 1867	703
May 31, 1866	701	June 30, 1867	697
June 30, 1866	695	July 31, 1867	708
July 31, 1866	701	August 31, 1867	694
August 31, 1866	683	September 30, 1867	698
September 30, 1866	686	October 31, 1867	692
October 31, 1866	694		

TABLE NINTH.

Prisoners Escaped and Recaptured during 1865, 1866, 1867.

Escaped.	No.	Recaptured.	No.
October, 1865		October, 1865	
November, 1865		November, 1865	
December, 1865		December, 1865	
January, 1866	3	January, 1866	
February, 1866		February, 1866	
March, 1866		March, 1866	
April, 1866	1	April, 1866	
May, 1866		May, 1866	
June, 1866		June, 1866	
July, 1866		July, 1866	
August, 1866		August, 1866	
September, 1866		September, 1866	1
October, 1866		October, 1866	1
November, 1866		November, 1866	
December, 1866		December, 1866	
January, 1867		January, 1867	
February, 1867		February, 1867	
March, 1867		March, 1867	
April, 1867		April, 1867	
May, 1867		May, 1867	
June, 1867		June, 1867	
July, 1867		July, 1867	
August, 1867		August, 1867	
September, 1867		September, 1867	
October, 1867		October, 1867	

TABLE TENTH.

Educational Abilities of Prisoners.

NATIVITY.	Read	Write	Both	Neither	Total
United States	213	195	195	30	243
England	42	38	38	4	46
Scotland	4	4	4	....	4
Ireland	59	51	51	26	85
Wales	3	3	3	....	3
France	9	9	9	....	9
Sweden	1	1	1	....	1
Germany	28	24	24	5	33
Italy	8	7	7	2	10
Portugal	2	2	2	1	3
Mexico	19	14	14	34	53
California	18	15	15	56	74
Chile	8	8	8	5	13
Brazil	....	....	....	1	1
West Indies	1	1	1	2	3
Manila	....	....	....	3	3
China	44	41	41	34	78
Austria	1	1	1	....	1
Prussia	2	2	2	....	2
Russia	1	1	1	....	1
Peru	....	....	....	1	1
British America	2	2	2	....	2
Poland	2	2	2	....	2
Australia	3	3	3	1	4
Isle of Man	1	1	1	....	1
Denmark	2	2	2	....	2
Greece	1	1	1	1	2
Canada	4	4	4	1	5
Switzerland	3	2	2	1	4
Argentine Republic	....	....	....	1	1
Belgium	1	1	1	....	1
Spain	1	1	1	....	1
Total	....	....	....	....	692

RECAPITULATION.

NATIVITY.	Total Read.	Total Write.	Total Both.	Total Neither	Total.
United States	213	195	195	30	243
Foreign	252	226	226	123	375
Native Californians	18	15	15	56	74
Totals	483	436	436	209	692

Total number of Prisoners..................692.

TABLE ELEVENTH.
Recapitulation for 1866.

DATE.	Total receipts	Total discharges	New trial and habeas corpus	Sent to Insane Asylum	Returned from Insane Asylum	Died and killed	Restored to citizenship by the Governor	Pardoned by the Governor	Pardoned by the President	Sentence remitted by the Secretary of War	Sentence remitted by the Secretary of the Navy	Escaped	Discharged by expiration of sentence	Discharged under the Act	Escapes recaptured	Pardons revoked	Prisoners received
November, 1865	28	15	1				1	2						11			28
December, 1865	29	19		1	1	1	2	1		1				14			28
January, 1866	21	23				3	1	1				3		17			21
February, 1866	9	19				1	2	3						11			9
March, 1866	26	10				1	1	1	1					6			26
April, 1866	34	10	3					4	6					4			34
May, 1866	28	26	2				3					1		13			28
June, 1866	11	17				1		2			1			12			11
July, 1866	21	15	1					3	1					11			21
August, 1866	8	26					6	2		2	2		2	12	1		8
September, 1866	18	15	1				8						1	4	1	1	16
October, 1866	25	17					1	4						11			24
Totals	258	212	8	1	1	8	25	23	8	3	3	4	3	126	2	1	254

TABLE ELEVENTH—Continued.
Recapitulation for 1867.

DATE.	Nov. 1866	Dec. 1866	Jan. 1867	Feb. 1867	Mar. 1867	Apr. 1867	May 1867	June 1867	July 1867	Aug. 1867	Sept. 1867	Oct. 1867	Totals
Total receipts	44	8	22	23	39	22	21	15	37	5	26	25	287
Total discharges	13	23	29	20	36	24	25	21	26	19	22	31	289
New trial and habeas corpus			1		2	4	1				1	2	11
Sent to Insane Asylum											3		3
Returned from Insane Asylum													
Died and killed	1	4	2		2	1	1	1	2	1	1		16
Restored to citizenship by the Governor	3	5	2	1	2	2	5	4	4	3	5	5	41
Pardoned by the Governor	3	3	3	2	3	4	4	3	2	2	3	5	37
Pardoned by the President													
Sentence remitted by the Secretary of War													
Sentence remitted by the Secretary of the Navy						6							6
Escaped													
Discharged by expiration of sentence	2					1			1				4
Discharged under the Act	6	9	21	17	27	13	8	12	17	13	12	16	171
Escapes recaptured													
Pardons revoked													
Prisoners received	44	8	22	23	39	22	21	15	37	5	26	25	287

TABLE TWELFTH.

Number of Prisoners confined in the different rooms and cells of Prison.

Main Prisons.	Description of Prisoners.	No.
Old Prison, cells 48 in number	Whites, Mexicans, and Californians	186
New Prison, No. 1, cells 198 in number	Whites, Californians, and Chinese	191
New Prison, No. 2, cells 198 in number	Whites, Californians, and Chinese	97
Old Prison basement—		
Room A	Whites and Mexicans	33
Room 1	Negroes and Indians	12
Room 2	Whites	29
Room 3	Whites	30
Room 4	Californians and Mexicans	36
Room 5	Whites	29
Room 6	Californians and Mexicans	29
Dungeon		2
Hospital and outside—		
Hospital		10
Outside		8
Total number of prisoners, October 31, 1867		692

TABLE THIRTEENTH.

Number of Terms.

Terms.	No.
Number of prisoners serving their first term	564
Number of prisoners serving their second term	89
Number of prisoners serving their third term	24
Number of prisoners serving their fourth term	13
Number of prisoners serving their fifth term	1
Number of prisoners serving their sixth term	1
Total	692

TABLE FOURTEENTH.

Occupation of Prisoners in the California State Prison, October 31st, 1867.

Occupation.	No.	Occupation.	No.
Shoe making	81	Cell tenders	17
Knitting	51	Doorkeepers	8
Saddle and harness making	138	Yard sweepers	6
Coopering	30	Mattress makers	2
Bookbinding	24	Lamplighter	1
Broom making	13	Lamp cleaners	2
Wagon making	20	Whitewashers	2
Brick making	75	Gatekeepers	4
Laundry	17	Turners	3
Water works	7	Cooks and waiters (outside)	32
Wood and coal yard	6	Butchers	3
Carpenters	7	Gardeners	5
Wheelwright	1	Tin shop	1
Blacksmithing	3	Barbers	3
Painting and glazing	3	Women	4
Kitchen and bakery	10	Trusties	3
Dining room	12	Reserve list	8
State shoe shop	8	Sick and in hospital	9
State tailor shop	6	Indigent	24
State harness shop	2	Unemployed	28
State room tenders	7		
Office men	6	Total	692

REPORT OF VISITING PHYSICIAN.

REPORT OF VISITING PHYSICIAN.

To the Honorable Board of Wardens of the California State Prison:

GENTLEMEN:—The following statistics of the Medical Department of the prison are respectfully submitted:

Diseases treated in the Hospital during the year 1867.

Month.	Disease.	No.	Month.	Disease.	No.
Jan'y...	Paralysis	1	April...	Paralysis	1
	Syphilis	1		Erysipelas	2
	Erysipelas	1		Neuralgia	1
	Iritis	1		Fumuculus	1
	Rheumatism	2		Rheumatism	1
	Pneumonia	1		Pneumonia	1
	Hæmoptysis	2		Hemorrhage of lungs	2
	Stricture	1		Stricture	1
	Chronic Diarrhœa	1		Chronic Diarrhœa	2
		11			12
Feb'y...	Paralysis	1	May.....	Paralysis	1
	Rheumatism	2		Syphilis	1
	Syphilis	1		Erysipelas	2
	Iritis	1		Incised wound of chest	1
	Pneumonia	1		Rheumatism	1
	Chronic Diarrhœa	1		Pneumonia	1
	Passive Hemorrhage	1		Hemorrhage of lungs	1
	Tumor on knee	1		Stricture	1
		9			9
March..	Paralysis	1			
	Carcinoma	1	June....	Paralysis	2
	Neuralgia	1		Syphilis	1
	Asthma	1		Dropsy of knee joint	1
	Fumuculus	1		Rheumatism	1
	Rheumatism	2		Pneumonia	1
	Pneumonia	1		Hemorrhage of lungs	2
	Hemorrhage of lungs	2		Asphyxia	1
	Stricture	1		Stricture	1
	Chronic Diarrhœa	2		Chronic Diarrhœa	1
		13			11

Diseases treated in the Hospital—Continued.

Month.	Disease.	No.	Month.	Disease.	No.
July.....	Paralysis	1		Phthisis	1
	Varacella	1		Ascites	1
	Parodiditis	1		Passive Hemorrhage	1
	Pneumonia	1		Chronic Diarrhœa	1
	Hemorrhage of lungs	3			
	Stricture	1			7
	Chronic Diarrhœa	1			
	Pleuritis	1	October	Rheumatism	1
				Iritis	1
		10		Phthisis	1
				Hemorrhage	1
August.	Paralysis	1		Pneumonia	2
	Rheumatism	3			
	Chronic Diarrhœa	1			6
	Hemorrhage	1			
	Tumor on knee	1	Nov.....	Iritis	.....
	Phthisis	2		Pneumonia	3
	Asphyxia	1		Hemorrhage	1
	Billious Fever	1		Phthisis	1
				Incised wound of face	1
		11			
					6
Sept......	Paralysis	1			
	Rheumatism	2			

Treated outside Hospital.	No.	Treated outside Hospital.	No.
January	78	August	112
February	78	September	62
March	71	October	62
April	73	November	68
May	53		
June	51	Total	780
July	72		

Deaths during the year 1867.

Date.	Disease.	No.	Date.	Disease.	No.
Jan. 17..	Syphilis	1	July 26..	Syphilis	1
Jan. 19..	Paralysis	1	July 29..	Hemorrhage of lungs	1
Mar. 9..	Phthisis	1	Aug. 11..	Hemorrhage of lungs	1
Mar. 28..	Phthisis	1	Sept. 28..	Dropsy	1
April 7..	Phthisis	1	Nov. 17..	Phthisis	1
May 24..	Erysipelas	1			
June 8..	Hemorrhage of lungs	1		Total	12

RECAPITULATION.

Number of cases treated inside hospital..	105
Number of cases treated outside hospital...	780
Total number treated for eleven months, ending November 30................................	885
Number of deaths during eleven months...	12
Number under treatment in hospital, November 30	7
Number under treatment outside hospital..	20
Total number under treatment, November 30	27

REMARKS.

Notwithstanding a large increase of numbers in this institution, I am happy in being able to state that the health of the prisoners since the date of my last report (of January first, eighteen hundred and sixty-six,) has been exceedingly good. Exceptions to the rule have been comparatively rare, and in most of these the maladies were admitted with the men. There have been no cases of epidemic or contagious disease, and the prevalent affections attendant upon change of seasons have been of a mild and manageable type. By far the greater number of cases treated outside of the hospital were of the most trivial character, there being many malingerers, men who simulate disease for the purpose of evading the slight tasks imposed upon them by prison discipline. Rheumatism, diarrhœa, and intermittent fever, embrace the remainder very generally. Those cases requiring constant attention were admitted to the hospital; nor do these furnish a correct index to the health of the prison, for of the deaths, twelve in number, seven resulted from pulmonary disease, the subjects of which were in an advanced stage when admitted; of the remaining five, two were of the worst forms of syphilis in Chinese subjects, admitted when in an incurable state; one from paralysis, and one from dropsy—both of the latter the result of former pernicious habits of life; leaving one only—that from erysipelas—that had its origin in the prison.

It is evident from the above statements how small was the percentage of mortality, and how largely influenced by anterior cases. Out of an average of over seven hundred (700) confined, twelve deaths took place.

During the year three patients have been sent to Stockton to be treated for insanity, there being no accommodations within the walls of the prison for the treatment of mental diseases.

There is no occasion at present for exception to the established regulations for preserving and promoting the health of the prisoners. It would be much easier to alter for the worse than to improve either the diet or the clothing. The causes of disease are mostly cut off, and a regularity of habit is enforced which goes far to insure an immunity from disease, and the natural hygienic conditions existing at this point enable the human system to resist the depressing influences of disease and medicine to an extent not observed elsewhere.

CHARLES BURRELL, M. D.,
Visiting Physician California State Prison.

COMMISSARY REPORT.

CONTENTS.

TABLE FIRST—Shows total cost of subsistence.

TABLE SECOND—Shows total cost of Prison improvements.

TABLE THIRD—Shows total cost of general use.

TABLE FOURTH—Shows total cost of clothing.

TABLE FIFTH—Shows total cost of shoes.

TABLE SIXTH—Shows total cost of bed and bedding.

TABLE SEVENTH—Shows total cost of stationery.

TABLE EIGHTH—Shows total cost of drugs and medicines.

TABLE NINTH—Shows total cost of wash-house.

TABLE TENTH—Shows total cost of ordnance.

TABLE ELEVENTH—Shows total cost of fuel.

TABLE TWELFTH—Shows total cost of forage.

TABLE THIRTEENTH—Shows total cost of tools, paint, tinware, iron, etc., charged to shops, and used in repairs, etc.

TABLE FOURTEENTH—General summary of the above.

TABLE FIRST.

Total cost of subsistence from November 1st, 1865, to December 1st, 1867.

Months.	Amount.
1865.	
November	$2,906 39
December	2,365 26
1866.	
January	2,366 59
February	2,193 21
March	2,531 49
April	2,820 90
May	2,759 42
June	2,627 95
July	2,873 56
August	2,829 18
September	2,759 78
October	8,367 98
November	3,634 03
December	3,065 85
1867.	
January	3,538 30
February	3,143 27
March	3,282 02
April	3,693 24
May	3,900 00
June	8,873 26
July	3,827 10
August	4,058 65
September	4,031 64
October	4,375 63
November	4,157 21
Total	$81,071 91

TABLE SECOND.

Total cost of lumber, iron, nails, lime, cement, asphaltum, carpets, upholstery, iron pipe, furniture, etc., issued from November 1st, 1865, to December 1st, 1867, for Prison improvements.

Months.	Amount.
1865.	
November	8478 13
December	290 92
1866.	
January	298 70
February	587 73
March	867 70
April	803 21
May	1,300 81
June	84 97
July	71 13
August	87 25
September	125 23
October	157 83
November	109 13
December	732 85
1867.	
January	55 55
February	137 06
March	103 67
April	185 10
May	171 12
June	119 77
July	1,021 54
August	225 11
September	316 31
October	145 31
November	181 79
Total	$8,157 42

TABLE THIRD.

Total cost of coal oil, lanterns, candles, brooms, stable utensils, crockery, stove furniture, tools, and materials, etc., etc, issued from November 1st, 1865, to December 1st, 1867, for general use of Prison.

Months.	Amount.
1865.	
November	$285 42
December	307 56
1866.	
January	243 15
February	285 31
March	409 42
April	391 33
May	312 07
June	196 30
July	157 69
August	169 26
September	183 92
October	168 29
November	208 46
December	258 99
1867.	
January	337 07
February	296 97
March	192 83
April	235 85
May	132 22
June	162 42
July	167 03
August	126 00
September	199 64
October	181 51
November	155 75
Total	$5,764 46

TABLE FOURTH.

Total cost of clothing from November 1st, 1865, to December 1st, 1867.

Months.	Amount.
1865.	
November	$783 58
December	776 48
1866.	
January	619 92
February	386 87
March	805 00
April	1,015 82
May	84 00
June	81 23
July	361 25
August	610 23
September	322 86
October	619 13
November	274 80
December	478 32
1867.	
January	315 68
February	848 79
March	431 65
April	756 02
May	181 03
June	653 98
July	743 55
August	364 72
September	753 29
October	291 00
November	365 84
Total	$12,980 04

TABLE FIFTH.

Total cost of shoes from November 1st, 1865, to December 1st, 1867.

Months.	Amount.
1865.	
November	$93 60
December	340 76
1866.	
January	214 80
February	170 68
March	88 29
April	190 76
May	72 53
June	153 71
July	236 87
August	51 75
September	84 00
October	114 27
November	140 49
December	100 87
1867.	
January	178 16
February	101 90
March	213 95
April	116 58
May	94 75
June	109 58
July	156 88
August	175 35
September	79 45
October	156 99
November	83 08
Total	$3,419 00

TABLE SIXTH.

Total cost of bed and bedding from November 1st, 1865, to December 1st, 1867.

Months.	Amount.
1865.	
November	$426 40
December	471 06
1866.	
January	200 00
February	....
March	215 78
April	247 62
May	288 20
June	213 50
July	17 12
August	128 48
September	315 12
October	....
November	435 96
December	89 04
1867.	
January	253 04
February	200 00
March	239 63
April	257 30
May	....
June	25 20
July	33 50
August	85 79
September	40 00
October	153 23
November	105 88
Total	$4,441 85

TABLE SEVENTH.

Total cost of stationery from November 1st, 1865, to December 1st, 1867.

Months.	Amount.
1865.	
November	$29 75
December	13 25
1866.	
January	23 75
February	29 50
March	22 00
April	51 00
May	28 13
June	21 50
July	
August	15 25
September	16 00
October	
November	75 50
December	9 00
1867.	
January	
February	81 00
March	
April	56 65
May	9 00
June	
July	33 50
August	5 75
September	22 50
October	17 00
November	
Total	$510 03

TABLE EIGHTH.

Total cost of drugs and medicines from November 1st, 1865, to December 1st, 1867.

Months.	Amount.
1865.	
November	$71 38
December	79 50
1866.	
January	218 50
February	72 00
March	51 88
April	117 63
May	122 25
June	136 51
July	27 00
August	76 45
September	21 25
October	61 68
November	24 26
December	73 85
1867.	
January	48 53
February	38 43
March	50 63
April	38 99
May	78 57
June	37 00
July	108 25
August	38 13
September	39 80
October	69 85
November	33 00
Total	$1,730 27

TABLE NINTH.

Total cost of materials furnished to wash-house from November 1st, 1865, to December 1st, 1867.

Months.	Amount.
1865.	
November	$40 14
December	25 00
1866.	
January	36 57
February	23 28
March	27 65
April	44 37
May	31 50
June	33 30
July	79 85
August	25 69
September	42 71
October	29 31
November	45 36
December	38 75
1867.	
January	29 25
February	28 14
March	62 15
April	32 00
May	50 69
June	23 71
July	73 30
August	37 50
September	44 05
October	21 55
November	36 36
Total	$960 18

TABLE TENTH.

Total cost of ordnance from November 1st, 1865, to December 1st, 1867.

Months.	Amount.
1865.	
November..	$8 25
December..	....
1866.	
January..	16 50
February...	21 00
March..	....
April..	....
May...	91 00
June...	....
July...	21 28
August..	8 25
September...	2 50
October...	7 50
November..	....
December..	....
1867.	
January..	....
February...	17 25
March..	....
April..	....
May...	....
June...	19 50
July...	....
August..	....
September...	....
October...	....
November..	5 25
Total..	$218 28

TABLE ELEVENTH.

Total cost of fuel from November 1st, 1865, to December 1st, 1867.

Months.	Amount.
1865.	
November	$296 87
December	....
1866.	
January	569 50
February	466 07
March	382 50
April	....
May	774 50
June	....
July	666 41
August	39 19
September	....
October	....
November	1,332 47
December	18 84
1867.	
January	32 02
February	18 72
March	1,292 30
April	210 05
May	655 16
June	....
July	21 28
August	....
September	....
October	....
November	1,756 75
Total	$8,582 37

TABLE TWELFTH.

Total cost of forage from November 1st, 1865, to December 1st, 1867.

Months.	Amount.
1865.	
November	869 55
December	87 74
1866.	
January	89 87
February	106 89
March	57 87
April	211 87
May	153 21
June	55 62
July	60 34
August	42 58
September	65 99
October	364 90
November	119 83
December	31 10
1867.	
January	118 90
February	91 72
March	118 44
April	18 46
May	79 85
June	90 63
July	389 67
August	80 29
September	333 63
October	297 12
November	170 20
Total	$3,305 72

TABLE THIRTEENTH.

Total cost of tools, paints, tinware, iron, coal, etc., used in paint shop, tin shop, and blacksmith shop, and not otherwise charged, from November 1st, 1865, to December 1st, 1867.

Months.	Amount.
1865.	
November	$43 37
December	88 50
1866.	
January	43 50
February	136 31
March	53 13
April	148 95
May	15 75
June	170 20
July	140 90
August	39 83
September	30 65
October	66 78
November	13 63
December	88 65
1867.	
January	36 89
February	77 83
March	63 35
April	74 87
May	177 57
June	
July	65 48
August	134 63
September	82 48
October	8 38
November	100 92
Totals	$1,902 55

TABLE FOURTEENTH.

General summary of the foregoing tables.

For what purpose.	Amount.
Subsistence	$81,071 91
Prison improvements	8,157 42
General use	5,764 46
Clothing	12,930 04
Shoes	3,419 00
Beds and bedding	4,441 85
Stationery	510 03
Drugs and medicines	1,730 27
Wash-house	960 18
Ordnance	213 28
Fuel	8,532 37
Forage	3,805 72
Paint shop, tin shop, and blacksmith shop	1,902 55
	$132,939 08
Profit and loss account for 22,400 pounds beef spoiled and thrown away in months of August and September, 1867	1,901 68
Total	$134,840 76

EXHIBIT

Showing number of pounds of provisions issued, including cost of same, from November 1st, 1865, to December 1st, 1867; also average of same per month.

Articles issued.	Total No. Pounds.	Average per month.
Beef	548,468	21,938.72
Hams and bacon	9,533	381.32
Codfish and mackerel	25,288	1,011.52
Flour	543,890	21,755.60
Potatoes and vegetables	523,018	20,920.72
Beans	148,970	5,958.80
Corn meal	19,841	793.64
Sugar	25,717	1,028.68
Tea	2,883	115.32
Coffee	5,532	221.28
Butter	15,664	626.56
Cheese	1,407	56.28
Pepper	1,158	46.32
Salt	51,065	2,042.60
Lard	3,190	127.60
Rice and hominy	6,100	244.00
Groceries, sundry	38,627	1,545.08
Totals	1,970,351	78,814.04

```
Total cost..................................................$81,071 91
Average per month..................................... 3,242 87
```

EXHIBIT

Showing number of pounds of provisions issued daily, including cost; also average to each person, including officers, employés, and prisoners, from November 1st, 1865, to December 1st, 1867.

Articles issued.	Pounds.
Beef	731.29
Hams and bacon	12.71
Codfish and mackerel	33.71
Flour	725.18
Potatoes and vegetables	697.85
Beans	198.62
Corn meal	26.45
Sugar	34.28
Tea	8.84
Coffee	7.37
Butter	20.88
Cheese	1.87
Pepper	1.54
Salt	68.08
Lard	4.25
Rice and hominy	8.13
Groceries, sundry	51.50
Total	2,627.05

Total cost per day $108 09
Average cost of rations for each person.......... 14.55
Average number of pounds to each person ....3 lbs. 8 oz.

EXHIBIT

Showing total amount of clothing issued, including cost, from November 1st, 1865, to December 1st, 1867; also monthly average of same.

Articles issued.	Number.
Whole number of pants issued..	2,415
Average per month..	96.40
Whole number of shirts issued	2,583
Average per month..	103.32
Whole number of coats issued	193
Average per month..	7.72
Whole number of hats issued..	270
Average per month..	10.80

Total cost of clothing...$12,930 04
Average per month... 431 00

Of this amount $1,579 10 was expended on discharged prisoners.

EXHIBIT

Showing total number of shoes issued and repaired, including cost, from November 1st, 1865, to December 1st, 1867; also monthly average of same.

Articles issued.	Number.	Cost.
Whole number of shoes issued..............................	2,298	
Average per month....................................	91.92	
Whole number of shoes repaired..........................	1,350	
Average per month....................................	54	
Total cost of shoes......................................	....	$2,609 00
Average per month..	....	104 36
Total cost of repairs....................................	....	810 00
Average per month..	....	32 40
Total cost of shoes and repairing.........................	....	3,419 00
Average per month..	....	136 76
Average cost of shoes per pair............................	....	1 13¼
Average cost of repairing per pair........................	....	60

EXHIBIT

Showing total amount of bed and bedding issued, including cost, from November 1st, 1865, to December 1st, 1867; also monthly average of same.

Articles issued.	Number.
Whole number of blankets issued	824
Average per month	32.96
Whole number of sheets issued	322
Average per month	12.88
Whole number of pillow cases issued	515
Average per month	20.60
Whole number of mattresses issued	421
Average per month	16.84
Whole number of pounds of pulu issued	485
Average per month	19.40

Total cost...$4,441 85
Average per month... 148 06

EXHIBIT

Showing total amount of soap, starch, soda, etc., issued to wash-house, including cost, from November 1st, 1865, to December 1st, 1867; also monthly average of same.

Articles issued.	Total No. lbs.	Cost.
Soap, in bars	7,939	$769 28
Starch	504	59 56
Sal soda	507	16 45
Potash	705	71 59
Blue	24	10 50
Sperm	8	4 80
Indelible ink, 5 dozen		10 75
Iron cauldron		10 00
Clothes pins, lines, washboards, etc.,		7 25
Total		$960 88

Average per month... $32 00

EXHIBIT

Showing total amount of ordnance and ordnance stores, from November 1st, 1865, to December 1st, 1867, including cost; also monthly average of same.

Article issued.	Cost.
Two Henry's rifles...	$65 00
Seventy pounds bar lead..	8 75
Four thousand Colt's pistol caps...............................	4 50
Six and one fourth kegs powder...............................	43 25
One case rifle powder...	12 50
Five hundred cartridges...	17 50
Six powder flasks...	6 00
One hundred cannon primers...................................	5 50
Three bags buckshot..	10 75
One ream envelope paper..	10 50
Shot pouch, powder flask, and wads........................	6 50
Sundries for repairs, etc..	22 53
Total..	$213 28

Average per month... $7 11

EXHIBIT

Showing total number of pounds of forage issued, including cost, from November 1st, 1865, to December 1st, 1867; also monthly average of same.

Articles issued.	Total No. of pounds.	Average per month.
Wheat..	20,317	812.68
Barley..	107,040	4,281.60
Hay..	80,480	3,219.20
Ground feed...	16,720	668.80
Corn meal..	10,420	416.80
Bran...	22,604	904.16
Oats...	4,971	198.84
Potatoes..	17,390	695.60
Oil cake meal...	535	21.40
Total..	280,477	11,219.08

Total cost $3,305 72
Average per month... 110 19

LIVE STOCK ON HAND.

Horses	6
Cows	4
Heifer	1
Boar	1
Old hogs	22
Pigs	155
Chickens	45
Ducks	50
Geese	9

Value of fuel, provisions, and stores on hand, November 30, 1867	$2,895 53

EXHIBIT

Showing total cost of sustaining a prisoner with subsistence, clothing, and bed and bedding, for one year.

Articles.	Value.
To subsistance	$53 10
To clothing	7 48
To shoes and repairing	2 36
To bed and bedding	86
Total	$63 80

Average number of officers and employés, from November 1, 1865, to December 1, 1867	49
Average number of prisoners during same time	694
Total	743

INVENTORY

Of furniture, bed and bedding, live stock, tools, etc., on hand at California State Prison, December 1st, 1867.

Description.	Number.
WARDEN'S QUARTERS.	
Carpet in parlor..	1
Carpet in south bed room...	1
Carpet in room west of parlor..	1
Carpet in room head of stairs...	1
Bedsteads, with hair mattresses, sheets, pillows, spreads, blankets, etc., complete..	3
Washstands, bowls, pitchers, towels, etc., complete.............	3
Small tables..	3
Looking-glasses...	3
Kitchen stove and fixtures complete.......................................	1
Dining table, crockery, table cloths, napkins, etc., complete..	1
Secretary...	1
Wardrobe...	1
CLERK'S OFFICE.	
Large office desk..	1
Large safe..	1
Table..	1
Settee...	1
Arm chairs...	4
Desk stool..	1
Stove and fixtures..	1
Window curtains..	2
Spittoon...	1
Looking-glass..	1
Lamp..	1
Carpet..	1
BEDROOM ADJOINING.	
Double bedstead...	1
Pulu mattress..	1
Straw mattress...	1
Bed spread...	1
Blankets, pair..	1
Sheets...	4
Pillow cases...	4
Wardrobe...	1
Chair...	1
Looking-glass..	1

INVENTORY—Continued.

Description.	Number.
Candlestick	1
Chamber	1
Carpet	1
Washstand and fixtures	1
COMMISSARY OFFICE.	
Office desk	1
Settee	1
Rocking chair	1
Arm chairs	4
Table	1
Stove and fixtures	1
Spittoon	1
Carpet	1
Water pitcher	1
Maps	2
Guard roll	1
Feather duster	1
Lamp	1
BED ROOM ADJOINING.	
Double bedstead	1
Pulu mattress, bolster, and pillows	1
Straw mattress	1
Spread	1
Pair blankets	1
Sheets	4
Pillow cases	4
Wardrobe	1
Table	1
Chair	1
Window curtain	1
Looking-glass	1
Washstand and fixtures	1
Carpet	1
COMMISSARY STORE.	
Office desk	1
Medicine case	1
Large cupboards	2
Small cupboards	2
Long tables	3
Clock	1
Letter press	1
Arm chairs	5
Desk stools	2
Washstand	1

INVENTORY—Continued.

Description.	Number.
Water pails	2
Tin wash basin	1
Pair platform scales	1
Pair counter scales	1
Five-gallon oil cans, with brass cocks	7

CAPTAIN OF GUARD'S ROOM.

Description.	Number.
Table	1
Sofa	1
Spittoon	1
Washstand and fixtures	1
Carpet	1
Chamber	1
Safe	1
Chairs	2
Candlestick	1
Double bedstead	1
Pulu mattress	1
Straw mattress	1
Spread	1
Sheets	4
Pillow cases	4

GATE KEEPER'S ROOM.

Description.	Number.
Bedstead, three quarter	1
Pulu mattress	1
Straw mattress	1
Spread	1
Blankets, pairs	3
Sheets	2
Pillow and case	1
Washstand and fixtures	1
Looking-glass	1
Carpet	1
Wash tub	1
Window curtains	2
Table	1
Lamp	1
Arm chairs	2

VISITORS' ROOMS.

Description.	Number.
Double bedsteads	2
Pulu mattresses and pillows	2
Straw mattresses	2
Washstands and fixtures	2
Carpets	2

INVENTORY—Continued.

Description.	Number.
Chambers	2
Bedspreads	2
Blankets, pairs	4
Sheets, pairs	4
Pillow cases	4
Looking-glasses	2
SITTING-ROOM.	
Marble top table	1
Sofa	1
Chairs	4
Looking-glass	1
Carpet	1
ROOMS AT LOWER GATE.	
Bedsteads	8
Bunk	1
Pulu mattresses	4
Straw mattresses	4
Chairs	5
Tables	3
Wardrobe	1
Sheets	8
Pillow cases and pillows	4
Tin wash basins	2
Tub	1
Desk	1
Buckets	2
Looking-glass	1
Lamp	1
Carpet	1
DAY GUARDS' ROOMS.	
Pulu mattresses	15
Straw mattresses	15
Sheets	28
Pillow cases	31
Pillows	28
Blankets, pairs	27
Blankets, single	5
Bed spreads	13
Bedsteads	4
Bunks	10
Chairs	22
Tables	5
Spittoons	8
Buckets	4

INVENTORY—Continued.

Description.	Number.
Candlesticks	5
Lamps	8
Sofa	1
Looking-glasses	2
Map	1
Stove	1
Window blinds	18

NIGHT GUARDS' ROOMS.

Description.	Number.
Pulu mattresses	15
Straw mattresses	15
Pulu pillows	15
Blankets, pairs	30
Sheets	30
Pillow slips	15
Bunks	15
Chairs	10
Roller towels	10
Single towels	24
Stair matting	1
Candlesticks	4
Window screens	3

ORDNANCE DEPARTMENT.

Description.	Number.
Six-pounder brass field pieces, with ammunition chest and gun carriages, complete	3
Twelve-pounder brass-mounted howitzer, with appurtenances, gun carriage, etc., complete	1
Minié rifles	22
Colt's revolvers (three in bad order)	36
Remington's revolvers	8
Mississippi yagers (bad order)	5
Pistol belts	46
Powder flasks	42
Cartridge boxes	70
Pistol holsters	48
Henry's rifles	16
Double-barrelled shot guns	3
Marine glasses	2
Spy glass	1
Lot ammunition	1

OFFICERS' DINING ROOM.

Description.	Number.
Table cloths	3
Castors	2
Soup plates	16
Dinner plates	22

INVENTORY—Continued.

Description.	Number.
Dessert plates	17
Cups and saucers	18
Goblets	12
Glasses	15
Milk pitchers	2
Water pitcher	1
Syrup pots	2
Sugar bowls	3
Tablespoons	36
Teaspoons	22
Knives	24
Forks	29
Salt dishes	3
Dining table	1
Side table	1
Chairs	12
Window screens	2
Broom	1

GUARDS' DINING ROOM.

Description.	Number.
Tables	2
Table cloths	4
Window curtains	4
Large dishes	9
Knives	32
Forks	28
Tablespoons	47
Teaspoons	29
Salt dishes	5
Soup plates	55
Dinner plates	37
Dessert plates	22
Vegetable dishes	28
Sugar bowls	5
Syrup cans	5
Castors	4
Water pitchers	3
Tin pails	3
Dinner bell	1

OUTSIDE KITCHEN.

Description.	Number.
Range	1
Water heater	1
Boilers	8
Sauce pans	22
Coffee pots	6
Tea pots	3

INVENTORY—Continued.

Description.	Number.
Dripping pans	10
Tin pans	20
Tin buckets	2
Knives	2
Dippers	2
Pudding moulds	2
Soup tureen	1
Steamer	1
Gridiron	1
Shovel	1
Basting spoons	6
Frying pans	3
Skimmers	3
Tin plates	12
Tin cans	3

OUTSIDE BAKE HOUSE.

Pie plates	18
Baking pans	6
Tin pans	6
Bakers' knife	1
Chair	1
Seives	2
Scales, pair	1
Sauce pans	2
Brush	1
Broom	1

VEGETABLE ROOM.

Buckets	2
Tubs	6
Chopping tray	1
Knife	1
Table	1
Tin pans	3
Coffee burner	1
Broom	1

BUTCHER SHOP.

Platform scales	2
Balances, pair	1
Bar scales, pair	1
Truck	1
Meat blocks	2
Meat table	1
Meat saws	2
Cleaver	1

INVENTORY—Continued.

Description.	Number.
Steak knife...	1
Skinning knives...	2
Steel..	1
Meat tanks..	4
Desk..	1
Oil stone..	1
Meat trays...	2
Ration box...	1
Meat hooks..	63
Barrels used for pickling meat...................................	4
Steak pins..	2
Scraper..	1
SLAUGHTER HOUSE.	
Windlass..	1
Bull ring and two ropes for same...............................	1
Block and tackle for hoisting......................................	1
Gammon sticks for hanging beef................................	12
Cleaver..	1
Saw for splitting down...	1
Spreaders, pairs...	2
Pritchets..	2
Beef hook..	1
Boiler for heating water...	1
Sledge...	1
Axe..	1
STABLE.	
Drays...	2
Carts..	2
Water cart...	1
Sprinkling cart...	1
Double-seat barouche..	1
Single buggy..	1
Dray harness, sets...	2
Barouche harness, set..	1
Single harness, set...	1
Saddles..	2
Riding bridles..	2
Spurs, pair...	1
Pitchforks..	2
Shovel..	1
Broom..	1
Hand saw...	1
Curry-combs...	3
Brushes...	3
Extra horse collars...	3

INVENTORY—Continued.

Description.	Number.
Cart harnesses	2
Blacksnake whip	1
Double pole for single buggy	1
Block and tackle	1
Water pails	2
Sprinkler	1
Chairs	3
SHOE SHOP.	
Shoe benches	10
Sewing machine	1
Shoe knives	16
Burnishers	2
Awl handles	5
Lasts, pairs	21
Forepart irons	10
Seat wheels	2
Crimping boards	3
Stitch wheel	1
Strip awl	1
Seam set	1
Heel planes	4
Heel shave	1
Awl handles	20
Rasps	9
Skirring knife	1
Rand files	4
Edge buffers	3
Size stick	1
Whetstones	5
Pincers, pairs	7
Punch	1
Soapstones	4
Shoulder sticks	6
Peg floats	4
Shoe hammers	14
Shoe tubs	2
Shoe pails	2
Water pails	2
Boot trees, sets	3
Shoe pegs, gallons	6
Shoe nails, pounds	18
Flower wheel	1
TAILOR SHOP.	
Sewing machines	2
Scissors, pairs	4

INVENTORY—Continued.

Description.	Number.
Goose iron	1
Press boards	5
Stove	1
Desk	1
Water pails	2
Square	1
Work tables	5
Stools	5
Thread, needles, and thimbles, lot	1
BLACKSMITH SHOP.	
Bellows, pairs	3
Anvils	4
Hand hammers	4
Sledge hammers	4
Drill machine	1
Mandrel	1
Tire setter	1
Tire roller	1
Swedge block	1
Plates, taps, and dies, sets	2
Plates, taps, and dies (old,) sets	4
Anvil tools, sets	2
Shoeing tools, set	1
Vices	3
Chair pattern	1
Files	5
Barrow wheels	3
Pipe tongues, pairs	5
Brace drills	2
Cross irons, pairs	40
Iron balls, lot	1
Old iron, lot	1
Iron, bundles	4
Shoe shapes, bundles	2
Iron, bars	4
Axles, iron	2
CARPENTER SHOP.	
Squares	7
Compasses, pairs	3
Hammers	3
Hatchets	2
Saws	10
Planes	28
Hollowed rounds and bevels	31
Sash, set	1

INVENTORY—Continued.

Description.	Number.
Chisels	15
Guages	6
Braces	2
Brace bits	31
Augurs	4
Thumb mortice guages	4
Screwdrivers	3
Spoke shave	1
Wood files	3
Saw set	1
Boring machine	1
Clamp screws	6
Hand screws	6
Oil cans	2
Oil stones	2
Drawing knife	1
Work benches	3

TINNERS' SHOP.

Turning lathe	1
Gouges	7
Chisels	4
Compasses	2
Hammer	1
Vice	1
Work bench	1
Saws	3
Hatchet	1

WAGON SHOP.

Work benches	4
Vices	4
Wheel horse	1
Assorted felloes	56
Planes	12
Spoke shaves	2
Drawing knife	1
Dividers, pairs	2
Hollow augurs	10
Assorted augur bits	25
Chisels and gouges	10
Bevel	1
Screwdrivers	2
Squares	3
Hammers	5
Hand saws	5

INVENTORY—Continued.

Description.	Number.
Hand axe	1
Oil stones	2
Small wrench	1
Rules	3
Braces	3
Files	7
Hand screws	5
Wallets	2
Scratch awls	2
HARNESS SHOP.	
Creasing machine	1
Rounding machine	1
Splitting machine	1
Vice	1
Square	1
Round knives	2
Pincers, pairs	12
Assorted edge tools	12
Awls	20
Loop irons	6
Files	3
Compass	1
Pliers, pair	1
Hammer	1
Mallet	1
Assorted buckles, gross	7
TIN SHOP.	
Large bench shears, pair	1
Large snipes, pair	1
Compasses, pairs	2
Square pliers	2
Square nippers	1
Mandrel	1
Large chisel	1
Stokes	3
Square head	1
Chisels	14
Punches	6
Rivet sets	2
Squares	2
Stake	1
Vice	1
Screwdrivers	2
Drill	1
Saw	1
Files	3

INVENTORY—Continued.

Description.	Number.
Mallets	3
Hammers	4
Soldering irons	3
Formers	4
Folders	2
Gutter bead	1
Roofing tongue	1

GUNSMITH'S SHOP.

Turning lathe, with rest and turning tools	1
Anvils	2
Vices	2
Tongs, pair	6
Drawing knife	1
Calipers, pairs	3
Compasses, pairs	2
Iron saw	1
Brace	1
Hammers	7
Screw plate, with taps	1
Drills	30
Pliers, pairs	2
Soldering irons	2
Wrenches	2
Sand, emery, and brush wheels	4
Square	1
Shears, pair	1
Pincers, assorted	30
Files	24
Grindstone	1
Bellows	1
Chisels	8
Heading tools	2
Steel brush	1
Ladle	1
Wire, rolls	2

GLAZIER'S SHOP.

Chisels	4
Diamond	1
Screw driver	1
Putty knife	1

LAMP DEPARTMENT.

Lanterns	21
Small lamps	12
Reflectors	10

INVENTORY—Continued.

Description.	Number.
Large lamps	21
Lamp trimmers, pairs	3
Looking-glasses	4
Oil cans	3
Chimneys (assorted,) dozen	3
MATTRESS SHOP.	
Sewing machine	1
Sail needles (assorted,) dozen	1
Benches	2
BARBER SHOP.	
Shears, pairs	2
Razors	6
Barbers' chairs	3
Stove	1
Buckets	2
Brushes	6
Towels, cups, etc., lot	1
TOOL SHOP.	
Stone hammers	48
Cutting hammers	20
Stone drills	11
Mortar hods	4
Whip saws	2
Cross-cut saw	1
Circular saw	1
Scythes and sneaths	2
Shovels	15
Picks	12
Wheelbarrows	9
Extra barrow wheels	4
Sledge hammers	12
Crowbars	9
Jackscrews	4
Trowels	7
Brick moulds	50
Hand trucks	2
Hand bars	2
Hand hooks	2
Truck, tongue, and axle	1
Asphaltum kettle	1
Derrick, block, and tackle	1
Sifter and scraper	1
Branding irons	2
Steel punch	1

INVENTORY—Continued.

Description.	Number.
Water barrels	5
Water hogshead	1
Axes	2
Plum bobs	3
Spirit level	1
Iron square	1
Stone punches	3
Cold chisels	3
Stone wedges, plugs, and feathers	12
Road scraper	1
Oakum press	1
Sail bench	1
Palms and needles	9
Marlinspikes	3
Fids	3
Caulking tools, set	1
Pitch mop	1
Pitch kettle	1
Oakum, bale	1
Tar brushes, buckets, and ladle	2
Spinning jenny	1
Whitewash brushes	3
Whitewash buckets	2

PAINT SHOP.

Description.	Number.
White lead, pounds	40
Turpentine, gallons	2
Black japan, gallons	2
Boiled oil, gallons	2
Varnish, gallons	2
Brown japan, gallons	1
Furniture varnish, gallons	1
Assorted paints, pounds	72
Pumice stone, pounds	3
Pallet knife	1
Putty knives	2
Flag stone	1
Benches	2
Table	1
Mixed paints, pounds	30
Assorted paint brushes	23
Paint buckets	12
Paint mill	1
Graining combs, set	1
Funnel	1
Chamois	1
Scoops	3
Square	1
Paint and oil cans, lot	1

INVENTORY—Continued.

LIST OF BLANKETS AND MATTRESSES INSIDE PRISON WALLS.

PLACE.	MATTRESSES.		BLANKETS.	
	New.	Old & worn.	New.	Old & worn.
Old prison.............................	366	24	669	83
Middle prison........................	186	7	334	49
South prison.........................	73	24	175	18
Hospital................................	14	....	24	....
Wash house...........................	....	....	15	2
Female department................	5	....	11	....
Totals........................	644	55	1,228	152

Description.	Number.
CAPTAIN OF YARD'S ROOM.	
Wardrobe...	1
Bureau..	1
Bedstead, blankets, sheets, etc.............................	1
Chairs...	3
Writing table and fixtures......................................	1
Washstand and fixtures...	1
Tables...	2
Water buckets...	2
Looking-glass..	1
Clock..	1
Coal box...	1
Coal bucket..	1
Map..	1
Spittoon..	1
Grate, poker, and shovel.......................................	1
Night lamp...	1
TURNKEY'S OFFICE.	
Writing desks and fixtures.....................................	2
Tables...	2
Washstands	2
Stamp and letter press..	1
Looking-glass..	1
Chairs...	3
Stools...	2
Water pitchers..	2
Bedstead, mattress, blankets, sheets, etc...............	1
Map..	1

INVENTORY—Continued.

Description.	Number.
Books of records, etc.	20
Spittoon	1
Grate, shovel, and poker	1
LIBRARY.	
Volumes, assorted	960
PRISON BAKERY.	
Bake oven	1
Bread tray	1
Scales, pair	1
Peels	2
Yeast tubs	2
Ferment barrels	2
Bread pans	20
Bread boxes	9
Flour sieves	2
Long pokers	2
Flour scrapers	2
Duster	1
Broom	1
Water buckets	2
PRISON DINING ROOM.	
Tables	57
Buckets	23
Bread trays	5
Water barrel	1
Swill tubs	3
Cupboards	2
Dippers	12
Tin plates	550
Large bread knife	1
Large bread pans	2
Brooms	6
HOSPITAL KITCHEN.	
Boilers	5
Sauce pans	3
Baking pans	3
Large tin pans	3
Chopping knife	1
Carving knife	1
Spoons	3
Small tin dishes	4
Water buckets	3

INVENTORY—Continued.

Description.	Number.
Water barrel..	1
Cupboard...	1
Locker..	1
Sink...	1
Broom..	1
Large cook stove and fixtures...............................	1
PRISON KITCHEN.	
Range and 4 boilers...	1
Large water cask..	1
Water tub..	1
Lockers...	3
Barrels..	8
Salt tub...	1
Steels..	2
Forks..	2
Buckets...	8
Wash tubs..	4
Meat trays...	2
Pans..	4
Bean tubs...	4
Stools...	8
Dippers...	6
Paddles..	3
Potato masher...	1
Sieves...	2
Strainers..	2
Pokers..	2
Shovel..	1
Large spoons..	2
Brooms...	2
Grease tub...	1
Coffee mills...	2
Carving knives..	8
Coal box...	1
LAUNDRY.	
Clothes press..	1
Flat irons...	6
Small tables..	2
Desks...	2
Clothes chest..	1
Wash tubs..	6
Wash boards...	6
Clothes pins, dozen...	5
Clothes lines, feet..	400
Large table..	1

INVENTORY—Continued.

Description.	Number.
s...	3
pe for hot water.............	1
neral use..	1
'..................	1
s..	3
l...	2
pipe................................	1
es, tier.....	1

FEMALE DEPARTMENT.

Description.	Number.
....	1
s..	3
id fixtures...	1
....	3
....	1
....	4

HOSPITAL.

Description.	Number.
....	1
s....,...	3
....	7
....	2
....	10
....	3
....	6
....	1
....	1
urnkey, for extracting teeth, pairs...............	2
tures... .	1
....	12
....	7
....	1
....	2
....	2

LIVE STOCK.

Description.	Number.
....	6
....	4
....	1
....	1
....	22
....	155
....	45
....	50
....	9

RECAPITULATION.

Ordnance Department—		
Mounted guns, carriages, etc.	$3,000 00	
Small arms and accoutrements	2,000 00	
Field glasses	75 00	
		$5,075 00
Officers quarters, guards', and reception rooms—		
Beds and bedding	2,000 00	
Furniture	1,000 00	
		3,000 00
Kitchen, bakery, and dining rooms of officers and guards		525 00
Live stock, wagons, etc.—		
Horses	600 00	
Cows	270 00	
Hogs and pigs	360 00	
Hens, ducks, and geese	75 50	
Carriages	360 00	
Carts, drays, and water wagons	185 00	
Saddlery and harness	300 00	
		2,150 50
Butcher shop and slaughter house		450 00
Cells and rooms inside of walls—		
Beds, bunks, and bedding	7,000 00	
Dippers, buckets, tubs, etc.	700 00	
		7,700 00
Library		180 00
Female prison		70 00
Hospital		140 00
Hospital kitchen		155 00
Prison kitchen and dining room		600 00
Prison bakery		100 00
Laundry		350 00
Lamp department		210 00
Tool house		500 00
Carpenter shop		150 00
Wagon shop		160 00
Turner's shop		40 00
Blacksmith shop		400 00
Gunsmith shop		400 00
Paint shop		150 00
Tin shop		50 00
Tailor shop		150 00
Shoe shop		150 00
Saddler shop		160 00
Mattress shop		30 00
Barber shop		25 00
Glazier's shop		15 00
Total		$23,085 50

REPORT

OF THE

JOINT COMMITTEE

ON THE

STATE PRISON.

REPORT

OF THE

JOINT COMMITTEE

ON THE

STATE PRISON.

D. W. GELWICKS.........STATE PRINTER.

REPORT.

To the Hon. the Assembly of California:

MR. SPEAKER: The undersigned Committees on State Prison beg leave to report that, in pursuance of the duty assigned them, they have visited the prison and made an examination of its condition.

In the pursuit of their investigations, several witnesses were sworn and examined, both at the prison and at San Francisco, and your committee submit the conclusions herein as founded upon the facts elicited by such examinations.

Your Committee had under investigation the various charges of speculation alleged by common rumor against the Warden and Commissary of the prison. They found no evidence to sustain such charges, and the facts show that whatever fault is to be found with the management at the prison is really with the system, and not with the officers. The buildings are not adapted to the classification, and at the same time the safe keeping of prisoners. The workshops are miserable structures, with no advantages for the economical employment of prison labor. There is not the necessary supply of water for manufacturing purposes and the proper cleansing of the cells and grounds of the prison. The prisoners are not properly fed. The diet should be more varied—the ration fixed and established by law. And the cooking department or kitchen should be under the direction of a free man, instead of a convict as at present.

Flogging should be abolished, and the discipline prescribed and made absolute by law. The tannery should be removed from its present location; in the crowded state of the prison yard it amounts to a nuisance. Supplies for the prison should be purchased by contract, open to all bidders by advertisement. There should be a resident Chaplain at the prison.

Upon the question of the erection of a branch prison, your Committee express the opinion that the State must of necessity, within a few years, prepare for the erection of such a building, and it is important when projected that the serious mistakes made in the building of the present prison buildings should be avoided. The two brick buildings erected during the years eighteen hundred and sixty-four and eighteen hundred and sixty-five, to meet the urgent necessity of increased cell room, are but poorly adapted to the safe keeping of prisoners. The testimony of officers of the prison is unanimous to the effect that these buildings are constructed of such materials as to afford no security for confining the large number of hardened criminals under their charge, necessitating the confining of this class entirely in the old building or stone prison. This building contains forty-eight cells and seven large rooms, and in these apartments are confined three hundred and eighty-four of the whole number of prisoners. The seven rooms mentioned each contain thirty or forty prisoners, while the two brick prisons, containing three hundred and ninety-six cells, are used for the confinement of but two hundred and eighty-eight, a large proportion of whom are Chinese, who seldom attempt escapes.

Thus it will be seen that the unfitness of the new brick buildings for the uses for which they were designed renders the crowding of the worst class of convicts into the secure cells and rooms of the old building and prevents that classification and separation of prisoners so desirable in carrying out reformatory measures. Your Committee have had propositions submitted for their consideration with reference to the establishment of a branch prison at the granite quarries owned by the Natoma Land Company.

The owners propose to cede to the State a site for a prison, with inexhaustible quarries and sufficient land for cultivation, in consideration of the sum of fifteen thousand dollars, to be paid for in convict labor. This location we regard as a desirable one for this purpose, being connected by the company's road with the Sacramento Valley Railroad. The supply of water is abundant for the most extensive manufacturing purposes, and the labor of the prisoners in working the quarries, it is claimed, would always yield a profitable return to the State. It is a question whether the diversion of one hundred convicts would not at the same time relieve the old prison, and such labor be profitably employed in laying the foundation for a new and permanent one. The last report of the Board of Prison Directors shows that on the first day of November, eighteen hundred and sixty-seven, there were fifty-one prisoners under sentence for one year, and one hundred for two years. Two hundred and twenty-one were twenty-five years old or less; sixty-six had not reached the age of twenty, and one was but sixteen years old. Five hundred and sixty-four were serving out their first term, many of them for their first offence against the law. When we consider the fact that in the same institution there are many who have grown old and are hardened in crime, some of them serving out their fourth or fifth terms, some means of separating these classes becomes a matter of serious importance. We call attention to the recommendations of Governor Low, in his last Biennial Message, upon this subject. The workshops are in a dilapidated condition. Originally badly designed and poorly built, they are totally unsuited to the profitable employment of prison labor. The evidence of the contractors and the officers of the prison is to the effect that the erection of new shops would largely increase the value of the privileges. The principal contractors testify that with convenient shops and store rooms, they would employ one-third more labor at an advanced rate of wages. In other words, give the contractors sufficient room, so arranged that they can supervise and control the force employed by them, and they will employ from one-third to one-half more labor, at fifty cents per day instead of thirty.

The increase of prisoners and constant enlargement of manufacturing pursuits within the prison necessitates the erection of new buildings adapted for the purpose. In this connection, your Committee remark that there is a great necessity for an increased supply of water for the proper cleansing of the cells and grounds of the prison, as well as for manufacturing purposes. Measures should be taken, in connection with the erection of new workshops, to procure an additional supply of water for all purposes in connection with the prison. To accomplish this, your Committee recommend the levy of a tax of five per cent. on each one hundred dollars of taxable property in the State to create a fund for the erection of new workshops and the obtaining of a sufficient supply of water.

The prisoners are not properly fed. In making this statement your Committee intend no reflection upon the officers in charge. No fault is found with the quantity of food; and it is admitted by all witnesses examined that, with the facilities at their command, the management has been admirable. In the erection of new workshops, the basement, as in the present building, would be appropriated for a kitchen; and this should be designed and arranged to provide for the proper cooking of the food. At present, everything is boiled; and it is in evidence before us that the prisoner in charge of the kitchen has been in the habit of skimming the fat from the boiled meat and afterward selling the same to such prisoners as were able to purchase from him.

One of the prominent evils of the present management your Committee believe to be the system of traffic in operation at the prison. Prisoners are engaged in selling to their fellow-convicts such articles as are in demand, the business being done under the superintendence of one of the officers, through whom the supplies are chiefly purchased. This gives ample opportunity for those who have gained considerable skill as mechanics to supply themselves with all needed comforts independently of the prison fare. And as the skill mentioned is generally possessed by old and habitual offenders, a discrimination is established in favor of those least entitled to the same, and against the most deserving.

One convict, having charge of a portion of the prison stores, is allowed to trade in the same kind of articles as those intrusted to him.

Another evil, directly connected with the last-mentioned, is the permitting the convicts to cook for themselves.

This promiscuous cooking in the shops and in the yard, and promiscuous mingling of prisoners, is, in the opinion of your committee, entirely wrong. The cooking and ration, as heretofore recommended, should be fixed by law, and, if necessary, additional guards should be employed in the yard to prevent the assembling of, and free intercourse between, convicts.

Many of the positions about the prison, involving some degree of trust and responsibility, are filled by convicts. This, under present circumstances, seems to be necessary for the safety of the prison, but the state of things requiring it should be remedied as soon as possible.

Your Committee submit, that in the short time allotted to them, a satisfactory report of the complicated financial accounts of the institution is simply impossible. In the performance of this duty, a committee should have full power and ample time to make a minute and unlimited investigation. This duty might be effectually performed by the committee hereinafter recommended to be appointed by the Governor.

Your Committee recommend that the ration should be fixed and established by law, and the kitchen placed under the direction of a free man.

Your Committee find, in their investigations, that gambling is practiced by the prisoners to a considerable extent. This evil originates, we believe, in the custom of permitting the prisoners, without restraint, the earnings received from contractors for overwork. Some idea of the magnitude of this evil may be gathered from the statement of one of the contractors examined, who testified that he had paid forty-five hundred dollars for overwork and in weekly stipends to the men employed by him in one year.

Your Committee believe that a regulation should be adopted requiring the greater amount of each convict's earnings for such overwork to be deposited with the Warden, and reserved for his discharge, allowing a small portion to be used for any proper purpose. The enforcement of such a regulation would effectually break up the gambling evil, and would be of great benefit to discharged prisoners.

In the matter of prison discipline, your Committee examined several witnesses—among others, the Visiting Physician. The testimony shows that the system of flogging is practiced as a mode of punishment. And although the testimony of the Physician, and all the officers of the prison examined, was unanimous in sustaining the necessity of this mode of punishment, with the present facilities for confining and guarding the prisoners—and the Physician also testifies that no case of severe flogging has come to his knowledge for several years—yet your Committee regard it as the relic of a barbarous age, and a practice that should be abolished and some mode adopted more in accordance with the usages of modern discipline, that the prison may be, as it should be in some measure, a reformatory institution.

Your Committee recommend the appointment of a Chaplain, believing, if the proper person be appointed, such an officer would be of great benefit in carrying out such reformatory measures as may be attempted.

They also recommend an appropriation of five hundred dollars ($500) for the increase of the Prison Library, said amount to be expended in the purchase of suitable books by the Chaplain of the prison, under the supervision of the Directors. The library at present consists of a small collection of books, valued in the inventory of prison property at one hundred and eighty dollars ($180).

The present commutation law has worked so well as a means of discipline that we recommend an extension of its provisions so as to allow to a convict, for constant good behavior, an increase of commutation in accordance with the length of his sentence. The law has been fairly tried in other States, and has, we believe, received universal commendation.

Your Committee have had their attention called to a matter that has been presented in the last Biennial Message of the Governor and in the report of the Board of Prison Directors. There are many men confined at the prison who have been sentenced for longer terms than the crime committed would seem to warrant. The disparity in sentences for the same crime by different Courts is an evil for which there seems no remedy. Many of these cases deserve investigation. It is conceded that the Executive has not time, in the multiplicity of his official duties, to make this investigation.

In connection with this subject, your Committee beg leave to submit that if the many reforms in prison matters deemed necessary and recommended by them in their report should receive the sanction of the Assembly, the Governor should be authorized to appoint a commission, with authority to make this investigation and sort out from the seven hundred prisoners all whose crimes have been adequately punished, or whose faithful labor and uniform good conduct give assurance of the sincerity of repentence. The recommendation of said commission to the Executive would be his warrant upon which to grant pardons.

This commission should also be authorized to visit any jail, prison or other house of detention in the State to collect information upon which to base a prison system, and submit the same to the next Legislature, with such suggestions and recommendations as may be necessary for the correction of the evils complained of. To this commission might also be intrusted the designing and superintendence of the erection of the new buildings for workshops.

Your Committee examined the armory and found some twenty of the yagers in bad condition. They should be disposed of at once and Henry's rifles substituted.

The net indebtedness of the prison, December thirty-first, eighteen hundred and sixty-seven, was thirty-four thousand one hundred and eighty-four dollars and ninety-five cents. The deficiency for the six months ending July first, eighteen hundred and sixty-eight, will amount to about forty thousand dollars. And your Committee recommend an appropriation of seventy-four thousand one hundred and eighty-four dollars and ninety-five cents to pay such indebtedness and meet the deficiency.

The Board of State Prison Directors estimate the appropriation necessary for the two years ending July first, eighteen hundred and seventy, at one hundred and fifty thousand dollars; and as there is no good reason to anticipate a decrease in the number of prisoners for that period, that amount will probably be required.

J. C. CRIGLER,
Chairman of Assembly Committee;

J. J. GREEN,
Chairman of Senate Committee.

Sacramento City, February 14th, 1868.

THIRTY-SECOND ANNUAL REPORT

OF THE

BOARD OF TRUSTEES AND OFFICERS

OF THE

OHIO INSTITUTION

FOR THE

EDUCATION OF THE BLIND,

TO THE

GOVERNOR OF THE STATE OF OHIO,

FOR THE YEAR 1868.

COLUMBUS:
COLUMBUS PRINTING COMPANY, STATE PRINTERS.
1869.

THIRTY-SECOND ANNUAL REPORT

OF THE

BOARD OF TRUSTEES AND OFFICERS

OF THE

OHIO INSTITUTION

FOR THE

EDUCATION OF THE BLIND,

TO THE

GOVERNOR OF THE STATE OF OHIO,

FOR THE YEAR 1868.

COLUMBUS:
COLUMBUS PRINTING COMPANY, STATE PRINTERS.
1869.

BOARD OF TRUSTEES.

FRANCIS C. SESSIONS, Esq., *Columbus*, Franklin County.
STILLMAN WITT, Esq., *Cleveland*, Cuyahoga County.
HENRY C. NOBLE, Esq., *Columbus*, Franklin County.

OFFICERS OF THE INSTITUTION.

SUPERINTENDENT,
G. L. SMEAD, M.A.

TEACHERS:
W. H. RICE, M.A.,   Mrs. A. E. HEYL,
Mrs. E. P. RICE,   Mrs. H. A. SMEAD,
GEORGE B. LINDSAY.

TEACHERS OF MUSIC:
H. J. NOTHNAGLE,   Miss ANNA M. BERGUNDTHAL,
A. L. BORER,   Miss CAROLINE C. HANNA.

TEACHER OF MECHANICS,
HENRY HAUENSTEIN.

PHYSICIAN,
J. W. HAMILTON, M.D.

STEWARD,
GEO. W. HEYL.

MATRON,
Miss OLIVE M. BROWN.

ASSISTANT MATRON,
Miss RUTH C. BARTLETT.

SEAMSTRESS,
Miss LIBBIE CARLISLE.

VISITORS' ATTENDANT,
Miss JANE MUNNELL.

REPORT OF THE TRUSTEES.

To His Excellency R. B. HAYES,
      Governor of Ohio:

The Trustees of the Institution for the Blind respectfully report, that the Institution under their charge is as prosperous as it can be under the present disadvantages growing out of the condition of the building. We sincerely regret that the Legislature, hitherto, have not granted our request for a new building for this Institution. We have exhausted all argument on this subject, and can only call the attention of the Legislature to our annual reports for 1866 and 1867, and to the careful report of our Superintendent, herewith submitted, as to the necessity for this building. We also regret to report that our former Superintendent, Dr. Asa D. Lord, so long connected with this Institution, felt constrained to resign his office, upon a call for his services made by the Trustees of the New York State Institution for the Blind at Batavia. In view of the long and faithful services of Dr. Lord as our Superintendent, we passed the following resolutions:

"*Resolved*, That it is with sincere regret that we receive the resignation of our Superintendent, Dr. Asa D. Lord, who has filled his office for the past twelve years to the entire satisfaction of the Trustees of this Institution, and to the acceptance of the public. His experience as an educator, his earnest devotion to duty, his integrity as an officer and man, and his high Christian character, entitle him to our confidence and esteem, and we cordially commend him to the Trustees of the New York State Institution for the Blind, and to the people of the State of New York, as a man eminently fit for the place to which he has been appointed; and we hereby tender him our best wishes for his future success.

"*Resolved*, That we accept the resignation of Dr. Asa D. Lord as Superintendent of the Ohio Institution for the Education of the Blind, to take effect on the 15th day of August, 1868."

We appointed Mr. George L. Smead Superintendent, in place of Dr. Lord, as he was the oldest teacher in the Institution, and a gentleman whom we deemed in every way qualified for the place. He has entered upon the duties with energy and intelligence, and we feel assured will do all he can to keep this Institution up to its high position. By the resignation of Dr. Lord, we lost the services of Mrs. Lord, who has acted as teacher in the Asylum while her husband was Superintendent. She was a lady every way qualified for the place, and we feel that the pupils, indeed, lost a mother when she left them. These changes have induced a few other changes in teachers and officers, necessary for the efficient organization of the Institution, and we hope to be able to report hereafter our usual prosperity.

The Steward herewith submits his report, and we feel confident that this office is as satisfactorily filled as in any similar institution.

We shall need for current expenses,

For the year	$25,000
For Salaries of Officers and Teachers	8,500

We shall also have to ask for an appropriation of twelve or fifteen thousand dollars to repair the present building, putting on a new roof and constructing suitable bathing arrangements for the pupils. If the plan of a new building can be settled at the present session of the Legislature, the bathing rooms might be made to conform to the building to be erected.

HENRY C. NOBLE,
F. C. SESSIONS,
STILLMAN WITT,
Trustees.

REPORT OF SUPERINTENDENT.

The session of school, which closed in June last, was prosperous as usual. Teachers and pupils co-operated to secure success in the course of study pursued. One hundred and forty-four pupils were in attendance during the year. Of these eighty-four were males and sixty females. Twenty-nine were new pupils. Up to this time in the present session, which began September 9th, one hundred and fifteen have been enrolled, of whom nineteen are new pupils. Thirty-eight, who are entitled to more time, are remaining away this year.

On the first of August last, Dr. A. D. Lord, for twelve years the efficient and beloved Superintendent of this Institution, resigned, to accept a similar position in the State of New York. His faithful labors here have placed this Institution among the first in the land. The blind of Ohio loved him as a father; and their gratitude, if it could be gathered in one heartfelt expression, would, I am sure, repay him for a lifetime devoted to the unfortunate.

His resignation involved that of Mrs. Lord, who so long has been a faithful teacher and loving mother to the pupils of this Institution.

Also, just before the commencement of the term, Miss M. C. Le Duc and Miss M. Tipton resigned their positions, involving a loss of valuable experience in our corps of teachers.

The vacancies have been filled by the appointment of Mrs. Smead, who teaches during the morning hours; Mr. W. H. Rice, Mrs. E. P. Rice and Miss C. C. Hanna. Mr. A. L. Borer, a recent graduate, has been employed as an additional music teacher. Miss Libbie Carlisle has been appointed seamstress, in place of Miss L. J. Post, resigned. The other officers and teachers remain in their positions, and we hope that the school may continue its prosperity.

Changes must take place from time to time in our corps of teachers; but the fact becomes more and more evident, that experience for a teacher of the blind is invaluable; not the mere experience of school-room routine, but of the patient, earnest work of adapting the instruction to the peculiar capacity of each scholar.

The course of study pursued last year comprised Reading, Spelling,

Writing, Arithmetic, Grammar, Geography, Physiology, Natural Philosophy, Chemistry, Physical Geography, Astronomy, Botany, Algebra, Mental Science, Moral Science, Logic and Music.

In the work department the females were engaged in sewing, knitting and bead-work; the males in broom making.

The girls also assisted in the domestic department of the household, making their own beds and washing dishes. While it is important that we should instruct our pupils so that they may gain a livelihood, it is also important that they learn those things which will make them useful and agreeable members of the family; for though many will support themselves, yet many others, especially of the females, will find homes with their friends, and their happiness will depend very much upon their disposition and ability to make themselves useful in the simple duties of the household.

The great and immediate want of this Institution is a new building. The present house was erected about thirty years ago. It was then poorly adapted to the purpose intended, as the wants of a large household of this kind were not well understood.

When completed it was supposed capable of accommodating sixty pupils and the necessary officers. Additions have since been made, which increase its capacity to one hundred. More than that number have occupied the building for several years. Yet, with the utmost crowding, not more than half of the blind of this State who are entitled to instruction here, can be admitted at one time, and much less than half can be safely accommodated.

There are in the State one hundred and seventy blind persons, entitled to the privileges of the Institution, whose cases I know personally. But those cases are from fifty-two counties. Taking the same ratio for the remaining thirty-six counties, and we should need to add sixty-eight more—making two hundred and thirty-eight who ought to be in the school or the work-shop to-day. Now, considering further, that in the counties represented at the Institution, there are probably many blind unkown to us, we shall see that the number is even greater than the above figures indicate.

It would be safe to say that, of the ten or eleven hundred blind of Ohio, there are two hundred and fifty who ought to be provided for in a State Institution.

Many of these, every year, are getting too old to be admitted to the school department, and must spend their lives in ignorance; and many in the county infirmaries, instead of supporting themselves, will remain a burden to the community, unless speedy provision is made for them. If we were assured that a new house would be furnished as soon as possible, the blind now unknown to us could be sought out and induced to come and receive the blessing offered them by the State.

The house is not only too small to meet the present and increasing wants of the blind, but is also very inconvenient. We have no suitable arrangements for cooking, washing, bathing and other necessary purposes; neither can we well introduce them into this building; and if we could, it would not be best, when we have such reasonable expectation of new and better accommodations. Indeed, this state of suspense has been a most serious hindrance to any improvement in our domestic apparatus.

We are also crippled in our school department—that for which the Institution was founded. The blind obtain with difficulty many ideas which the seeing catch at a glance; hence, for the blind, apparatus to illustrate the different brances taught is all the more necessary. We are deficient in this respect because we have no suitable place to keep in safety what we might otherwise obtain for this purpose.

We need more school rooms, sitting rooms, and reading rooms for pupils.

Music is a very important department in the education of the blind. We need more instruments, but can not have them, because we have no suitable rooms to put them in.

Physical exercise is essential to health in any school. In a school for the blind special attention should be given to gymnastics; but we have no hall in which to practice.

The question of health is a serious one. Our pupils, having less vigor than the average, feel very sensitively any influence tending to depress the tone of their physical systems; therefore they should be surrounded by the best possible conditions for insuring health.

Sixteen years ago, the physician then in attendance at this Institution, reported among the causes of an epidemic that prevailed in the house, a deficiency of sleeping apartments, requiring too many to be crowded in one room. During the year for which that report was made, the attendance averaged only about sixty. Last year there were, at one time, as many as one hundred and thirty pupils in the Institution. Within the sixteen years mentioned, the capacity of the building has not increased as the inmates have increased. If, then, there was a deficiency of sleeping apartments with only sixty pupils, much more now does this cause of ill health press upon us.

But it may be asked, why fill the house so full? We answer: By reducing the number we fail still more than now in educating all the blind of the State. It is a balancing of two evils, and to tell just the point where one becomes the greater and the other the less, is a difficult thing. And then, too, the applicants themselves are very urgent; they show the best of reasons for entering the Institution, their need and desire of instruction. It is hard to say to a blind man of twenty: "We cannot admit you now; you must wait till next year;" for next year he will be twenty-one, and too old to be admitted to the school department. It is harder still to say to some children of nine or ten years of age: "You can not come now; we have no room; wait till you are older;" for the poor child may have no opportunities for instruction at home; the parents may be ignorant and vicious, exerting the worst of influences. Perhaps the child may be an inmate of some infirmary, surrounded by the lowest of the low. Can we help reaching out the beneficent hand of the State to such applicants, even though the blessings it offers may not be unmixed with evil.

The physician above mentioned also reported bad ventilation as a fruitful cause of disease. Our appliances for this purpose have been increased since that time. Perhaps the ventilation is as good as can be made under the circumstances, but it is not adequate in the crowded condition of the house.

An insufficient supply of water and a lack of bathing apparatus was also mentioned as an aggravating cause of the epidemic referred to.

We have now several underground cisterns which furnish a sufficient quantity of water for ordinary purposes; but, in case of fire, this supply would soon be exhausted.

Our sewers have, of necessity, too little inclination for effective drainage; but in erecting a new building, we should grade and elevate the grounds, and place tanks in the attics, so as to furnish a head of water with which to clear the sewers. We are in immediate need of bathing apparatus, but nothing really efficient for so many can be put in without steam works. These would involve too great an expense for an old house like this. Our washing is now done in one of the wings, under rooms which must be occupied as sleeping apartments. The vapors from this are injurious; but we have no other place to perform this necessary work.

If a new building could be commenced the coming spring, the engine-house might be erected at once, furnishing rooms for washing and laundry purposes, and machinery to facilitate the work.

The danger in case of fire has been referred to in a previous report of the Trustees. We cannot retire at night without solicitude upon this point. In an old building like this it is impossible to make complete provision for safety. The furnaces and the building are not adapted to each other. The basement is too low, making it difficult to remove the wood work far enough from the heating apparatus. In a cold day we do not dare to heat the house sufficiently for fear of fire. If such a calamity should occur, our stairways are so narrow, and attics so inconvenient of access, that loss of life would be imminent.

We know that the cost of an edifice for this purpose will add somewhat to the taxation of the people of this State. The friends of pupils, and citizens of the State, often visit us to see what can be done for the blind. I never yet heard from any of these persons a complaint of taxation for such purposes; but many have declared their willingness to pay their proportion of any amount needed for such a beneficent object. The parent of a blind child often feels like this: "I have other children, who can see. I will deny myself, for them, as only a parent can; but for my afflicted child I will care the most tenderly; its misfortune brings it the closer to my heart." The State, in her free schools, expresses a similar sentiment: "We have children who rejoice in all their senses; them we will educate—the rich and poor alike; but for those afflicted with a life-long misfortune we will provide the more carefully. To compensate for their deprivation we will furnish increased facilities for education. If possible, we will enable them to compete successfully with their more fortunate fellow men."

Experience has proved that the work of educating the blind is a work worth doing—worth doing for the sake of economy, worth doing for the sake of humanity—and in any event worth doing well. For the full and complete performance of this work we need a new building. We need it now, because the present one is too small; because it is very unsuitable for the purpose, and because the blind are increasing in number. We need it for the health and safety of the inmates. The State is able to furnish it. The people are willing to be taxed for it. The blind are worthy of it. These reasons force themselves upon us now. The evils resulting from delay are increasing, and will increase, until the blind are placed on a par with the other unfortunate children of the State.

In conclusion, we would express our thanks to the people of the State who have sustained this Institution, trusting that their bounty may be extended until all the blind shall receive a share.

We are truly grateful to our Heavenly Father that most have been exempt from illness; that the sick have been restored to health, and that no calamity has befallen our household.

Respectfully submitted,

G. L. SMEAD,
Superintendent.

COLUMBUS, Nov. 21, 1868.

PUPILS INSTRUCTED DURING THE YEAR 1868-9.

MALES.

Name.	Post Office.	County.
John Adams	Zanesville	Muskingum.
Charles J. Adkins	Newtown	Hamilton.
Samuel Banker	Iron Furnace	Scioto.
Edward Benbow	Cleveland	Cuyahoga.
John W. Bender	Columbus	Franklin.
Julius E. Bliss	Ashtabula	Ashtabula.
Albert D. Borer	Findlay	Hancock.
David P. Bovee	Dublin	Franklin.
Daniel Brennan	Carthage	Hamilton.
Robert Brice	Ashland	Ashland.
William H. Brock	Cuyahoga Falls	Summit.
George M. Close	Mitchell's	Jefferson.
Robert Coen	St. Mary's	Pleast's, W.Va.
Patrick Coleman	Spring Valley	Greene.
Gurdon E. Cook	Copley	Summit.
Jeremiah Cronin	Springfield	Clarke.
Henry W. Couden	Cincinnati	Hamilton.
John F Crumholtz	Portsmouth	Scioto.
Burtis H. Dennison	Black River	Lorain.
Michael Fahey	Lima	Allen.
Samuel Farmer	Lowell	Washington.
Byron Fish	Cleveland	Cuyahoga.
Wilson H. Fulford	Dayton	Montgomery.
William Garwood	Kenton	Hardin.
Henry Good	Lockbourne	Franklin.
George E. Gore	Pharisburg	Union.
John C. Griggs	Lowell	Washington.
John W. Gurnea	Urbana	Champaign.
S. Addison Hagerman	Huntersville	Hardin.
John S. Hall	Highland	Ritchie, W.Va.
Charles Hamstead	Greenland	Grant, W. Va.
John Harmount, Jr	Williamsport	Pickaway.
John Harmon	Columbus	Franklin
James L. Harper	Malaga	Monroe.
George Heinlein	Bridgeport	Belmont.
Emuel Herman	Independence	Cuyahoga.
George H. Hodgkins	Columbus	Franklin.
Charles B. Hutchins	Logan	Hocking.
John J. Kelley	Urichsville	Tuscarawas.
William H. Leamon	Walnut Hills	Hamilton.
Thomas M. Lilly	Columbus	Franklin.
Adam Long	Hanging Rock	Lawrence.
Frank Lumb	Neptune	Mercer.
Isaac Lynn	Willetsville	Highland.
George W. Major	New Middletown	Mahoning.
John P. Martin	Nelson	Portage.
James McCombs	Warren	Trumbull.
Jesse B. McMillen	Dunkirk	Hardin.
Sylvester McMillen	Dunkirk	Hardin.
William E. Mortier	Elmore	Ottawa.
William O'Donnell	Cincinnati	Hamilton.

Pupils Instructed during the year 1868-9—Continued.

Name.	Post Office.	County.
Charles D. Patterson	Peru	Huron.
George S. Pelley	Columbus	Franklin.
Charles A. Pessarge	Columbia	Hamilton.
Thomas G. Popham	Democracy	Knox.
James Reardon	Storrs	Hamilton.
Thomas B. Runyan	Columbus	Franklin.
George C. Russell	Kirtland	Lake.
Charles Simms	Crestline	Crawford.
J. C. Smith	Pyrmont	Montgomery.
Walter B. Smith	Collamer	Cuyahoga.
Frank Syler	Columbus	Franklin.
Peter Thatcher, Jr	Cleveland	Cuyahoga.
Frank C. Thomas	Stow	Summit.
Charles Vaughn	Cincinnati	Hamilton.
John S. Van Cleve	Urbana	Champaign.
John E. Walker	Cleveland	Cuyahoga.
Martin Walt	Columbia	Hamilton.
Willie S. Weeks	Hilliard's	Franklin.
John C. Welton	Cincinnati	Hamilton.
Adam Zeh	Avon	Lorain.

FEMALES.

Name	Post Office	County
Mary F. Alger	Bristolville	Trumbull.
Helen M. Allen	N. Fairfield	Huron.
Mary A. Alexander	Cincinnati	Hamilton.
Carrie Betsel	Cleves	Hamilton.
Abby M. Butler	Rome	Franklin.
Sabra A. Callin	Rochester	Lorain.
Alice M. Close	N. Fairfield	Huron.
Martha Cook	Cleveland	Cuyahoga.
Elizabeth P. Daly	Ironton	Lawrence.
Catherine T. Davis	Utica	Licking.
Fanny Davis	Utica	Licking.
Maria Dillon	Captina	Monroe.
Louisa Driftmyer	Woodville	Sandusky.
Ann Driver	Minersville	Meigs.
Rosina Ernst	Pleasant Ridge	Hamilton.
Isabel Farmer	Lowell	Washington.
Martha A. Fox	Hanoverton	Columbiana.
Mary Friedenour	Newark	Licking.
Melissa S. Gibson	Dayton	Montgomery.
Ada M. Hackett	N. Fairfield	Huron.
Kate M. Henderlick	Reynoldsburg	Franklin.
Ella M. Hopwood	Dresden	Muskingum.
Mary E. Hull	Warren	Trumbull.
Anna Hunciker	Cincinnati	Hamilton.
Mary Jackson	Cincinnati	Hamilton.
Frederika Karg	Dayton	Montgomery.
Emma C. Keefer	N. Fairfield	Huron.
Mary A. Kelley	Pisgah	Butler.
Rhoda McCrory	Mungen	Wood.
Maggie McGrath	London	Madison.
Matilda E. Malott	Perrin's Mills	Clermont.
Maggie Y. Merriam	Chillicothe	Ross.
Mary Murphy	Delaware	Delaware.
Julia Morgan	Palatine	Marion, W.V.
Anna M. Nation	Mechanicsburg	Champaign.
Sarah J. Neal	Cincinnati	Hamilton.
Ida M. Newburn	Washington	Guernsey.
Mary J. Nowman	Nebraska	Pickaway.

Pupils instructed during the year 1868-9—Continued.

Name.	Post Office.	County.
Rosabel Penuell	New Alexandria	Jefferson.
Mary J. Popham	Democracy	Knox.
Statira Potter	Portage	Wood.
Rachel Quick	Delta	Fulton.
Mary A. Reed	Tallmadge	Summit.
Florence E. Richards	Marietta	Washington.
Sarah Ridenour	Elida	Allen.
Catharine Sauders	Cincinnati	Hamilton.
Mary A. Sigar	Hilliard's	Franklin.
Mary Smith	Cleves	Hamilton.
Celestia Terrell	Cleveland	Cuyahoga.
Anna S. Vigus	Lilly	Scioto.
Mary E. Wainwright	Blanchester	Clinton.
Lizzie M. Walter	Orrville	Wayne
Sarah E. Warner	Columbus	Franklin.
Sarah A. Watson	Chambersburg	Montgomery.
Mary E. Wing	Dublin	Franklin.
Frances A. Wooley	Middleburg	Summit.

INDUSTRIAL DEPARTMENT.

MALES.

Ferdinand L. Bartlett	Toledo	Lucas.
Madison Been	Columbus	Franklin.
John D'Arcy	Columbus	Franklin.
Michael Callaghan	Columbus	Franklin.
John Gallagher	Soldiers' Home	Montgomery.
William M. Laven	Xenia	Greene.
Norman Miller		Medina.
Patrick Owens	Cincinnati	Hamilton.
Noah W. Ratcliff	Bellaire	Belmont.
William Reynolds	Lockbourne	Franklin.
Ira Sproul	Cleveland	Cuyahoga.
George Walter	Soldiers' Home	Franklin.
Samuel Whiston	Columbus	Franklin.

FEMALES.

Matilda M. Britton	Hilliard's	Franklin.
Mima Datson	East Cleveland	Cuyahoga.
Sarah G. Farris	Van Wert	Van Wert.
Mary Thomas	Delaware	Delaware.

School Department—Males 71, females 56 127
Industrial Department—Males 13, females 4 17
                                                            144

PUPILS NOW PRESENT WHO WERE ABSENT LAST YEAR.

MALES.

A. E. Bigelow	Cleveland	Cuyahoga.
Thomas Cahill	LaGrange	Lorain.
Leonidas Homan	Caledonia	Marion.
Fredcrick Kilzer	Columbus	Franklin.

FEMALES.

Eliza Briscoe	Geneva	Ashtabula.
Lizzie Brown	Cleveland	Cuyahoga.
Lizzie Canavan	Cleveland	Cuyahoga.
Clem. A. C. Dwyer	Fredericktown	Knox.
Sarah A. Frazee	Cincinnati	Hamilton.

Pupils instructed during the year 1868-9—Continued.

Name.	Post Office.	County.
Sarah B. Hall	Cincinnati	Hamilton.
Ann E. Ibberson	Norwalk	Huron.
Arabella Jordan	Hamilton	Butler.
Flora Kilzer	Columbus	Franklin.
Mary L. Melott	Sardis	Monroe.
Isabel Palmer	New Alexandria	Jefferson.
Senna Schooley	Sabina	Clinton.

Males 4, females 12. Total, 16.

NEW PUPILS.

MALES.

Michael Aker	Delaware	Delaware.
Wilbur H. Clark	Weymouth	Medina.
Thomas Cowper	Cleveland	Cuyahoga.
David Dolby	Sylvania	Lucas.
Jonathan Foreman	Murdoch	Warren.
Lewis Hutten	LaGrange	Jefferson.
Edmund Jefferson	Dayton	Montgomery.
Jacob Kautz	Cincinnati	Hamilton.
Thomas Lunney	Soldiers' Home	Montgomery.
Lewis May	Cincinnati	Hamilton.
John V. Moore	Cincinnati	Hamilton.
Andrew J. Parker	New Harrisburg	Carroll.
William Selsor	S. Solon	Madison.
John W. Shively	Delaware	Delaware.

FEMALES.

Mary J. Driver	Minersville	Meigs.
Anna M. Little	New Waterford	Columbiana.
Mrs. W. H. Noble	Cleveland	Cuyahoga.
Sarah E. Reynolds	Union Furnace	Hocking.
Sarah A. Stewart	Zanesville	Muskingum.

Males 14, females 5. Total, 19.

Whole number in attendance during the fiscal year ending Nov. 15, 1868: Males 102, females 77. Total 179.

STATISTICS OF THE INSTITUTION.

The following chapter is inserted each year with the necessary additions, for the convenience of those who have not access to a file of our reports. The table presents a summary of the progress of the Institution. The statement of expenditures are taken from the reports of the proper officers. The actual expenses for each of the last twelve years are found by deducting from the whole sum paid out, the sums received by the Steward from other sources than the State Treasury:

Year.	Expenses.	Reports.		No. of Pupils.		
		No.	By whom made.	Enrolled.	Admitted Yearly.	Total.
1837	$7,907 51	1	The Trustees	11	11	11
1838	14,103 67	2	The Trustees	20	4	15
1839	13,196 22	3	The Trustees	21	7	22
1840	11,871 16	4	Mr. Chapin	35	6	28
1841	10,155 29	5	Mr. Chapin	50	19	47
1842	9,664 68	6	Mr. Chapin	56	16	63
1843	9,263 39	7	Mr. Chapin	58	17	80
1844	9,229 09	8	Mr. Chapin	65	12	92
1845	9,463 83	9	Mr. Chapin	68	17	109
1846	10,957 96	10	Chapin & Penniman	73	15	124
1847	9,937 12	11	Mr. Penniman	68	16	140
1848	10,569 20	12	Mr. McMillen	73	17	157
1849	10,446 95	13	Mr. McMillen	67	14	181
1850	10,630 50	14	Mr. McMillen	72	14	185
1851	11,101 93	15	Mr. McMillen	69	14	199
1852	11,952 09	16	Mr. Harte	80	21	220
1853	11,916 13	17	Mr. Harte	69	11	231
1854	11,828 66	18	Mr. Harte	64	14	245
1855	13,331 80	19	Mr. Harte	64	22	267
1856	14,319 32	20	Mr. Lord	60	13	280
1857	15,996 47	21	Mr. Lord	93	30	310
1858	18,887 95	22	Mr. Lord	105	22	332
1859	16,202 19	23	Mr. Lord	120	34	366
1860	16,626 24	24	Mr. Lord	120	17	383
1861	16,885 91	25	Mr. Lord	120	24	407
1862	15,294 42	26	Mr. Lord	120	25	432
1863	17,849 85	27	Mr. Lord	120	30	462
1864	19,891 38	28	Mr. Lord	135	39	501
1865	26,301 86	29	Mr. Lord	137	40	541
1866	27,694 58	30	Mr. Lord	150	44	585
1867	31,003 18	31	Mr. Lord	145	38	623
1868	33,346 35	32	Mr. Smead	144	29	652

PHYSICIAN'S REPORT.

OHIO INSTITUTION FOR THE BLIND,
November 30, 1868.

To the Trustees:

It is very gratifying to be able to report that the present year has been characterized by the prevalence of a very remarkable degree of good health. Not a single case of serious illness occurred within the year, nor have the pupils suffered to any extent from the minor diseases that have been prevalent among them, such as catarrhal, diphtheritic, and malarious difficulties. This is all the more remarkable because the past year has been attended with decidedly more than an average amount of sickness in the community at large. Much of this is undoubtedly due to the watchfulness and care of those in the immediate charge of the hygienic interests of the Institution.

Respectfully,
J. W. HAMILTON, M.D.,
Physician.

REPORT OF THE STEWARD.

The following statements present an exhibit of the finances of the Institution and its relations to the State Treasury, a summary of the receipts and disbursements, and a classified list of all purchases for the Institution during the year. The sum of $1,906.01, received from other sources than the Treasury, deducted from the total of disbursements, leaves $23,923.48 as the sum expended by the State for current expenses.

Respectfully submitted,

G. W. HEYL, *Steward.*

CURRENT EXPENSES.

Appropriation for first quarter of 1868	$5,000 00	
Partial appropriation for the year 1868	5,000 00	
Appropriation for the year 1868	13,750 00	
		$23,750 00
Drawn by Steward during the year		23,750 00

SALARIES.

Balance in treasury, Nov. 15, 1867	$3,334 64	
Appropriation for first quarter of 1868	2,000 00	
Partial appropriation for the year 1868	1,302 86	
Appropriation for the year 1868	4,857 00	
		$11,494 50
Drawn by Steward during the year		9,421 87
Leaving in the Treasury, Nov. 15, 1868		$2,072 63

Summary of Receipts and Disbursements for the year ending Nov. 15, 1868.

Balance from last year	$440 01	Paid wages of help	$2,224 10	
Received from Treasury	23,750 00	Repairs and improvements	4,701 51	
" for boarding	250 00	Groceries and provisions	11,616 18	
" for brooms, etc.	992 70	Miscellaneous items	5,497 19	
" for bead-work	382 06	Mechanical department	1,790 43	
" for hogs	181 25		$25,829 49	
" for horse	75 00			
" for sewing machine	25 00	Balance on hand	266 53	
	$26,096 02		$26,096 02	

REPAIRS AND IMPROVEMENTS.

Hardware, glass and nails	$236 97
Carpenter work, gates and cooperage	234 95
Paints, painting and glaizing	135 03
Repairing and repainting carriages	136 85
Blacksmithing	85 81
Sand, lime and gravel	289 94
Furniture and repairs	532 33
Whitewashing and plastering	138 97
Pianos, instruments, etc.	1,373 47
Harness work	68 85
Wells, plumbing, etc.	148 66
Lumber	176 16
Tinware and tinning	229 22
Sewer-pipe and cement	44 68
Furnace, stoves and repairs	472 43
Cleaning vaults	52 50
Gum hose	36 25
Paving gutter on west side of grounds	308 47
	4,701 54

GROCERIES AND PROVISIONS.

Meat, fresh and salt	3,469 63
Poultry and fish	173 13
Butter	1,321 12
Lard	545 69
Flour and meal	1,747 54
Cheese	110 63
Eggs	94 30
Rice and hominy	67 27
Coffee and tea	832 53
Sugar and molasses	1,291 83
Vinegar and cider	39 80
Salt, pepper and spice	67 70
Apples, peaches and berries	307 59
Beans	46 64
Soda, cream tartar and hops	18 70
Tomatoes, cucumbers, etc.	118 93
Bread, crackers, etc.	639 59
Indigo, starch, etc.	55 30
Potatoes	654 53
Candles	7 73
	11,616 18

MISCELLANEOUS ITEMS.

Coal, 6,000 bushels	$725 00
Wood	746 66
Gas for the year	311 04
Ice, two seasons	96 60
Drugs and medicines	183 60
Crockery	94 64
Trees, shrubs and seeds	15 00
Postage and revenue stamps	90 69
Books, stationery and printing	353 35
Binding	20 72
Freight	34 99
Hay, straw and feed for stock	841 28
Soap, hard and soft	311 87
Horses	350 00
Stock hogs	56 04
Cow	56 00
Mattresses	157 00

Feathers	$46	85
Sheets, blankets, &c	212	20
Dry goods, carpets, &c	626	03
Curtains, blinds, &c	52	60
Sewing machine	85	00
	$5,497	19

MECHANICAL DEPARTMENT.

Broom corn	$1,240	05
" handles	173	57
" wire and twine	50	01
" hammers and needles, &c	37	00
Brass wire for bead work	15	10
Paid pupils for bead work (overwork)	273	75
	$1,790	48

Persons employed in the Institution during 1867–8.

Name.	Occupation.	Compensation.	
Asa D. Lord	Superintendent	$1,200 00	per annum
G. L. Smead	Teacher	1,000 00	"
Mrs. A. E. Heyl	"	500 00	"
Miss M. E. DeLuc	"	500 00	"
Mrs. E. W. Lord	"	500 00	"
G. B. Lindsay	"	400 00	"
H. J. Nothnagle	" of music	1,000 00	"
Miss Anna M. Bergundthal	" "	100 00	"
Miss M. A. Tipton	" "	200 00	"
Henry Hauenstein	" of mechanics	900 00	"
Dr. J. W. Hamilton	Physician	300 00	"
G. W. Heyl	Steward	800 00	"
Miss O. M. Brown	Matron	400 00	"
Miss R. C. Bartlett	Assistant Matron	300 00	"
Miss Laura J. Post	Seamstress	4 00	per week.
Miss Jane Munnell	Visitors' Attendant	100 00	per annum
Jacob Rau	Foreman, etc	35 00	per month.
Andrew Volk	Gardener	30 00	"
James Oliver	Porter	10 00	"
Mary E. Board	Cook	3 00	per week.
Susan Rench	Baker	3 00	"
Mary Lane	Laundress	3 00	"
Mary Callihan	"	3 00	"
Mary Conway	"	2 50	"
Kate Kean	Chambermaid	2 50	"
Kate Cunningham	"	2 50	"
Elizabeth Seger	In dining room	2 50	"
Eve Lang	" "	2 50	"

SUGGESTIONS.

To the Parents and Guardians of Blind Children and Youth:

The age at which it is best for children to enter the Institution, depends very much upon the circumstances of the families to which they belong. If they can be under good influences at home, can have the care of mother and sisters, can take exercise in the open air, can be taught the use of words, can learn to count, and to perform some of the operations in arithmetic, and commence learning to read, it is unquestionably better for them to remain at home till they are ten, or perhaps twelve years old; but if they cannot receive proper care, and be taught some of these things, they should come at the age of eight or nine years. Those who enter at this early age need not necessarily attend every year until their pupilage expires. After learning to read, and making a good beginning in other studies, they may spend a year at home now and then, and by a little aid from their friends, may be constantly improving, or, at least, be prevented from forgetting what they have learned.

The following are some of the things which may be learned at their homes as well as after they enter the Institution:

1. To count and number, and to add, subtract, multiply and divide, etc.
2. The multiplication table.
3. To spell common words, beginning with monosyllables.
4. The meaning of common words.
5. The letters in raised print.
6. Items of general information: every blind child of six or seven years old, should know the points of the compass, the name of the town, county, and State in which he lives, the number of counties in the State, and of States in the Union, etc.
7. Facts in geography and history may be added as they can be understood.
8. Hymns, verses of Scripture, and select passages of prose and poetry, which they can understand, should be committed to memory; these will furnish them subjects of thought when they are alone, of conversation when they are in company.
9. Singing common tunes, or playing some simple instrument.
10. There is no reason why a blind child should not commence attending the district or other school with his seeing brothers and sisters, and take part in the exercises in spelling, mental arithmetic, geography, etc.; indeed, in everything except reading.

Blind children can learn everything which can be taught by conversation, and by giving them an opportunity to examine and handle objects, just as well as those who have sight; and there is no reason why their education should not be commenced as early as that of seeing children is. Indeed, instead of being neglected because they are blind, they should be taught with more care. During the last ten years, the parents of a number of blind children have written to me as here requested, and then pursued the course above recommended; the result is that their children enter the institution with as much knowledge and discipline as they could acquire in one or two years of tuition here, and their future progress is much more easy and rapid than that of those who have had no such training at home.

I will furnish a copy of the Alphabet, in raised print, to the parents of any blind child who will give me their names and post-office address, and shall take great pleasure in giving information which they may wish in relation to books or other things pertaining to the instruction of which children at home, or in regard to their admission to the Institution. For such information, please address G. L. Smead, Columbus, O.

After pupils have entered the Institution, it is important that they should be present every day while they profess to attend. There is but one session in the year. On account of the discomfort and the greater risk of health, etc., to the blind from traveling in winter, it has never been customary to have a vacation or recess at the holidays, and parents are earnestly advised not to encourage their children to think of visiting home at that time. We observe as holidays, Thanksgiving, Christmas, New Year and May-day; these we endeavor to make as pleasant to the pupils as possible. Between Christmas and New Year, the classes go on as at other times, and scholars cannot be absent for a week or more then, without great loss to themselves and great inconvenience to Teachers; much greater than would be the case with other scholars, because here the instruction is given almost entirely by the Teacher, and the scholar who is absent cannot make up the missing lessons by studying them from books. The only possible way is for the Teacher to sit down and do all the work over again. If this is not done, the pupil must suffer the inconvenience of his loss during the remainder of the term.

It has been our constant aim to secure to our pupils the greatest possible amount of benefit from the limited time allowed them here. For this purpose, after our younger pupils have attended one or two years, they are advised to remain at home a year or more, and if practicable, to attend school with their seeing brothers and sisters. Many have done this, and, instead of forgetting what they had acquired here, have learned half or two-thirds as much as they would have done in our classes. Beside the advantage gained from their great maturity when they return, and the consequent ability to understand better what is here taught, and to appreciate the valuable opportunities the Institution affords, these children learn much by thus associating with other children; the tendency to imitate manners or habits peculiar to the blind is obviated.

The same plan has been pursued by our older pupils, especially those who expect to engage in teaching; and it has been found that, by remaining at home a year or more, before spending the last year of their pupilage, reviewing and digesting what they had learned, ascertaining their deficiencies, etc., they are able, when they return, to accomplish as much during their last year as they might have done in two, had they not allowed their minds thus to mature.

The blind are, for the most part, to spend their lives among those who have sight. It should be the aim of all who have the oversight of them to render them as much like the seeing as possible. They should be carefully guarded against forming any habits which will be disagreeable to others. The blind are always noticed by strangers, and their manners and habits observed more particularly than those of other persons; hence it is a very great kindness to them to prevent them from acquiring unsightly habits, or to correct them, if such have been formed.

Parents should be especially careful to prevent their boys from forming the habit of using tobacco; its influence on all who begin to use it before reaching maturity is specially injurious, but it is even more so to the blind than to most others. Be assured it is no kindness to them to be allowed to form any such habits.

Much effort has been used to make the opportunities here provided known to the adult blind, and to induce them to enter as soon as possible after the loss of sight. The importance of beginning, as soon as may be, to labor as blind men, cannot easily be over-estimated. Every month's delay renders it more difficult for them to learn, and makes them more awkward, to say nothing of the moral influence of idleness, and the feeling of helplessness and dependence which must attend the person who feels that he is doing nothing for himself or others.

It has been customary to encourage our workmen to locate in the neighborhood in which they are acquainted, rather than to look to the Institution for employment, or to seek it in large towns. The wisdom of this plan is proved by the experience of every year. A village of a few hundred inhabitants, with the surrounding country population, will usually furnish employment for a broom maker, during the year; and the adjacent country will, in most parts of the State, produce all the broom corn he will need, so that he can obtain his material at very little cost for transportation. For the last twelve or fifteen years hardly an individual of ordinary force of character, who has pursued this course, and labored with perseverence and industry, has failed to make a respectable livelihood; while many have succeeded as well as the average of seeing persons.

The experience of nearly two hundred men warrants the statement, that any blind man, who has energy, and is disposed to be industrious, can, in a short time, learn to make corn brooms, and become able to support himself. The machinery necessary to carry on this business costs only fifty dollars. There are now in the State more than a hundred blind persons who are earning from $200 to $600, or more, each year, instead of being supported in idleness, at a cost to their friends of $200 to $300 per year.

ACKNOWLEDGMENT.—For the following papers and periodicals, sent gratuitously to the Institution, the proprietors will please accept the thanks of officers and pupils:

Cincinnati Weekly Gazette, Dollar Times, Ladies' Repository, Western Christian Advocate, Presbyter, Journal and Messenger, Christian Press, Religious Telescope (Dayton), Cleveland Herald, Geauga Democrat, Stark County Democrat, Highland News.

The publishers of these papers, and those of others, who are willing so to do, will confer a great favor by forwarding their publications during the coming year.

TERMS OF ADMISSION, ETC.

Applications for admission should be addressed to the "Superintendent of the Institution for the Blind, Columbus, Ohio," and should state the name, residence, and post-office of the applicants parent or guardian, and the supposed cause of blindness. Applicants must be between the ages of eight and twenty-one years; they can attend for such a portion of seven years as their abilities and improvement seem, in the judgment of the Trustees and Superintendent, to warrant.

Satisfactory testimonials, signed by two or three respectable citizens, must also be furnished, embracing the facts set forth in the following form:

"The undersigned, citizens of ——— county, in the State of Ohio, represent to the Trustees of the Institution for the Blind of said State, that they are acquainted with ——— ———, a blind boy, who resides in said county, and that they believe him to be of suitable age, bodily health, mental faculties, and moral character, to receive instruction.

"Dated at ———, this ———, A. D. ———."

Persons over twenty-one years of age, if free from bad habits, can enter the Institution for one year to learn a trade. Persons of this class have an opportunity to hear instructive reading in the evening; they are expected to be present at morning and evening worship, and to attend church on the Sabbath, like the other pupils. A man of active mind, and some acquaintance with the use of tools, can learn to make corn brooms in three or four months; some have done it in half that time. Those who have recently lost their sight, and who wish to learn a trade, should come here as soon as possible; every month's delay renders it more difficult to learn it.

For residents of the State the school is free, no charge being made for board or tuition; but parents and guardians must provide their children with good and suitable clothing and pay their traveling expenses, and should also deposit with the Steward a small sum for occasional expenses. For pupils residing out of the State the terms are one hundred and twenty dollars per annum, payable half yearly in advance.

The term commences on the second Wednesday of September, and closes the third Wednesday in June. The proper time for admission is at the commencement of the term.

Vacation continues twelve weeks—from the close of the term in June until the second Wednesday in September. Pupils are expected to spend the vacation at home, or with their friends.

When boxes or packages are sent to pupils, a letter should, at the same time, be sent by mail, stating distinctly how the same is to come, whether by *stage* or *express*, or as *freight*, and by what route.

All letters to pupils should have after the name this address—
(Blind Asylum),
Columbus, Ohio.

OF THE

TRUSTEES AND SUPERINTENDENT

OF THE

Arkansas Institute for the Blind

LOCATED AT ARKADELPHIA

APRIL, 1868.

LITTLE ROCK, ARK.:
JOHN G. PRICE, PUBLIC PRINTER
1868.

OF THE

TRUSTEES AND SUPERINTENDENT

OF THE

Arkansas Institute for the Blind

LOCATED AT ARKADELPHIA.

APRIL, 1868.

LITTLE ROCK, ARK.:
JOHN G. PRICE, PUBLIC PRINTER
1868.

OFFICERS OF THE INSTITUTE.

TRUSTEES:

HARRIS FLANAGIN, *President.* W. P. NEELY, *Treasurer*
J. L. WITHERSPOON, *Secretary.* T. A. HEARN
I. W. SMITH, I. B. McDANIEL,
W. A. TRIGG, H. B. STUART.
A. G. HEAVN.

OTIS PATTEN, *Superintendent.*

Mrs. S. M. PATTEN, } *Teachers.*
Miss ANNA B. PATTEN

Miss ANNA C. GREEN, *Teacher of Music.*

Mrs. L. E. LATHROP, *Matron.*

THOS. ROWLAND, M. D., } *Physicians.*
JOHN R. McDANIEL, M. D.

TRUSTEES' REPORT.

To His Excellency the Governor of the State of Arkansas:

The Trustees of the Arkansas Institute for the education of the Blind, would respectfully report, That after the close of this school as stated in the Report of the Superintendent, in September, 1863, the furniture and other property of the Institute which was liable to waste and destruction, on account of the unsettled condition of the country incident to the war, were sold by the Trustees, and the proceeds applied to settling the debts of the Institution, all of which were paid off and discharged.

After the close of the war, in the fall of 1866, the trustees met, reorganized and re-elected Mr. Otis Patten, Superintendent, who was thereupon duly notified, and he came to Little Rock in December, 1866, and by his exertions and exhibitions obtained from the Legislature, then in session, an appropriation of $8,000 to purchase suitable buildings, and provide furniture, books, and apparatus for the Institution; $1,200 for salary of Superintendent and $200 a year for each blind pupil.

When the above appropriation was received we proceeded to purchase the property known as the late residence of Dr. James K. Rogers, in the suburbs of the city of Arkadelphia, for the sum of $4,000 comprising a large one story frame building, with ten rooms, and about six acres of ground, a plat of which is herewith transmitted with this report for your inspection. The deed for said property was duly executed and recorded in the Recorder's Office of Clark County.

This property is in a beautiful and convenient location, and well adapted for a public institution. You will see by reference to the accompanying plat that the State does not yet own, but should by all means have lots A F, and the undivided one half interest in the two northern acres west of lot A. These can be purchased for $350, which is a very reasonable price. The Trustees should also have authority to give in exchange a deed for the small fraction in S W corner of lot C, for the fraction in N E corner of lot D; this would place the whole property in proper shape, and is necessary to the convenience and beauty of the location.

There were many repairs needed upon the buildings in order to adapt them to the use of the Institution, and we have expended out of the aforesaid appropriation the sum of $800 for the same.

It is desirable that the grounds belonging to the Institute be fenced, and we would respectfully ask an appropriation of $800 to do this and purchase the additional lots above named.

The Institution is in great need of a pair of mules and a two-horse wagon, and some cows to furnish milk and butter for the pupils, and for this purpose would ask an appropiation of $650.

We would also ask for an appropriation of $1000 to purchase another piano and additional books and apparatus for the use of the school, and $2,000 to finish repairs upon the building and to construct some temporary rooms for workshops, and sleeping and dining rooms. These rooms can be so constructed that they can be moved, and will answer for out-buildings to the main building when the same shall be built.

We would also fully endorse what the Superintendent says in his report as regards the appropriation of $200 a year for each pupil. It will not be denied by any one at all conversant with such matters, that $200 per year will not pay for board and washing alone, and they would be astonished if told, that in addition to this, the pupil is taught and trained, and all the expenses of assistant teachers and matrons, etc., had to be paid out of this small amount.

The Trustees do not think, under the circumstances, that they would be considered extravagant in asking that the above appropriation be increased to $300 per year for each pupil, and that the same be drawn quarterly in advance, as recommended by the Superintendent.

We herewith transmit a statement of receipts and expenditures, showing a balance against the Institute of $1,770, which is respectfully submitted.

By reference to the very able and extensive report of the Superintendent, it will be seen that there are about 250 blind persons in this State that should be accommodated in this school, and that with the present number (28) the school is very much crowded, and indeed so much so, that it is very inconvenient and uncomfortable for pupils and teachers, and also unhealthy, and we would therefore earnestly recommend that the Legislature make provision for a building that will suitably accommodate 100 pupils and the necessary teachers and employees, and such a building as will be an honor to the State, and a matter of just pride to all her citizens, and in asking or naming any sum for this purpose, we do not wish to ask any appropriation that would be considered extravagant or unnecessary. Of course such a building and the improvement of the grounds is a work of time, and the appropriation should be made biennially, as it should be needed, after the plan has been decided upon. The foundation of the building should be of stone (which can be procured near this place) and the body fo the building of brick. The foundation for the whole building and the walls and roof should be finished in the next year.

After full and mature deliberation, we are of opinion that in order to do this it will require an appropriation of $25,000. This sum may at first appear large and unnecessary, but experience will in the end show the wisdom of the appropriation, and all right-minded men and citizens will applaud an appropriation made in a liberal spirit by a generous and noble young state for the comfort, relief, happiness and education of her poor, unfortune blind. This is a matter, however, of suggestion which we submit to the honorable Legislature of Arkansas, believing that they will do what is right for, and act a noble and generous part towards this most unfortunate class of her citizens, and who, of all others, appeal to them by all those considerations and feelings which melt the eye of pity, or soften the heart with generous emotions.

In conclusion, we, as Trustees, would ask for the very able, clear and historical report of our worthy Superintendent, that full and careful consideration which it eminently deserves, and we here cheerfully bear testimony to the untiring zeal and devotion, and the ability, capacity, and energy which he has at all times shown since he became Superintendent of this school. Its struggles, its trials, its vicissitudes, with all of which he was connected, form a noble chapter in the history of his life, and we unite with him in rejoicing that this Institution emerged from all its difficulties and trials, and now rests secure under the fostering care of the State of Arkansas.

We cannot conclude without adding our tribute to the capacity, efficiency and energy of Mrs. Susan M. Patten, as an assistant teacher and manager of the pupils, and also to Miss Anna C. Greene, the music teacher, and Miss Anna Patten, also an assistant. They are both very efficient and capable, and deserve a much higher salary than they and the Matron now get, and which is all that the school can now afford in its present straitened condition financially.

With feelings of deepest solicitude for the future welfare and prosperity of this noble charity, which we have done all we could to sustain and build up in sunshine and in storm, we commit its destiny to the guardian care and protection of the Legislature of Arkansas, confident that they will generously and nobly maintain what we conceive to be the most commendable of charities, and what will prove in the end an untold blessing to this poor, sightless and unfortunate class.

We have the honor to be,
 Very respectfully,
  Your ob'd't servants,
   H. FLANAGIN, *President.*
   JAMES L. WITHERSPOON, *Secretary.*
   M. D. NEELY, *Treasurer.*

WM. H. TRIGG,
H. B. STUART,
T. A. HEARD, } *Committee.*
J. B. McDANIEL,
I. W. SMITH,

STATEMENT

OF THE EXPENSES AND RECEIPTS OF THE ARKANSAS INSTITUTE FOR THE BLIND, FOR FIFTEEN MONTHS, ENDING MARCH 31st, 1868.

DR.			CR.	
To amount paid for house and grounds	$4,000 00	By amount received from the State of Arkansas to procure buildings and grounds, purchase furniture, books, school apparatus and musical instruments, tools and stock for work-shop, and pay other expenses of re-opening the Institution	$8,000 00	
To repairs	866 33			
To furnishing	2,460 79			
To provisions	3,017 51			
To salaries	1,483 30			
To books, school apparatus and piano	525 65			
To traveling expenses and cost of exhibitions	585 09			
To stationery, postage, and text books	72 88	By amount received from the State for current expenses of quarter ending March 31, 1867	400 00	
To medicine	32 95			
To servant hire and labor	422 95	By amount received from the State for current expenses of quarter ending June 30, 1867	850 00	
To fuel	150 00			
To shop expenses	422 48			
		By amount received from the State for current expenses of quarter ending September 30, 1867	1,200 00	
		By amount received from the State for current expenses of quarter ending December 31, 1867	1,450 00	
		By amount received from the State for current expenses of quarter ending March 31, 1868	1,450 00	
		By receipts from work-shop	184 00	
		By borrowed money	600 00	
		By receipts from exhibitions, contributions and all other sources	101 67	
Total	$14,040 32	Total	$14,235 97	
		Balance in treasury April 1, 1868	$ 195 74	

There were unpaid claims against the Institution April 1st, for salaries and servants hire for the preceding quarter for repairs, books, provisions, etc., amounting to about $1,170 00
Borrowed money 600 00

Total $1,770 00

Seven hundred dollars of this amount is for provisions purchased in New Orleans, and not received at the first of April, making a deficit for past expenses of $1,070.

Vouchers for every dollar of the above expenditures have been carefully filed, and are at all times subject to the inspection of any person or persons authorized to examine them. While everything that our means would allow has been done to promote the comfort, health, and improvement of the pupils, rigid economy has been observed. Not a dollar has been spent, not a peck of potatoes, nor a paper of pins purchased for the Institution without a voucher, which voucher must be examined and approved by the Board of Managers, and a warrant drawn for the same by the Secretary and signed by the President, before being paid out of the Treasury.

SUPERINTENDENT'S REPORT TO THE TRUSTEES.

GENTLEMEN: As it is desirable that our Reports should present a connected history of the Institution, for the benefit of those who may come after us, this one will extend back over a space of five and a half years, to October, 1862, when our last published report was made. There were at that time connected with the Institution thirteen pupils—seven males and six females. During the ensuing year seven others were admitted, and one young man, who entered for a short time to learn broom making, was discharged, leaving nineteen—eight males and eleven females—connected with the Institution at the time of its suspension in September, 1863. Early in that year it became evident that, owing to the high prices of provisions and all articles of household consumption, the appropriation from the State (which before the war, when paid in gold, was barely sufficient to sustain the Institution,) would, now that it was received in a depreciated paper currency, prove entirely inadequate to that object; and it would have been necessary to suspend the school several months sooner had we not had a monopoly of the broom trade. After much exertion, I succeeded in procuring a supply of broom-corn from distant parts of the State, transporting the most of it two hundred miles, nearly one-half the distance in wagons. Having procured broom-corn, a new difficulty soon presented itself. There was neither broom-wire nor twine in the country. Several of our female pupils had learned to spin, and we might have manufactured twine out of cotton, but we had only one pair of cards, for which I paid forty-two dollars and a half, and these were in constant use either by pupils or servants, manufacturing clothing for the household. Fortunately we had a quantity of small wire, procured for bead fancy-work, which, by doubling and twisting and redoubling several times, we made sufficiently strong to tie brooms, of which we made and sold more than one thousand from October, 1862, to September, 1863. In this manner and by the use of hitherto unheard of expedients for supplying the deficiencies resulting from the wear and tear of bedding and table furniture, we managed to get along quite comfortably, without increasing the old debt of the Institution, contracted before we receeived State aid, until September, 1863, when Price's army fell back to Arkadelphia.

Our supplies of groceries were nearly exhausted, and could not be replaced. Flour had risen to $20 per hundred weight, salt $10 per bushel, and other articles in proportion. Bacon was not to be had at any price. Our only dependence for meat for a family of twenty-five persons had, for months, been the shanks and livers bought of the negroes who butchered for the Confederate government works, located here, with now and then a half-months ration of beef purchased of a workman. Even this meager supply now failed, all parts of the beef being needed for the soldiers. Our bedding, now much worn and reduced, a part of it having been taken to clothe indigent pupils, was entirely insufficient for cold weather. Only two hundred dollars in Confederate money remained with which to lay in food and provisions for winter and pay all other expenses of the Institute until January, and no one could tell what might be the condition of the country at that time.

Under these circumstances, by authority of your Board, I closed the school, and with some difficulty, owing to the disturbed condition of the country, succeeded in sending the pupils home, with the exception of three whose friends lived beyond the military lines. For these I procured boarding with kind families, who promised to see that they were cared for till they could be sent home ; and having placed the records, vouchers, and other valuable papers, including an inventory of all property belonging to the Institute (in value one thousand dollars) in safe hands, and procured a careful family to move into the rented house we had occupied, to take care of the furniture and other effects of the Institution, on the seventh of October, I left with my family, in a farm wagon, for Louisville, Ky., where we arrived safely on the 23d ; having, without arms or any weapon of defense, other than the shield of faith, performed a journey of near one thousand miles, by land and water, through a country swarming with soldiers from both armies.

On reaching Louisville, I was immediately tendered the position of teacher in the Kentucky Institution for the Blind, which I had resigned some years before.

I feel constrained to acknowledge the hand of our Heavenly Father in the wonderful manner in which our Institution was preserved and sustained through four years of trial.

The first two years we were without State aid and entirely dependent upon private benificence; and during the two succeeding years we were surrounded by privation and want, yet we never suffered for the necessaries of life, and sometimes enjoyed its luxuries; and, when this part of the country was to become the arena for contending armies—one of which already environed our very premises—the same kind hand protected us. restraining the passions of men and permitting us to depart, unmolested and in peace, to our various and some of them far distant destinations.

RE-OPENING OF THE SCHOOL.

In November and December, 1866, I visited Little Rock, in compliance with your request, and gave an exhibition before the Legislature then in session, with two blind pupils from the Indiana Institution, brought with me for that purpose ; and, having procured an appropriation, re-opened the Institution at Arkadelphia, early in 1867.

From that time to March 31st, 1868, thirty-five pupils—fourteen males and twenty-one females—have been admitted. Three have been honorably discharged, two have left in an irregular manner, one has remained at home, and one has died, leaving twenty-eight—ten males and eighteen females—now connected with the school. Of these, fifteen are orphans, and eleven half-orphans, only two having both parents living.

The past has been a prosperous year to the Institute. The officers and teachers have been faithful and zealous in the discharge of their arduous duties, and have cordially co-operated with the Superintendent in promoting the interests of the school. Their success has been manifest in the rapid progress of pupils in their studies, and in their great improvement in general deportment.

The pupils have manifested a zeal in the pursuit of knowledge which has been very gratifying to their teachers and which has astonished visitors to the school. I take great pleasure in commending their general good conduct, few cases deserving censure having occurred.

Though some of our pupils enter the school dejected and crushed by recent misfortune, and others, very naturally, have to go through a short season of home-sickness, they soon become interested in their studies and accustomed to school routine, and it would now be difficult to find a more cheerful or happier household than ours.

During the last year, ten pupils—three males and seven females—have made a public profession of religion, and united with the Methodist, Presbyterian, and Baptist churches.

In September last, Mr. S. F. Christie and wife resigned their positions as work teacher and matron. The latter post has been filled by Mrs. L. E. Lathrop, a lady of experience, who comes recommended by the Superintendent of the Missouri Institution at St. Louis. A temporary arrangement was made with Mr. Christie to remain in charge of the workshop to the end of December, when he left, the funds of the Institution being insufficient to afford him a salary that would support his family. Though totally blind from early childhood, Mr. Christie is an excellent mechanic, and under his instruction our boys learned to make brooms which will compare well with those of Northern manufacture.

We have recently been obliged to take part of the workshop for the boys to sleep in, so that before active operations can be resumed in this department, we must have more room as well as means to employ a competent teacher and purchase stock. This interruption of the workshop is greatly to be regretted, as to many of the blind the skill there acquired must be their only hope for self support.

The following is the shop account for the 31st of March, embracing both male and female departments:

Dr.		Cr.	
To amount for machinery, tools, material and overwork for pupils	$422 48	By work sold	$184 00
To balance	167 72	Brooms on hand	26 60
		By Beadwork on hand	25 00
		Raw material on hand	34 25
		By machinery and tools	320 35
	$590 20		$590 20

The above does not include a large amount of work done for the house, such as making mattrasses, brooms, bedding, and a considerable amount of carpentering done by the teacher of the work department.

Had we been able to get material, and to retain our teacher, the balance in favor of the shop would have been considerably larger, though it is doubtful whether it will ever prove a source of much pecuniary profit to the Institution.

It must be remembered that only the older boys can work in the shop, that, besides being blind apprentices, they are students, who spend only a part of the afternoon (five days in the week) in the shop; that their movements are necessarily much slower than those of seeing persons, and that in learning they waste material and make much unsaleable work. Add to this that soon as they become expert in their trade they wish to go out and set up for themselves. Under all these circumstances, the older institutions consider that the work department does well if it pays its way.

Our pupils have made good progress in music, under the instruction of Miss Anna C. Green, a young lady of superior musical ability. Eight have taken lessons on the piano, one on the guitar, and the whole school have been instructed in vocal music in two classes. The performances of the choir and of the juvenile singing class, do credit both to teachers and scholars. Several of the boys practice upon the violin.

Our classes have been rendered more interesting, and the labors of the teachers made more pleasant and profitable, by grading the school. The pupils are now distributed into three divisions, viz: Primary, taught by Miss Anna B. Patten; Intermediate, by Mrs. S. M. Patten, and Senior, by the Superintendent. For the branches taught in the several divisions see circular (Appendix B.)

The members of the Senior division were in school several years before the Institution was suspended. They also constitute a normal class, the members of which, it is hoped, will ere long be able to render valuable assistance in teaching.

The following classes have received daily instruction, viz: in reading, five; in mental arithmetic and spelling, three each; in geography, vocal music, and gymnastics, two each; in written arithmetic, algebra, English grammar, writing, science of familiar things, history and lessons on animals, one class each.

We have introduced the practice of gymnastics, taught by Miss Anna Patten, feeling that, as a healthy exercise and system of physical training, its importance in a school for the Blind can hardly be overrated. It has all the advantages claimed for dancing, and many others, without the objectionable features of that amusement, and all reasons which are causing its introduction into the best schools for the seeing, apply with greater force to the blind.

Though many pupils come to us in feeble health, the cause of blindness affecting the whole system, yet no severe case of protracted illness has occurred. Death has once visited our household, and in a very sudden and distressing form. George W. Martin, an intelligent, cheerful boy of thirteen years, who promised to become an ornament to the school, was accidentlly drowned, on the eighth of June last, while bathing in the Ouachita river with his teachers and fellow-pupils, as had been their usual practice in the summer season ever since the Institution was first opened. A messenger was immediately dispatched to the bereaved friends in Ouachita county, and the afflicted father arrived in time to see the remains of his son consigned to the earth. He visited the Institution, and after observing its arrangements remarked to several gentlemen that if he had another blind child he would send him here. This sad occurrence makes more apparent than ever the necessity of erecting a bath house on the river, which may be used without the possibility of accident. The female then, as well as the male pupils, could enjoy the luxury of river bathing.

Our thanks are due to Drs. Rowland and McDaniel for prompt medical attention whenever needed by the pupils. Hitherto their services have been rendered gratuitously. The number of pupils however is now so large, and the calls upon them so frequent, that it is hardly to be expected that they will long continue to devote so large a portion of their time to the Institution without compensation. As it is highly important that the Blind under our care should have prompt and skillful medical attention whenever needed, it will be necessary to make provision to meet this additional expense.

It may be interesting to inquire what has become of the nineteen pupils who were connected with the Institute at the time of its suspension. Eight of them have returned to school. One is supporting himself by tending a grist-mill in Pike county, and, though totally blind, I am told that he gives general satisfaction. Two of the young men bought the stock on hand in the work-shop at the time the school was suspended, and carried on the broom and mattrass business here. Two, who are too old to return to school, are with their friends. Both can read by touch, and both have the whole or a part of the sacred Scriptures in raised print. Three have removed from the State and three have not been heard from. Of those who have returned to school, the eldest two, one male and one female, (both orphans), have supported themselves—the former by teaching singing, tuning pianos and repairing clocks, and the latter by spinning and plaiting straw hats, both of which, she learned at the Institution.

I would call the attention of the Board to the crowded condition of our house. Though the building, purchased for the Institute a little more than a year since, is probably better adapted to the purpose than any other in the place, and accommodated the school very well while there were but few pupils, it is entirely too small for our present number. The comfort and health of the inmates, as well as a proper separation of the sexes, require an enlargement of accommodations. The hall passing through the centre of the building is the only room large enough to accommodate the household at once. This, besides being a constant passway from one part of the house to the other, we are obliged to use for the triple purpose of chapel, school-room, and dining-room. Our sleeping-rooms are much crowded, and we have neither sick-rooms or bath-rooms. Many of our pupils are young men and women at a very susceptible age. A marriage between two blind persons would be a calamity we could not too deeply deplore, yet with our present limited accommodations, we have none but moral means to prevent attachments being formed. The house should be sufficiently large and so constructed that an entire seperation of the sexes could be effected. It should also be sufficiently spacious to accommodate all the blind of the state, who are suitable subjects to be received into the Institution, and who may wish to avail themselves of its privileges.

There are probably in Arkansas not far from two hundred and fifty white blind persons, of suitable age to attend school. I have, during the last fifteen months, obtained the names or sex, and residence of one hundred and and seven in twenty-five counties. If the other counties are equally represented, and I know no reason why they should not be, there are in the State no less than two hundred and forty-eight blind persons, who are legally entitled to enter the Institution. Should only two in every five of these wish to avail themselves of the privileges of the school at the same time, we should need a building capable of accommodating one hundred pupils, together with their teachers and atten-

The following extract from the report of the Wisconsin Institute for the Blind, just received, is as applicable to Arkansas as Wisconsin:

"It may not be inappropriate to mention here some of the things that it is necessary to provide for, in preparing to accommodate one hundred blind pupils. It is plain that their condition, and the peculiar methods of their instruction, require special adaptation in the building they are to occupy.

"The scholars learn almost altogether from the lips of the teacher, instead of from books, therefore several classes cannot, as in common schools, be engaged in study at once in the same room. This makes five or six school rooms necessary. Some of these should be tolerably spacious. It must not be forgotten that we must provide space in our school-rooms, not only for pupils, teachers and apparatus, but also for numerous visitors. In fine weather every day brings a number, some singly, and some in parties of a dozen or more. They wish to see how the Blind are taught, and how much they can learn. Not only may the public fairly claim the right to see the operations of the Institution, but it is for its advantage that they should do so. They are, therefore, always welcome; but it cannot be denied that, when the room is small and the class large, they are sometimes in the way. The only way to prevent this, is to make the rooms of ample size. Great quantities of costly and bulky apparatus are required. Places must be provided where this will be kept safe from accident, and yet be so perfectly accessible as to insure its being brought immediately into use when the occasion arises. These should not be mere closets, but have space enough to allow the teacher, in many cases, to take the class to the apparatus instead of moving it. The great amount of attention given to music, makes it necessary to devote ten or twelve small rooms exclusively to that purpose. Then there should be three or four comfortable, home-like sitting-rooms, besides the school-rooms, which will partially answer for the same object. None of these apartments, except perhaps the music-rooms, should be very far from the ground; because it is unwise to bring in the natural objection to going up and down long flights of stairs, and to strengthen the natural inclination of blind persons to stay in the house, instead of moving freely about in the open air."

In addition to the above named apartments, there should be ample and spacious sleeping-rooms, sick-rooms and bath-rooms for both sexes, kitchen, laundry, dining-rooms and store-rooms and covered galleries, where the pupils may exercise in unpleasant weather. This building should be of brick or stone, and made comfortable in winter by hot air, or steam heating apparatus, both for the security of the building, and to prevent accident to the blind inmates. Open fire places and stoves are alike dangerous in a household of blind persons, while the uneven heat of the latter is positively unfavorable to health. Every mother of a blind child knows with what anxiety she watches over the unfortunate one during winter to prevent accident by fire. Each member of the family is constituted a guardian of the sightless one. The danger is greatly increased in a family composed mostly of blind persons who cannot watch over each other.

The appropriation made by the last Legislature for the current expenses of the Institution, has proved insufficient, notwithstanding rigid economy. Nothing has been purchased that could well be dispensed with. The Institution has never owned a carpet, and never but one rocking chair. All such luxuries, so far as we have had them, having been furnished by the Superintendent at his own expense.

Our supply of books, maps, and all kinds of school apparatus, as well as musical instruments, is entirely inadequate. Though quite a number of our pupils can read the Sacred Scriptures by touch, we have only one entire copy of the Bible, and only two copies of the New Testament in raised letters.

Our Matron and Teachers have been employed at very low figures, while their duties have been arduous. Their ability and zeal deserves a better remuneration, and would command it elsewhere. Even with the most rigid economy, it was hardly to be expected that with the prevailing high prices, two hundred dollars in paper could be made to perform the office of two hundred dollars in gold before the war.

It is doubtful whether any boarding-house in Arkadelphia would feed and lodge our pupils for two hundred dollars per year, to say nothing of tuition, washing and other expenses It must be borne in mind that the instruction of the Blind is more expensive than that of any other class. Books and all kinds of school apparatus must be prepared at great expense expressly for their use, and adapted to the touch. A Bible for the seeing can be had for fifty cents, while a Bible for the Blind, printed by the American Bible Society, and therefore the cheapest book, in raised letters, costs twenty dollars in New York. A slate for the seeing can be bought for twenty-five cents, while the metalic slate frame, with moveable type for the Blind, costs at least ten times that amount. The same may be said of maps and other school apparatus.

The Blind also require more teachers than the same number of seeing persons. One teacher of the seeing can easily instruct twenty-five or thirty pupils, but not so with the teacher of the Blind. When illustrations are addressed to the eye, a room full can often be reached at once; but when addressed to the touch it is often necessary for the teacher to give his whole attention to each pupil separately, thus occupying with one scholar the time that might be devoted to a whole class if they could see.

The great importance of teaching the Blind music and handicraft as a means of future support adds much to the expense of their instruction.

I would recommend that you ask of the Legislature a sufficient appropriation to put our school on an equal footing with similar institutions in other states. Much might be saved could we draw the appropriation for current expenses at the commencement, instead of the close of the quarter, and thus be enabled to purchase all our supplies at the lowest cash prices. We are often obliged, in order to obtain credit, to pay twenty-five or even a greater per cent. more for articles of absolute necessity than if we had the cash.

The following statistics of a few institutions will show what other states are doing for the Blind:

ARKANSAS INSTITUTE FOR THE BLID—REPORT.

Name of Institution.	No. Pupils	Annual Appropriation.	Cost of Building & Grounds.
Wisconsin	48	$16,000 00	Unknown.
Missouri	59	15,000 00	$50,000 00.
Kentucky	55	Annual allowance of 13,700 $25,000 00	About $100,000 00.
Indiana	96	300 00 per pupil	$100,000 00.
Maryland	29	25,000 00	140,000 00.
Louisiana Deaf Dumb and Blind	77	200 00 per pupil.	Upwards of $200,000 00.
Arkansas	28		$4,000 00.

In addition to the above the Legislature of Kentucky has recently appropriated twenty thousand dollars ($20,000) to pay debts and meet other necessary expenses of the Institution, and a committee of the Legislature of Wisconsin has recommended an appropriation of sixty thousand dollars ($60,000) to enlarge the building for the Blind. Virginia, North Carolina, South Carolina, Georgia, Mississippi and Texas, as well as all the Northern States, have also made liberal provision for the blind, but I have failed to receive definite statistics from their several institutions.

By a wise provision of the Act passed by the last Legislature of Arkansas, our Institution is placed upon the common school plan, and thrown open alike to the rich and poor, instead of, as formerly, requiring the former to pay, and the latter to obtain a certificate of pauperism from the County Court. The advantages of the new plan are so many and so great that I believe that most, if not all, the Institutions for the Blind in the Mississippi Valley, after trying the old system a while, have adopted it. It is owing, in a great measure, to this change that our school has filled up so rapidly during the past year. For though all of the thirty-five pupils who have been admitted, with perhaps a single exception, could have come in under the old law, very few of them would probably have come, if, in order to do so, they had been obliged first to get a certificate of poverty from the County Court. Of twenty-seven pupils received under the old law, only two paid for their board and tuition.

The number of blind who are able to pay is so small that it is hardly worth while to make a distinction calculated to produce bitter feelings between the two classes of pupils, and to keep out of the school many who are fairly entitled to its privileges. Under the old plan it was often difficult to determine who was, and who was not, able to pay. For example, Mr. A. is an industrious farmer, owning a small tract of moderately fertile land. By working early and late he manages to live comfortably and to make both ends meet, but he has a large family, and cannot in justice to his other children spare two or three hundred dollars year after year to support his blind child at the Institution. The County Judge doubts whether, in such case, he is authorized to give a certificate of inability to pay, and the unhappy blind boy remains at home, heartily wishing that his father was either richer or poorer.

B. is an orphan boy with an estate of a few hundred dollars, only the interest of which can be used till he is of age. This is sufficient to support him among his relations in the country, and with economoy would clothe and pay his travelling expenses to and from the Institution, but no more; yet, according to the letter of the old law, he could not get a certificate because he had an estate and he was doomed to grope through

Such cases were not uncommon under the old system, and some of the most promising blind children in the state were thus kept from school. The rich and those of moderate means help to support the Institution by their taxes, and may justly claim its privileges for their blind children. Under the present law all may feel that they are alike the favored children of the Commonwealth.

Some provision should be made for clothing destitute pupils and paying their traveling expenses. A large majority of our pupils, and probably of all the blind in the state, are orphans or half orphans. Of the fifty-four who have received instruction in the Institution since its organization in 1859, only six have both parents living. Many have no friends able or willing to clothe them. In a few instances counties have made provision for clothing, but some come to us without a change of garments, and without money and with their travelling expenses unpaid. We cannot see them suffer, but to provide for them is a heavy tax either upon the Institution or Superintendent. This should be done by the counties where the persons resides, and where their circumstances are known; and it should be arranged that the Institution would be at no trouble or expense in collecting, and so that there would be no delay in getting the clothes. If a blind child comes to us in mid-winter without shoes or stockings, which has occurred more than once, it is hard to be obliged to wait till his county act in the case. The difficulty may be obviated by the passage of a law authorizing the Superintendent to provide for those whose friends either through inability or neglect fail to do so, and present the bills, properly attested, to the Auditor, who shall draw his warrant on the Treasurer for the amount, the same to be charged to the several counties, who, in turn, shall pay to the State, and have power to collect from the friends, if they have the ability to pay. A plan like this has been adopted for the benevolent institutions of Indiana and works well.

The following newspapers have been sent gratuitously to the Institution, for which the publishers have our thanks: Arkansas Christian Advocate, Weekly Arkansas Gazette, Arkansas Weekly Republican, The Conservative, The Southern Standard, Christain Observer, Richmond, Va.; and the Deaf and Dumb Casket, Raleigh, N. C.

Permit me, gentlemen, in closing this report to express my appreciation of your kindness and courtesy to myself, both as an officer of the Institute and personally, through all the years of our intercourse. May Heaven richly reward your many acts of kindness to me and mine.

APPENDIX A.

CATALOGUE OF PUPILS.

NAME.	AGE.	RESIDENCE.	CAUSE OF BLINDNESS.
Lewis White	7	Little Rock	Congenital.
Sarah E. Shockley*	21	Van Buren	Small Pox.
Martha J. Williams*	24	Sebastian County	Sore Eyes.
Jane Hicks	17	Fort Smith	" "
Lsuisia J. Brooks	16	Benton	" "
Melinda Henry†	21	Hot Springs County	" "
William H. Griffin	21	" "	Conginital.
James M. Cloud	18	Rockport	Fever.
John F. Tyler	7	Clark County	Congetinal.
Josaphine Manly	18	Pulaski County	Unknown.
Francis M. Locke	9	Little Rock	Sore Eyes.
Lavisa C. Elliott	14	Dallas County	Scarlet Fever.
E. Monroe Switzer	19	Montgomery County	Accident.
Commodore Riffe*	15	Ouachita County	Sore Eyes.
Francina Riffe	13	" "	" "
John W Bellah	19	Richmond	Amaurosis.
George W. Martin ‡	13	Ouachita County	Fever.
Rebecca J. Mitchell	19	Pike County	Anraurosis.
Georgiana Brooks	10	Saline County	Congenital.
Robert G. Ward	25	Yell County	Unknown.
Lorena E. Miller	11	" "	Sore Eyes.
Caroline Rhoades	25	" "	" "
John Parks	17	" "	Whooping Cough
Lucinda Lawrence	21	" "	Sore Eyes.
Agnes Sinclair	17	Johnson County	" "
Louisia J. Burnet	15	" "	" "
Sophronia Bright	23	Saline County	" "
Mary J. Wortham	20	" "	Congenital.
Louisia H. Riffe	16	Clark "	Sore Eyes.
Robert Herron §	19	Yell "	Cataract.
Charles B. Pruitt	17	Franklin "	Fever.
William C. Brown ‖	16	Sebastain "	" "
Clendora A. J. Scott	17	Yell "	Sore Eyes.
Emily Eastwood	16	J8huson "	Congenital.
Elizabeth Kirtry	17	" "	Sore Eyes.

* Honorably discharged. † Remained at home. ‡ Died. § Left in an irregular manner

APPENDIX B.

CIRCULAR OF THE ARKANSAS INSTITUTE FOR THE BLIND.

LOCATION AND OBJECT.

This Institution, first organized in February, 1859, at Arkadelphia, Clark County, conformably to an Act of the Legislature, was re-opened in February, 1867, after a suspension of three and a half years.

It occupies about eight acres of ground, beautifully situated on a high bluff overlooking the Ouachita river, and within the limits of the city. It has for its object the moral, intellectual, and physical training of the young blind of both sexes.

ORGANIZATION AND MANAGEMENT.

This, like all similar institutions in this country, is organized under three seperate departments, viz: the School, the Industrial and the Household Department, each performing its respective office of ministering to the improvement and comfort of the pupils.

The general government of the Institute is entrusted by the Legislature to a board of ten Trustees, while the immediate control and management of its several departments is confided to a Superintendent chosen by the Board.

The Superintendent is assisted in the Household Department by an experienced Matron, whose duty it is to administer the domestic concerns, having the care of the female pupils when out of school, and the direction of the servants in their various duties. It is also her duty, under the direction of the Superintendent, to see that the sick are properly cared for, and the clothing of both sexes kept in repair.

The other departments of the school are filled with competen teachers appointed by the Board of Trustees, upon the nomination of the Superintendent, but who are directly responsible to the latter for the faithful discharge of their respective trusts.

PLAN OF EDUCATION.

The plan of education pursued at the Institute is designed to be thoroughly practical, comprehending all that is necessary for such a development of the mental and physical powers of the blind as is best calculated to place them upon an equal footing with seeing persons in their capacity for usefulness and self-maintainence.

The course of instruction, therefore, embraces, in addition to the ordinary school course, the science and practice of vocal and instrumental music; several appropriate mechanic arts, moral and religious culture and such other training as serves to establish becoming habits, energy of character, business tact, etc.

The following are the principal branches of the course:

PRIMARY DIVISION.—Spelling, Reading, Mental Arithmetic, Vocal Music, Gymnastics and Handicraft.

INTERMEDIATE.—Reading, Writing, Dictionary, Mental Arithmetic, Primary Geography; Primary Grammar, Written Arithmetic, Gymastics, Vocal and Instrumental Music and Handicraft.

SENIOR.—Written Arithmetic, Advanced Geography, English Grammar and Analysis, Algebra, Geometry, Natural Philosophy, Moral Philosophy, Physiology, Rhetoric, Logic, Astronomy, Vocal and Instrumental Music.

Reading is taught by means of raised letters, which are traced by the fingers. Several presses on both sides of the Atlantic are employed in embossing books for the blind. The following are some of the books which have been printed for their use in America: The Bible, in eight quarto volumes, Watt's Psalms and Hymns, Pilgrim's Progress, Dairyman's Daughter, Milton's Poetical Works, Select Library, Encyclopedia for the Blind, Dictionary for the Blind, English Reader, Blind Child's Book, in three parts, Fables and stories for children, Kneass' Introductory Primer, Kneass' Second Reader, Philosophy of Natural History and others.

Writing is performed with a lead pencil, the paper being placed upon a card with parallel grooves, which serve to keep the lines straight. The principles of Aritmetic and Algebra are taught orally, and the problems are solved either mentally or upon a frame, with moveable figures and signs answering as a substitute for the slate and pencil.

Most of the other branches are taught orally, and by the aid of maps and diagrams adapted to the touch. Music occupies a prominent place in the course of instruction, because it is not only a source of great enjoyment and improvement to those shut out from the visible creation, but to many whose talents enable them to pursue it as a profession it will afford the means of an honorable independence.

In the mechanical department our male pupils have been taught to make mattrasses and brooms. The females learn to knit and sew and to make fancy bead work. This department affords to the pupils exercise conducive to health and physical development, besides giving them a trade by which they may be enabled to support themselves after finishing their course in the Institution. There is no school on Saturday, that day being allowed the pupils for recreation. On Sabbath they attend church and sunday-school at places of their own or their friends selection; no sectarian influence being exerted in the Institution.

DOMESTIC ARRANGEMENTS.

The Institution is conducted, as nearly as possible, after the model of a well regulated private family. The pupils reside in the same house with the Superintendent and Teachers, and everything that our means will allow is done to promote their health and happiness. A plain, but wholesome and plentiful diet, clean and comfortable beds, frequent bathing and exercise in the open air, prompt medical attention, and kind nursing in cases of sickness, and the constant sympathy of friends whose pleasure is to minister to the welfare of their unfortunate charge, are some of the means used to promote these ends.

AGE OF PUPILS.

From ten to fourteen is the most favorable age for entering the Institution, provided the pupil have judicious care and training at home prior to that age. But this is not always the case, and as there are many who lose their sight after that age, or having lost it earlier do not find an opportunity of going to school at the proper time, the regulations of the Institute allow of the admission of all proper applicants who are not under six or above twenty-six years of age.

It must be borne in mind, however, by the friends of blind children, that though they have the privilege of sending them to the Institute at a later period than the one mentioned as the best, yet it is of the highest importance that they should be sent within that period, for as they grow older their neglected powers lose their susceptibility for cultivation, rendering the training more and more difficult, until they become wholly incapacitated for receiving such an education as will fit them for a life of usefulness, independence and happiness. It is not uncommon to witness results of this kind, arising out of the morbid tenderness with which a blind child is regarded by his friends, they being unwilling to trust him to the care of strangers lest some harm should befal him. Indeed every years experience but serves to indicate more clearly the lamentable prevalence of this unjust neglect, as there are constantly applying for admission into the several Institutions of the county, those whose melancholy lot it is to lead a life of hopeless ignorance and dependence, but who might, with proper training in early youth, have become happy and useful members of society, maintaining themselves comfortably and respectably.

TERM OF INSTRUCTION.

This is not limited to any definite number of years, but is determined in each individual case, by the acquirements of the pupil, and consequent fitness for graduating.

The length of each ones term, will depend upon his aptness to learn and the extent of the course pursued.

SCHOOL SESSION.

There is but one session in the year, commencing on the fourth Wednesday in September, and closing on Wednesday after the first Tuesday in July. During vacation, the pupils have an opportunity of visiting their homes, and replenishing their clothing.

ADMISSION OF PUPILS.

The State, wisely regarding this Institution as a part of a system of public instruction, has thrown it open to the Blind of Arkansas between the ages of six and twenty-six years, who, if of proper character and capacity, are received, boarded and instructed at the expense of the Commonwealth.

Application for the admission of pupils into the Institution, should be addressed to the Superintendent, and should state the name, age and cause of blindness of the person for whom application is made; also at what age he or she became blind, and whether the blindness is partial or total; what are his or her personal habits and moral character, and what is the post office address of the parent or guardian. No person of confirmed immoral character, or having any infectious or offensive disease, will knowingly be received into the Institute.

Pupils should come provided with a supply of comfortable clothing, which should be replenished, from time to time, as may be necessary. Each article should be marked with the owners name, to prevent confusion or loss; and each pupil should be provided with a small sum of money which, if thought best, may be deposited with the Superintendent to meet such industrial expenses as mending shoes postage, etc.

It is important that all pupils should be present at the commencement of the session, or as soon after as posssble, and remain until its close. Letters to the pupils should be addressed to the care of the Institute.

www.ingramcontent.com/pod-product-compliance
Lightning Source LLC
Chambersburg PA
CBHW032001300426
44117CB00008B/859